16448

Dickens
Interviews and Recollections

Volume I

Also by Philip Collins

A Christmas Carol: The Public Reading Version (*editor*)
A Dickens Bibliography
Charles Dickens: *David Copperfield*
Charles Dickens: The Public Readings (*editor*)
Dickens and Crime
Dickens and Education
Dickens's *Bleak House*
Dickens: The Critical Heritage (*editor*)
English Christmas (*editor*)
From Manly Tears to Stiff Upper Lip: The Victorian and Pathos
James Boswell
Reading Aloud: A Victorian Métier
The Impress of the Moving Age
Thomas Cooper, the Chartist

DICKENS

Interviews and Recollections

Volume 1

Edited by

Philip Collins

First published 1981 by
THE MACMILLAN PRESS LTD
London and Basingstoke
Companies and representatives
throughout the world

ISBN 0 333 26254 9

Printed in Hong Kong

To Jean and Arthur Humphreys
with love and gratitude

Contents

List of Plates

Acknowledgements

Dr Michael Slater and Dr Andrew Sanders, past and present editors of the *Dickensian*, have been generous in advice and in giving me permission to reprint material from their journal, as have their contributors, Professors K. J. Fielding, Jerome Meckier and John R. DeBruyn. The trustees of the Dickens House Museum have allowed me to publish manuscript material and to reproduce portraits from their collection, and the Curator of Dickens House, Dr David Parker, has been most helpful in giving me access to its riches. Other illustrations appear through the kindness of the Forster Collection (Victoria and Albert Museum), the National Portrait Gallery, and the Mander and Mitcheson Collection.

Other friends and colleagues have helped by answering enquiries or securing material for me: Professor Sylvère Monod, Professor F. W. J. Hemmings, Professor Kathleen Tillotson, Dr John Podeschi, Miss Eva Searl, Mr Iain Crawford, Mr Charles Leahy and Mr Richard Foulkes. Like all students of Dickens, I am much in the debt of the editors of the Pilgrim Edition of *The Letters of Charles Dickens*, the annotation as well as the text of which has been invaluable. The staff of Leicester University Library have been energetic in obtaining materials for me, and the Epsom Library and the Eastgate House Museum, Rochester, have answered enquiries. I salute and thank my predecessors in this biographical field, whose researches have greatly eased mine: notably Frederic G. Kitton, William R. Hughes, Robert Langton and W. J. Carlton. I thank also the patient and skilful typists who have coped with my second and third as well as my first thoughts: Mrs Doreen Butler, Mrs Sylvia Garfield, Miss Anne Sowter, Mrs Pat Taylor and Mrs Brenda Tracy.

For permission to reprint copyright material I thank the editors of *The Times Literary Supplement*, *Harper's Magazine* and *University* (Princeton, N. J.), and the following publishers: Oxford University Press and the Clarendon Press for the extracts from the Pilgrim Edition of *The Letters of Charles Dickens*, ed. Madeline House, Graham Storey and Kathleen Tillotson; *The George Eliot Letters*, ed.

Gordon S. Haight; Arthur A. Adrian's *Georgina Hogarth and the Dickens Circle*; and Gordon N. Ray's *Thackeray: The Age of Wisdom, 1847–1863*; John Murray (Publishers) Ltd for the extracts from James Milne's *A Window in Fleet Street*; Frederick Muller Ltd for the extracts from Gladys Storey's *Dickens and Daughter*; William Heinemann Ltd for the extracts from Sir Henry Fielding Dickens's *The Recollections of Sir Henry Dickens, Q. C.*; Harvard University Press, and Belinda Norman-Butler, literary executor for the Estate of William Thackeray, for the extracts from *The Letters and Private Papers of William Makepeace Thackeray*, ed. Gordon N. Ray; the Belknap Press of Harvard University Press for the extracts from *The Journal of Richard Henry Dana, Jr, 1841–60*, ed. R. F. Lucid.

Every effort has been made to trace all the copyright-holders, but if any have been inadvertently overlooked the publishers will be pleased to make the necessary arrangement at the first opportunity.

List of Abbreviations

The following abbreviations are used in the editorial matter.

Dickens Circle J. W. T. Ley, *The Dickens Circle: A Narrative of the Novelist's Friendships* (1918).

Dkn *The Dickensian* (1905–).

Life John Forster, *The Life of Charles Dickens* (1872–4), ed. J. W. T. Ley (1928). Book and chapter, as well as page, references are given.

N *The Letters of Charles Dickens*, ed. Walter Dexter (the Nonesuch Edition), 3 vols (1938).

P *The Letters of Charles Dickens*, ed. Madeline House, Graham Storey and Kathleen Tillotson (the Pilgrim Edition), 4 vols issued so far (Oxford, 1965–77).

Pen and Pencil *Charles Dickens: By Pen and Pencil, including Anecdotes and Reminiscences Collected by his Friends and Companions*, ed. Frederic G. Kitton (1890); with *Supplement* (1890).

Speeches *The Speeches of Charles Dickens*, ed. K. J. Fielding (Oxford, 1960).

Introduction

This book has been both a joy and an anguish to compile: a joy because Dickens is such a vivid, active and fascinating man, in whom I continually delight; an anguish because, even with two volumes allowed me, I have had to omit so many aspects and so many lively and intelligent accounts of him. His friend and colleague Edmund Yates aptly commented, 'I have always held that Dickens was an exception to the general rule of authors being so much less interesting than their books',[1] and, though not everybody took to Dickens, I have never come across anyone who, meeting or seeing him, wrote him off as dull, uninteresting or negative. Moreover, his personality and multifarious activities are intimately and intricately connected with his art, as his commentators have shown. I tried to illustrate this in an essay called 'How Many Men was Dickens the Novelist?', where I argued that it was impossible to isolate the Novelist from the many incarnations of the Man – the parent and family man, the journalist and editor, the philanthropist and public man, the brilliant after-dinner speaker, the amateur actor, theatrical director and public reader, even the author (as he intended to be) of a cookbook: and this list of his activities is far from exhaustive.[2]

Into all these activities, public and private, artistic and practical, he threw himself wholeheartedly. It was, wrote his friend and biographer John Forster,

> one of the secrets of Dickens's social charm that he could . . . allow each part of him its turn; could afford thoroughly to give rest and relief to what was serious in him, and, when the time came to play his gambols, could surrender himself wholly to the enjoyment of the time, and become the very genius and embodiment of one of his own most whimsical fancies. . . . He did even his nothings in a strenuous way.
>
> (*Life*, II, viii, 155; VI, iii, 495[3])

His amateur theatrical activity may provide a first example of this.

Even Forster was surprised to discover, during the first of Dickens's adult ventures of this kind in England (*Every Man in his Humour*, 1845), how talented, competent and energetic his friend was:

> But greatly as his acting contributed to the success of the night, this was nothing to the service he had rendered as manager. It would be difficult to describe it. He was the life and soul of the entire affair. I never seemed till then to have known his business capabilities. He took everything on himself, and did the whole of it without an effort. He was stage-director, very often stage-carpenter, scene-arranger, property-man, prompter, and bandmaster. Without offending any one he kept every one in order. For all he had useful suggestions, and the dullest of clays under his potter's hand were transformed into little bits of porcelain. He adjusted scenes, assisted carpenters, invented costumes, devised playbills, wrote out calls, and enforced as well as exhibited in his proper person everything of which he urged the necessity on others. (*Life*, v, i, 383)

Similarly, in his 'Splendid Strolling' chapter about the 1847–8 theatricals, Forster marvels at Dickens's vitality and animation:

> In the enjoyment as in the labour he was first. His animal spirits, unresting and supreme, were the attraction of rehearsal at morning, and of the stage at night. At the quiet early dinner, and the more jovial unrestrained supper, where all engaged were assembled daily, his was the brightest face, the lightest step, the pleasantest word. There seemed to be no need for rest to that wonderful vitality. (*Life*, vi, i, 469)

This is just one of what Forster later calls 'the many examples I have given of his untiring energy both in work and play' (*Life*, vi, vi, 535). Some of Dickens's friends and acquaintances were daunted by this restless activity, and total commitment even to his relaxations, and found it very wearing. He glanced at this himself in his narrative 'The Lazy Tour of Two Idle Apprentices' (1857), based on a holiday jaunt which he ('Francis Goodchild') took with his friend Wilkie Collins ('Thomas Idle'). 'Having done nothing to fatigue himself for a full quarter of an hour, Francis began to fear that he was not in a state of idleness', and Thomas Idle protests, 'You *can't* play. You don't know what it is. You make work of everything. . . .

A man who can do nothing by halves appears to me to be a fearful man' ('The Lazy Tour', *Christmas Stories*, ii, 684; iv, 723[4]). Friends found it difficult, likewise, to match, let alone enjoy, the relentless pedestrianism that was his most regular daily relaxation – a steady four miles an hour, with a fifteen to twenty mile walk in prospect. But Dickens also 'did nothing by halves' in his benevolent activities, as indeed in everything else. Humphry House, describing his years of work for Urania Cottage, the home for outcast women financed by Angela Burdett Coutts, justly remarks, 'This grind of charitable business would be astounding in any man: it is scarcely credible in the greatest English creative genius of his time.'[5] Well might Lord Shaftesbury, who knew him, and found him sometimes an ally, sometimes an enemy, exclaim, 'The man was a phenomenon, an exception, a special production. Nothing like him ever preceded. Nature isn't such a tautologist as to make another to follow him.'[6]

Shaftesbury had been reading Forster's *Life of Dickens*. His exclamation might equally have been provoked by reading the novels (not that he seems ever to have done that). But my concern, in contributing to this 'Interviews and Recollections' series, is, like Shaftesbury's in the journal entry just cited, biographical. How Dickens's writings struck contemporary critics, and the reading public, has been surveyed and illustrated elsewhere.[7] The present collection depicts the man behind the books, but many items will of course refer to his writing habits, sources of inspiration, artistic personality, and much else germane to the novels and other writings. For, as Forster remarked, 'His literary work was so intensely one with his nature that he is not separable from it, and the man and the method' throw a singular light on each other' (*Life*, IX, i, 712) – a sentence which, like Yates's quoted in my opening paragraph, might serve as epigraph to the present book. The material, I have said, is extremely abundant; and it is so for several reasons: most obviously, because Dickens achieved immediate national (and soon international) fame with his first novel, *Pickwick Papers* (1836–7), at the age of twenty-four – and not merely fame, for he enjoyed a popularity and an affectionate regard unique in English literary annals. When, in 1858, he was contemplating a supplementary career as a public reader, he referred in several letters to 'that particular relation (personally affectionate and like no other man's) which subsists between me and the public' (*N*, iii, 15), and he did not deceive himself. To quote one member of his readings audiences, the American Moncure D. Conway, at the end of his performance 'it was not mere applause that followed, but a passionate outburst of love for the man'.[8] His critical fortunes waxed and waned, but his popularity was unchallenged through-out his life: so thousands of readers – and even illiterate non-readers who were aware of his works – wanted to see or meet him, and often, if they did so, they recorded their impressions.

Moreover, he lived a very public life, and in an age of publicity: there were far more newspapers and periodicals during his lifetime than ever before, and his appearances on various platforms, as orator or performer, gave journalists many opportunities to report, and report upon, him. His two visits to the United States, in 1842 and 1867–8, exposed him to the curiosity and the candour of the American press, often to his indignation or embarrassment, and American citizens were assiduous – not to say intrusive – in making the best of this once-in-a-lifetime chance to see the Immortal Boz. They were zealous, too, in recording their impressions, as the editors of the Pilgrim *Letters* (vol. 3) covering the 1842 visit demonstrate through their numerous quotations from published or manuscript sources. Forster quotes one example, an account of Dickens at a party in Cincinnati by a young woman (name unknown) who confessed to 'considerable disappointment in the personnel of my idol': his manner was 'easy, negligent, but not elegant. His dress is foppish; in fact, he was overdressed. . . . He appeared a little weary, but answered the remarks made to him – for he originated none – in an agreable manner' (*Life*, iii, vi, 258n). It is piquant to compare Dickens's account of the same evening: he and his wife were 'introduced to at least one hundred and fifty first-rate bores, separately and singly. I was required to sit down by the greater part of them, and talk! . . . I really think my face has acquired a fixed expression of sadness from the constant and unmitigated boring I endure' (*P*, iii, 194). A sadder comparison can be made, again from America but from the 1867–8 readings tour, between the outer and the inner man. 'His photographs give no idea of his genial expression', reported one newspaper. 'To us Mr. Dickens appears like a hearty, companionable man, with a good deal of fun in him.' But that day Dickens – who was very ill and in low spirits – was writing home, 'I am nearly used up. Climate, distances, catarrh . . . have begun to tell heavily upon me. . . . Sleeplessness besets me.'[9] Here, in the old-trouper tradition, he was concealing 'how ill all's here about my heart' – but it is important that he had it in him thus to play a public part. A final American contrast might be made between the judgements of his Boston publisher and host, James T. Fields, and of his wife Annie. Fields applied to Dickens what was said of Garrick, that he was 'the *cheerfullest* man of his age' (Forster did so too); and Fields continued, 'In his presence there was perpetual sunshine, and gloom was banished as having no sort of relationship with him.' Annie Fields does not quite contradict him, but she adds a dimension of analysis when she writes, 'wonderful, the flow of spirits C. D. has for a sad man'.[10] Both she and her husband knew Dickens intimately, and both were intelligent observers; but which of these recollections more fully represents the man?

This was the first age of photography, as a quotation from an American journalist has already reminded us, so Dickens belongs to the first generation of celebrities thus recorded for posterity. That journalist, it will be recalled, remarked that 'His photographs give no idea of his genial expression.' This is worth remembering, since we form our mental picture of Dickens largely from such apparently authentic evidence. It is indeed remarkable, when one thinks of it, that in no photograph, painting or drawing (to my recollection) is Dickens seen smiling, let alone laughing: and there are many hundreds of contemporary pictures of him in the Dickens House collection alone. Thus one vitally important dimension of the physical appearance of our greatest comic author – who was, often enough, a man of conspicuous geniality – is altogether missing from the visual record. Some photographs of him are reproduced in this work, and a few paintings. Even before photography had made such headway, his face was familiar, notably through the portrait of him by Maclise used as the frontispiece of *Nicholas Nickleby* (1839).Thus, when on holiday in Broadstairs in 1840, he could only 'preserve his incognito' at a place of entertainment by 'not venturing into the glare of the lights, as his face was too well known'.[11] The currency of photographs, later, made it even more likely that he would be widely recognised wherever he went, and this fact accounts for many other recorded recollections of him. (It must also have added a spice of danger, if his visits to the young actress Ellen Ternan, in Streatham or Stroud or wherever, had the illicit clandestine purposes that have been alleged.) 'To walk with him in the streets of London', recalls his son Henry, 'was a revelation; a royal progress; people of all degrees and classes taking off their hats and greeting him as he passed.'[12] A few samples of such chance encounters, when he was recognised by strangers, may be quoted here, the first from a few weeks before his death, when he was observed 'walking in Kensington Gardens with a little girl very plainly dressed – obviously the child of some friend in humble circumstances – with whom he was chatting and romping as if he were himself a child'.[13] Or here he is, in Liverpool in 1869, an occasion recorded by his companion and not by those who recognised him: during his walk to the railway station, 'he was repeatedly stopped by persons of the working classes wanting to shake hands with him, and all of them eager to thank him for the pleasure his books had afforded them. This, however, was not a new experience to him in the large manufacturing towns.'[14] These two glimpses of Dickens are very pleasing and meritorious – but 'we have had too many honeysuckle lives of Milton', as Dr Johnson said, and I must not give too unremittingly saccharine a flavour to my collection (though most of the items quoted will be favourable to him, not – I trust – through my over-partiality, but because, bating his faults, he predominantly impressed people as a good, attractive and kindly man). So my other two samples shall be more acerbic. The first – if true – presumably illustrates my 'spice of danger' comment. 'Charles Dickens was once by chance my fellow-traveller on the Boulogne packet', writes the anonymous author of *Gossip of the Century*, and

> travelling with him was a lady not his wife, nor his sister-in-law, yet he strutted about the deck with the air of a man bristling with self-importance: every line of his face and every gesture of his limbs seemed haughtily to say – 'Look at me; make the most of your chance. I am the great, the *only*, Charles Dickens; whatever I may choose to do is justified by that fact.'

And her account continues with Dickens's further self-importance at the Custom House when the officer fails to recognise, or be over-awed by, him.[15] The other quizzical glimpse occurs in the recently discovered diaries of Arthur J. Munby, a young London solicitor at this time:

> *Tuesday, 10 May, 1864.* Near Covent Garden this afternoon I met Charles Dickens, walking along alone and unnoticed. A man of middle height, of somewhat slight frame, of light step and jaunty air; clad in spruce frockcoat, buttoned to show his good and still

youthful figure; and with brand new hat airily cocked on one side, and stick poised in his hand. A man of sanguine complexion, deeply lined & scantly bearded face, and countenance alert and observant, scornful somewhat and sour; with a look of fretfulness, vanity; which might however be due to the gait and the costume. Thus he passed before me, and thus, in superficial casual view, I judged of him. Anyhow, how unlike the tall massive frame, the slow gentle ways, the grave sad selfabsorbed look, of Thackeray![16]

Other such momentary encounters will be quoted, but inevitably most of my extracts will come from authors who knew Dickens more closely. I have already quoted from Forster, his closest friend and adviser throughout his career as a novelist. His *Life* has often been criticised as ill ordered and as devoting too much attention to the biographer and not enough to other friendships and other sources of evidence; but I regard Dickens as singularly fortunate in his official biographer. None of the weighty official biographies of eminent Victorian authors so well stands up to frequentation, unless it be Mrs Gaskell's *Life of Charlotte Brontë* or Hallam Tennyson's *Memoir* of the Poet Laureate. Forster was deeply intimate with his subject, and was an astute observer and a practised writer. I shall quote him sparingly, however, in my selections below, because the *Life* will be familiar to students of Dickens, and should be at the head of the reading list of others who, having perused my volumes, want to learn more about the novelist. Many of Dickens's other friends and associates were practised authors and journalists too, of course, and wrote about him, or were notable actors or artists who became the subject of biographies which contain reminiscences or relevant letters. Two early biographers who were not acquainted with Dickens deserve special mention for their productive zeal in seeking out people who were, but were not likely to write down their reminiscences: Robert Langton, author of *The Childhood and Youth of Dickens* (1883; revised and enlarged, 1891), and Frederic G. Kitton, compiler of *Dickensiana* (1886) and *Dickens by Pen and Pencil* (1890) and author and editor of many other books about Dickens. Other such early studies using interviews with people who knew Dickens include Adolphus William Ward's *Dickens* (1882) and William R. Hughes's *A Week's Tramp in Dickens-land* (1893). These interviews, or responses to biographers' letters of enquiry, are particularly valuable on his childhood and early life before his days of fame, and on his function as a neighbour and squirearchal figure during his final years at Gad's Hill.

Of 'interviews' – half of this series' title – with Dickens himself, there are few. This was not a common journalistic form in the England of his day. Most of the interviews known to me, indeed, are by overseas visitors, mainly Americans, who formally called upon him or had good opportunities of meeting him, usually though not always with a view to publishing their discoveries. Occasionally an American newspaper, during his visits, reported snatches of what must have been interviews: thus, the *New York Tribune* (3 Dec 1867) reported 'on the best authority' – presumably Dickens, though it might have been his readings manager, George Dolby – that he put at least two months' thorough rehearsal into every new item in his repertoire.

But, if 'interviews' are scanty, published and unpublished 'recollections' are many, partly, as has been remarked, because he was so famous and beloved throughout his career and because he led a much more public life than most authors, on platforms and as an editor, but also because he lived mostly in London and generally lived very sociably. In the first flush of his popularity he frequented the great houses more than he did later; he hated being lionised and, as Forster says, 'what is called society . . . did not suit him, and he set no store by it' (*Life*, viii, ii, 635). But few of his friends or members of his social circle were obscure persons. In an item below, 'The Company He Kept' (i, 105–10), I exemplify the range of his acquaintance, and it may be illustrated here by a list of his recorded engagements during the final months of his life in 1870.[17] He was busy giving his farewell readings and writing *Edwin Drood*, and these activities always reduced his availability for society; moreover, his health was failing and he had to cancel some engagements, and he was at his country retreat, Gad's Hill, for periods during these five months. He lamented that he had got himself into such a 'complicated state of engagements that my life is positively made wretched' (*N*, iii, 775). Still, he packed a lot in. He breakfasted with Gladstone, and met Disraeli at dinner in May, and both of them heard him give his last public speech, at the Royal Academy Banquet; it was, said Gladstone, 'one of the most finished perform-ances of its kind' he had ever heard. He gave other public speeches, at the Newsvendors' Benevolent and Provident Institution dinner and as prize-giver at the Birmingham and Midland Institute. More privately he was dining with friends – Forster, Carlyle, Landseer,

Millais, the Honourable Mrs Richard Watson, and younger colleagues such as Edmund Yates and Percy Fitzgerald – was lunching with George Eliot (attending Sunday service at the Priory, as he happily put it), but having to decline an invitation from Tennyson because of his reading commitments. At the poet Locker-Lampson's, he met Dean Stanley, who was to bury him at Westminster Abbey a few months later. Stanley invited him to the Deanery, where the guests included Lord John Russell, the only Prime Minister with whom he was close friends. At the Army and Navy Club, Colonel Hamley (Commandant of the Staff College) gave a dinner for him, where the guests included Spencer Walpole, the statesman, and J. L. Motley, the American Minister in London. Lord Houghton gave a dinner at which he was specially wanted, to meet the King of the Belgians and the Prince of Wales: 'I never saw Mr Dickens more agreable', his hostess recalled (*Life*, xi, iii, 832). Dickens was the Prince's favourite novelist, as he was the Queen's too, and on 9 March she received him at Buckingham Palace. They discussed – of all subjects – the 'servant-problem', as if they were a pair of middle-class housewives, and went on to talk about America, the price of provisions, the cost of meat and bread. He knew about such things, and what to do with them. One of his more surprising literary plans at this time was that 'great scheme for writing a cookery book'. This he announced at a dinner at Lady Molesworth's (the great old Tory hostess) where he 'simply bubbled over with fun and conversation'; and, taking her and Lord Redesdale to the theatre at the end of May, he was still 'in high spirits, brim-full of the *joie de vivre*. His talk had all the sparkle of champagne, and he himself kept laughing at the majesty of his own absurdities, as one droll thought followed another.'[18] He attended a royal levee, dined at the American embassy, and of course gave various dinners at Hyde Park Place to return some of this hospitality. Most notably he gave a very grand reception on 7 April: his first return to general society after his separation from his wife twelve years before, noted one guest. All the most prominent people in town were there (wrote another), literary, artistic, and fashionable; the supper was sumptuous, 'profusion without ostentation'. The music was provided by the leading performers of the day – Hallé and Lady Thomson at the pianofortes, Joachim on the violin, Santley and Cummings and the London Glee and Madrigal Union among the vocalists.

Most of the people mentioned in that account of his 1870 social engagements were eminent enough to write their memoirs, or to have their biographies written or their letters or journals published, and almost all of them have recorded their memories of Dickens on this occasion or on others. So the evidence about Dickens, over the years, accumulates in enormous quantity; and, as has been noted, there are, besides, the many impressions of him recorded by journalists or strangers who saw him in the street or attended one of his readings. One other category of witness deserves special mention – members of his family.

Here the record is patchy, with hardly anything surviving from Dickens's elders and coevals, but a good quantity from his children and even from one grandchild, Mary Angela Dickens, who was aged seven when he died. It is frustrating that his parents wrote, or were recorded as saying, almost nothing about their famous son, except John Dickens's reply to an enquiry about where the novelist had been educated: 'Why, indeed, Sir – ha! ha! – he may be said to have educated himself!' (*Life*, I, iii, 47). Thus we have no account, except Dickens's own, of those crucially formative experiences of his boyhood, his shame over his father's imprisonment and his anguish at being *déclassé* by being sent out to manual work in a blacking-warehouse. It would have been fascinating, too, to hear John Dickens's reactions to his fictional appearance as Mr Micawber: he must have recognised himself, so many of the character's circumstances being literally his own; but Elizabeth, his wife, may be forgiven for not realising that the foolish Mrs Nickleby was based upon herself, though Dickens particularly enjoyed her scepticism as to whether 'such a woman' ever existed (*Life*, III, viii, 280).[19] A few family letters survive, often acrimonious, but, among his brothers and sisters, only Fanny left any record of their childhood – and that was scanty, being confined to her having been 'brought up in the Established Church, but I regret to say, without any serious ideas of religion' (she had become an extremely pious Congregationalist, and with her husband, Henry Burnett, had abandoned her former 'worldly' life). Burnett was one of the people whose recollections Kitton obtained, but Fanny had died many years earlier.[20]

Dickens's wife Catherine maintained a dignified silence about their marriage and its breakdown, but charged their daughter Katey to deposit in the British Museum his letters to her, trusting that thus posterity would see that he 'had once loved her'.[21] Catherine's unmarried sister Georgina Hogarth, who shocked many observers by staying with Dickens after the separation, was more forthcoming, though she never wrote at length about him. She co-edited the *Letters* (1880–2), which contain some narrative of his life, helped Forster, Ward, Langton, Kitton and other early biographers, and generally acted as guardian of the sacred memory. But it is his children who provide much the fullest picture of the domestic Dickens. Three of his sons – Charles, Alfred and Henry – wrote·about him, quite extensively though with some suppressions. His elder daughter, Mary (Mamie), published several books and articles, repetitive but informative, though her piety towards her beloved father so exasperated Dame Una Pope-Hennessy that she described Mamie's amiability as verging on imbecility.[22] Dickens, who gave inventive and sometimes elaborate nicknames to his children, had sagely called her 'Mild Glo'ster'. The other daughter, Katey, was named '(from a lurking propensity to fieriness), Lucifer Box' (*P*, III, 331) – a prescient judgement on the girl, then less than three years old. She was more independent and rebellious, and more capable; indeed, she of all the children most resembled their father in ability and force of character. She had her father's face, Mamie their mother's. Katey even resembled her father in having a slow pulse and in being short-sighted. (Curiously, one does not think of Dickens as bespectacled, but in private he was so: Percy Fitzgerald, in 1913, could 'see him now . . . , the strained eyes, peering through the gold-rimmed glasses, always of strong power; the face bent down to the manuscript which lay on the table'.[23])

Katey (later Mrs Charles Collins, and then after Collins's death Mrs Perugini) wrote a moving account of her father's last days, reprinted below (II, 354–8), and a few other scraps, and she edited an anthology, *The Comedy of Dickens* (1906). But her major report on her father was made posthumously, through the record of her conversations with a friend, Gladys Storey, which the latter published in *Dickens and Daughter* (1939). Miss Storey also records,

It is known only to a few that Mrs. Perugini wrote a life of her father, clearing her mother of false accusations made at the time of their separation. This manuscript Mrs. Perugini burnt. 'I told only half the truth about my father,' she said, 'and a half-truth is worse than a lie, for this reason I destroyed what I had written. But the truth *must be told* when the time comes – after my death.' Mrs. Perugini feared for the truth to 'come out' during her lifetime, even after her death, lest those who revealed it – not being in possession of the true facts – would 'get them all wrong'.

So it was that the author gave a promise to Mrs. Perugini to undertake the fulfilment of her wish, hearing from her own lips the unvarnished truth as set down in this book. Mrs. Perugini remained as irrevocably desirous that the truth should be revealed, as her mother was anxious that her husband's letters to her should – after her death – be given to the British Museum for the world to read. Mrs. Perugini said that she could sum up the mistakes in her father's life on one half-sheet of note-paper, and that she would commence with the words: 'What could you expect from such an uncanny genius?'[24]

Miss Storey's reliability was much attacked at the time, for Katey's reported sayings about her father were much less 'honeysuckle' than those by other members of the family. Certainly Miss Storey is inaccurate in some of her factual statements, as several commentators have shown: most lately, Mary Lazarus in an appendix to her book *A Tale of Two Brothers: Charles Dickens's Sons in Australia* (1973). But I take her report to be substantially correct, and of great interest, and I quote it below (1, 151–5). It is sad, however, that Katey's biography, even telling 'only half the truth', was destroyed, for in intelligence and independence it would have surpassed any of the other family accounts of Dickens – and the sadder because her destroying the manuscript for the reason stated, instead of turning it into cash, was a mark of the integrity that she would have brought to her task.

The arrangement of this collection is broadly chronological – only broadly so, because many reminiscers jump inside a paragraph from one period of Dickens's life to another. The chronology observed is of course that of his career, not of the date of the items' publication. Brief glimpses of him are sometimes grouped together under one heading, such as 'Boz Emergent' or 'In the Chair'. Items mainly dealing with a particular phase of his career, such as his work as a magazine editor or his life at Gad's Hill, are printed successively. But these topics are also mentioned in other items, so the reader consulting this collection with a particular topic or aspect in mind should check the index. For readers unfamiliar with the detail of Dickens's career, a chronology has been provided. Here and in some headnotes to items about Dickens's earlier years, whenever dates remain conjectural I have gratefully accepted the sagacious surmises of the Pilgrim *Letters* editors.

In selecting items for reprinting, I have sometimes given the benefit of the doubt to relatively inaccessible ones, partly because the interested general reader can hardly be expected to lay his hands on them, and partly to make this collection the more useful to specialist readers, who will be familiar with the more obvious sources. As was mentioned above, John Forster's *Life* has been sparingly cited, for these reasons: it is accessible and indispensable.

The Pilgrim text is cited for letters up to 1846, and the Nonesuch Edition for letters thereafter; see the List of Abbreviations for the style in which references are given. In the reprinting of items, typographical errors have been silently corrected and book-titles, etc., have been regularised into italic.

'Suggestions for Further Reading' are given at the end of volume II. These are confined, as is the present collection, to biographical aspects of Dickens.

PHILIP COLLINS

Leicester
April 1979.

NOTES

1. Edmund Yates, *Recollections and Experiences* (1885 edn) p. 331.

2. Philip Collins, 'How Many Men was Dickens the Novelist?', in *Studies in the Later Dickens*, ed. Jean-Claude Amalric (Montpellier, 1973) pp. 145–68.

3. References to Forster's *Life of Dickens*, and to collections of Dickens's letters, will be given thus in the text. See List of Abbreviations.

4. References to Dickens's fiction give chapter (and, if relevant, book) numbers, with page references to the Oxford Illustrated Edition of his works (1947–58).

5. *All in Due Time* (1955) p. 235.

6. Edwin Hodder, *Life and Work of the Seventh Earl of Shaftesbury* (1886) III, 298.

7. See, for example, Amy Cruse, *The Victorians and their Books* (1935) ch. 8, 'Dickens'; George H. Ford, *Dickens and his Readers* (1955); *Dickens and Fame 1870–1970* (centenary number of *The Dickensian*, 1970); *Dickens: The Critical Heritage*, ed. Philip Collins (1971).

8. Moncure D. Conway, *Autobiography* (1904) II, 7.

9. *Portland Transcript*, 4 Apr 1868; *N*, III, 640. I have used this comparison, and the Fields one which follows, in my essay cited in note 2 above.

10. James T. Fields, *Yesterdays with Authors* (1872) p. 241; *Life*, II, viii, 162; Annie Fields quoted by Arthur A. Adrian, *Georgina Hogarth and the Dickens Circle* (1957) p. 126.

11. Eleanor E. Christian, 'Reminiscences of Dickens', *Englishwoman's Domestic Magazine*, x (1871) 340.

12. Henry Dickens, *Memories of my Father* (1928) p. 17. On Dickens's instant recognisability, see G. A. Sala and Charles Kent, below, II, 197–8, 242. 'You could always pick out Dickens, in the Strand, by his red waistcoat, with a heavy watch-chain across it', James Milne was told – *A Window in Fleet Street* (1931) p. 187.

13. *Leeds Mercury*, 10 June 1870, obituary article.

14. George Dolby, *Charles Dickens as I Knew Him* (1885) p. 400.

15. [Julia Clara Byrne], *Gossip of the Century* (1892) I, 225.

16. *Munby: Man of Two Worlds*, ed. Derek Hudson (1972) p. 191.

17. The remainder of this paragraph is derived from my essay 'Dickens in 1870', *Times Literary Supplement*, 4 June 1870, p. 606.

18. For references, see below, II, 349–51, 'At Lady Molesworth's'.

19. The only comment by John Dickens on the Micawber characterisation that is known to me is second-hand and comes from R. Shelton Mackenzie, who reports that John Dickens's acquaintances recognised Micawber as a portrait of him, and that 'He considered himself rather complimented in thus being converted into literary "capital" by his son' – R. Shelton Mackenzie, *Life of Charles Dickens* (Philadelphia, n.d. [1870]) pp. 203, 37. Mackenzie is unreliable but, for a biographer writing as early as 1870, he is decidedly knowledgeable; thus he also reports, correctly, that Elizabeth Dickens was the original of Mrs Nickleby (p. 200).

20. James Griffin, *Memories of the Past: Records of Ministerial Life* (1883) ch. 8, on the Burnetts. Cf. Henry Woodcock, 'The Religious Side of Charles Dickens and his Sister Fanny', *Aldersgate Primitive Methodist Magazine*, Mar 1901, pp. 106–10, 204–6, 284–8.

21. Kate Dickens Perugini, Foreword to *Mr and Mrs Charles Dickens: His Letters to Her*, ed. Walter Dexter (1935) p. xi.

22. Una Pope-Hennessy, *Charles Dickens 1812–1870* (1947 edn.) p. 435.

23. Percy Fitzgerald, *Memories of Charles Dickens* (1913) p. 77. A pair of his spectacles is preserved at the Bleak House Museum, Broadstairs.

24. Gladys Storey, *Dickens and Daughter* (1939) p. 91. On the evidence available to her, see David Parker and Michael Slater, 'The Gladys Storey Papers', *Dkn*, LXXVI (1980) 2–19.

A Dickens Chronology

1812   Born at Portsmouth, 7 Feb, eldest son of a Naval Pay Office clerk. Moves to London, 1816, and to Chatham, 1817; first schooling there. Family moves to London (Camden Town), winter 1822–3; no school then, because family in financial straits.

1824   Working in Warren's blacking-warehouse, Feb to (?) June. Father in Marshalsea Debtors' Prison, Mar–May.

1824–7   At Wellington House Academy, in the Hampstead Road.

1827–8   Working as a clerk in solicitors' offices.

1829–36   Short-hand reporter, first at Doctors' Commons (lawcourts), then on various newspapers, notably the *Morning Chronicle* (from 1834). Much time in Parliamentary press gallery. Applies for an audition, as an actor, at Covent Garden, 1832; also contemplates emigrating.

1833–6   Publishing stories and essays in magazines and newspapers, mostly collected in *Sketches by Boz* (two series, 1836).

1836   Marries Catherine, daughter of Scottish man of letters, George Hogarth, 2 Apr; they live in chambers at Furnival's Inn. 31 Mar, first number of *Pickwick Papers* published; runs till 30 Oct 1837. (NB. All his novels were serialised before appearing in book form.) Three plays performed in London, 1836–7.

1837   *Oliver Twist* (to 1839), published in *Bentley's Miscellany*, which Dickens edits 1837–9. First child born (Charley); over the years, until 1852, seven surviving sons and two daughters born. Moves to 48 Doughty Street (now the Dickens House). First public speech.

1838   *Nicholas Nickleby* (to 1839).

1839   Moves to Devonshire Terrace.

1840   *Master Humphrey's Clock* (to 1841): contents are mainly *The Old Curiosity Shop* (1840–1) and *Barnaby Rudge* (1841).

1841   Receives the Freedom of the City of Edinburgh: his first public honour.

1842   Visits the USA and Canada, with his wife, Jan–June. *American Notes* (Oct), *Martin Chuzzlewit* (1842–4).

1843   *A Christmas Carol.* Further Christmas books published: *The Chimes* (1844), *The Cricket on the Hearth* (1845), *The Battle of Life* (1846), *The Haunted Man* (1848).

1844   July, leaves London for Genoa, where he and the family live for one year.

1845   First of the amateur theatricals (Jonson's *Every Man in his Humour*).

1846   Founding editor of the *Daily News* (21 Jan until his resignation, 9 Feb). *Pictures from Italy.* May, leaves with family for Lausanne and Paris, until Feb 1847. *Dombey and Son* (to 1848).

1847   Begins 'Splendid Strolling' (amateur theatrical tours in provinces).

1849   *David Copperfield* (to 1850).

1850   *Household Words* begins, 30 Mar; Dickens 'conducts' it weekly till 28 May 1859. Contributes many essays and Christmas stories, etc., to it, and to its successor, *All the Year Round.*

1851   Moves to Tavistock House.

1852   *Bleak House* (to 1853). Begins regular family holidays in Boulogne.

1853   First public readings: *A Christmas Carol*, Birmingham, 27–30 Dec. Further such readings, in aid of charities, till 1858.

1854   *Hard Times* serialised in *Household Words.*

1855   *Little Dorrit* (to 1857). October, living in Paris with his family, until May 1856. Other such periods of residence in France in later years.

1856   Buys Gad's Hill Place, near Chatham, but does not begin living there until June 1857. Also maintains Tavistock House residence, until 1860.

1857   Meets the actress Ellen Ternan, then aged 18, and is clearly infatuated. It is possible, but unproven, that in later years she becomes his mistress.

1858   First 'paid' public readings, from 29 Apr. Separates from his wife in May; she never meets him again. Provincial reading tour, Aug–Nov, after London season. In later years gives occasional Christmas or Easter seasons in London, and undertakes provincial tours (with odd nights in London), Oct 1859, Oct 1861–Jan 1862, April–June 1866, Jan–May 1867, Oct 1868–Apr 1869; also American tour 1867–8 and 'Farewell' readings, 1870. Altogether about 472 performances.

1859   Closes down *Household Words*, and substitutes *All the Year Round* (30 Apr 1859 until his death). *A Tale of Two Cities* serialised in its opening numbers.

1860   Sells Tavistock House; has rooms at the *All the Year Round* offices, and in later years sometimes rents a London house, but now mostly lives at Gad's Hill. *The Uncommercial Traveller* published in *All the Year Round*, with additional items in later years; also serialises in it *Great Expectations* (1860–1). Is writing much less fiction, or journalism, in the 1860s, partly because the public readings take up his time and energy, and provide him with sufficient income.

1863   In Paris, Oct–Feb; gives public readings, for charity, there.

1864   *Our Mutual Friend* (to 1865).

1865   In bad railway accident at Staplehurst, 9 June; finds railway travelling irksome after this experience.

1867–8 Ill health becoming evident. American reading tour, Nov 1867–Apr 1868. On return, begins his extensive 'Farewell' readings tour, abandoned when he collapses, Apr 1869.

1870   'Farewell' readings in London, 11 Jan–15 Mar. Apr, *Edwin Drood* serialisation begun (novel never completed). 9 June, dies suddenly at Gad's Hill; buried in Westminster Abbey.

'My Dear Collins': a Message from Novelist to Biographer

CHARLES DICKENS

From his letter to Wilkie Collins, 6 June 1856, *N*, II, 777–8. Paul Forgues (see below, I, 65–6), whom Collins might wish to 'prime' about Dickens, was editor of the *Revue des deux mondes*. Dickens's not over-modest account of his earlier life indicates what he wanted to be known and thought about himself. In another letter to a journalist who was writing a memoir of him he further disclosed, 'Do you care to know that I was a great writer at 8 years old or so – and worked many childish experiences and many young struggles, into Copperfield?' (to Mary Howitt, 7 Sep 1859, *N*, III, 122). For an earlier sketch of his life, for a German journalist in 1838, see *P*, I, 423–4.

My dear Collins, – I have never seen anything about myself in print which has much correctness in it – any biographical account of myself I mean. I do not supply such particulars when I am asked for them by editors and compilers, simply because I am asked for them every day. If you want to prime Forgues, you may tell him without fear of anything wrong, that I was born at Portsmouth on the Seventh of February, 1812; that my father was in the Navy Pay Office; that I was taken by him to Chatham when I was very young, and lived and was educated there till I was twelve or thirteen, I suppose; that I was then put to a school near London, where (as at other places) I distinguished myself like a brick; that I was put in the office of a solicitor, a friend of my father's, and didn't much like it: and after a couple of years (as well as I can remember) applied myself with a celestial or diabolical energy to the study of such things as would qualify me to be a first-rate parliamentary reporter – at that time a calling pursued by many clever men who were young at the Bar; that I made my début in the gallery (at about eighteen, I suppose), engaged on a voluminous publication no longer in existence, called *The Mirror of Parliament*; that when *The Morning Chronicle* was purchased by Sir John Easthope, and acquired a large circulation, I was engaged there, and that I remained there until I had begun to publish *Pickwick*, when I found myself in a condition to relinquish that part of my labours; that I left the reputation behind me of being the best and most rapid reporter ever known, and that I could do anything in that way under any sort of circumstances, and often did. (I daresay I am at this present writing the best shorthand writer in the world.)

That I began, without any interest or introduction of any kind, to write fugitive pieces for the old *Monthly Magazine*, when I was in the gallery for *The Mirror of Parliament*; that my faculty for descriptive writing was seized upon the moment I joined *The Morning Chronicle*, and that I was liberally paid there and handsomely acknowledged, and wrote the greater part of the short descriptive *Sketches by Boz* in that paper; that I had been a writer when I was a mere baby, and always an actor from the same age; that I married the daughter of a writer to the signet in Edinburgh, who was the great friend and assistant of Scott, and who first made Lockhart known to him.

And that here I am.

'A Terrible Boy to Read'

MARY WELLER AND OTHERS

From Robert Langton, *The Childhood and Youth of Charles Dickens*, enlarged edn (1912) pp. 25–6, 34–9, 44, 57. Mary Weller (born 1804), later Mrs Gibson, was the servant – at prosperous times one of the two servants – in the Dickens household at Chatham, c. 1817–22, and is probably recalled in 'Nurses' Tales' (*Uncommercial Traveller*) and other writings. She remarked on the family's increasing financial difficulties that in the later Chatham days there were 'no such juvenile entertainments' as she describes here. Her recollections are followed, in this item, by others from the Chatham period collected by Langton; Mr Tribe was the son of a local innkeeper, Mrs Godfrey was the sister of Dickens's schoolmaster Mr Giles.

Mrs. Gibson says: 'Little Charles was a terrible boy to read, and his custom was to sit with his book in his left hand, holding his wrist with his right hand, and constantly moving it up and down, and at the same time sucking his tongue. Sometimes Charles would come downstairs and say to me, "Now, Mary, clear the kitchen, we are going to have such a game", and then George Stroughill would come in with his Magic Lantern, and they would sing, recite, and perform parts of plays. Fanny and Charles often sang together at this time Fanny accompanying on the pianoforte. Though a good and eager reader in these days (about 1819) he had certainly not been to school, but had been thoroughly well taught at home by his aunt and mother, and' (adds Mrs. Gibson, speaking of the latter) 'she was a dear, good mother, and a fine woman.'

'A rather favourite piece for recitation by Charles at this time was "The Voice of the Sluggard" from Dr. Watts, and the little boy used to give it with great effect, and with *such* action and *such* attitudes.' . . .

Little Charles Dickens lives in Mrs. Gibson's memory as 'a lively boy of a good, genial, open disposition, and not quarrelsome, as most children are at times.' . . .

It was [at the Mitre Inn, Rochester] (the families of Mr. Dickens and Mr. Tribe being on visiting terms) that little Charles used occasionally to sing, in a clear treble voice, some of those old songs which he was always fond of, and which he has since recalled many times in his writings. Sea-songs were at this time his especial favourites, and at a memorable party here, Mr. Tribe well remembers Charles and his sister Fanny mounted on a dining table for a stage, singing what was then a popular duet [*Long Time I've Courted You, Miss*, some stanzas of which Langton quotes]. . . .

At birthday parties, Twelfth Night parties, and ordinary evening parties, at the Mitre, at Ordnance Terrace, and elsewhere, and in juvenile picnics in the hayfield in front of the terrace (now swallowed up by the Chatham Railway Station), the accomplishments of Charles and his sister were often utilised to amuse the company.

The mention of the comic singing to his friend, Mr. Forster, many long years afterwards, was accompanied with a modestly expressed fear that 'he must have been a horrible little nuisance to many unoffending grown-up people who were called upon to admire him' [*Life*, I, i, 6]. The evidence is, however, all the other way, and Mr. Tribe, Mrs. Gibson, Mrs. Godfrey (a sister of Mr. William Giles, his schoolmaster), and others, can remember perfectly that these songs were warmly applauded by all, and justly so, for they were admirably sung. . . .

Mr. Giles had been educated at Oxford, was an accomplished scholar, and a very conscientious, painstaking man. He seems to have been much struck (could not fail to have been so) with the bright appearance and unusual intelligence of his little pupil, and, giving him every encouragement in his power, even to making a companion of him of an evening, he was soon rewarded by the marked improvement that followed. Charles made rapid progress, and there is no doubt whatever that his wonderful knowledge and felicitous use of the English language in after life was, in a great measure, due to the careful training of Mr. Giles, who was widely known as a cultivated reader and elocutionist.

Mrs. Godfrey, the eldest sister of Mr. Giles, a venerable lady, now (1882) in her eighty-ninth year, residing at Liverpool, has kindly given me her recollections of Charles Dickens as a school-boy. She was some fifteen or sixteen years older than Charles, and was, consequently, well able to form an opinion of the appearance, manners, and capabilities of her brother's little pupil. Her recollection of him is, that he was a very handsome boy, with long curly hair of a light colour, and that he was of a very amiable, agreeable disposition. He was capital company even then (at nine or ten years of age), and she saw a great deal of him.

'Not Particularly Studious'

SEVERAL SCHOOLFELLOWS

The sources of this composite item are given in the Notes. When someone asked Dickens's father where his famous son had been educated, he replied – to Dickens's lasting joy – 'Why, indeed, Sir – ha! ha! – he may be said to have educated himself!' (*Life*, I, iii, 47). His schooling was indeed modest and interrupted. In Chatham he attended the Rev. William Giles's school; on his arrival in London (winter 1822–3) the family could not afford to send him to school. After the blacking-warehouse period – Feb to (?) June 1824 – an improvement in the family's fortunes enabled him to be sent to the Wellington House Academy – June 1824 to (?) Mar 1827. Schoolfellows from the Academy provide the material for this item. Dickens gives fictionalised accounts of it, and of its irascible headmaster Mr Jones, in Mr Creakle's school (*David Copperfield*) and in 'Our School' (*Reprinted Pieces*); see Philip Collins, *Dickens and Education* (1963) pp. 7–14, 114.

[Owen P. Thomas informed John Forster that he was Dickens's fellow dayboy at this 'Classical and Commercial Academy', and his playmate out of school.]

You will find a graphic sketch of the school by Mr. Dickens

himself in *Household Words* of 11 October 1851. The article is entitled 'Our School'. The names of course are feigned; but, allowing for slight colouring, the persons and incidents described are all true to life, and easily recognizable by any one who attended the school at the time. . . .

My recollection of Dickens whilst at school is that of a healthy looking boy, small but well-built, with a more than usual flow of spirits, inducing to harmless fun, seldom or ever I think to mischief, to which so many lads at that age are prone. I cannot recall anything that then indicated he would hereafter become a literary celebrity; but perhaps he was too young then. He usually held his head more erect than lads ordinarily do, and there was a general smartness about him. His week-day dress of jacket and trousers, I can clearly remember, was what is called pepper-and-salt; and instead of the frill that most boys of his age wore then, he had a turn-down collar, so that he looked less youthful in consequence. He invented what we termed a 'lingo', produced by the addition of a few letters of the same sound to every word; and it was our ambition, walking and talking thus along the street, to be considered foreigners.

[Elsewhere, Thomas writes:] When I at length met him again [in 1854], I found him as agreeable and friendly as he had been so many years before as a boy. Mr. Dickens intimated to me, when speaking of our old school, that it had been in his power to render service to Mr. Jones, as well as to Mr. Manville [the Latin master]. Mr. D. *never* omitted anything it was in his power to do for old friends, 'he was a man, take him for all in all' that we shall (hardly) 'look upon his like again'. . . .

I rather differ from Dr. Danson [see next extract] when he says that C. D. did not, he believes, learn Latin there, because all the senior boys (and C. D. became one) learned the elements of that language, or at least, were supposed to do so, there being an efficient Master always.[1]

[Another schoolfellow, Dr Henry Danson, also sent his reminiscences to Forster.]

Mr. Jones's school . . . was considered at the time a very superior sort of school, one of the best indeed in that part of London; but it was most shamefully mismanaged, and the boys made but very little progress. The proprietor, Mr. Jones, was a Welshman; a most ignorant fellow, and a mere tyrant; whose chief employment was to scourge the boys. Dickens has given a very lively account of this place in his paper entitled 'Our School', but it is very mythical in many respects, and more especially in the compliment he pays in it to himself. I do not remember that Dickens distinguished himself in any way, or carried off any prizes. My belief is that he did not learn Greek or Latin there, and you will remember there is no allusion to the classics in any of his writings. He was a handsome, curly-headed lad, full of animation and animal spirits, and probably was connected with every mischievous prank in the school. I do not think he came in for any of Mr. Jones's scourging propensity: in fact, together with myself, he was only a day-pupil, and with these there was a wholesome fear of tales being carried home to the parents. His personal appearance at that time is vividly brought home to me in the portrait of him taken a few years later by Mr. Laurence. He resided with his friends, in a very small house in a street leading out of Seymour-street, north of Mr. Judkin's chapel.

Depend on it he was quite a self-made man, and his wonderful knowledge and command of the English language must have been acquired by long and patient study after leaving his last school. . . .

His chief associates were, I think, Tobin, Mr. Thomas Bray, and myself. The first-named was his chief ally, and his acquaintance with him appears to have continued many years afterwards. At about that time Penny and Saturday magazines were published weekly, and were greedily read by us. We kept bees, white mice, and other living things clandestinely in our desks; and the mechanical arts were a good deal cultivated, in the shape of coach-building, and making pumps and boats, the motive power of which was the white mice.

I think at that time Dickens took to writing small tales, and we had a sort of club for lending and circulating them. Dickens was also very strong in using a sort of lingo, which made us quite unintelligible to bystanders. We were very strong, too, in theatricals. We mounted small theatres, and got up very gorgeous scenery to illustrate the *Miller and His Men*[2] and *Cherry and Fair Star*. I remember the present Mr. Beverley, the scene painter,[3] assisted us in this. Dickens was always a leader at these plays, which were occasionally presented with much solemnity before an audience of boys, and in the presence of the ushers. My brother, assisted by Dickens, got up the *Miller and His Men*, in a very gorgeous form. Master Beverley constructed the mill for us in such a way that it could tumble to pieces with the assistance of crackers. At one representation the fireworks in the last scene, ending with the destruction of the mill, were so very real that the police interfered, and knocked violently at the doors. Dickens's after taste for theatricals might have had its origin in these small affairs.

I quite remember Dickens on one occasion heading us in Drummond-street in pretending to be poor boys, and asking the passers-by for charity – especially old ladies; one of whom told us she 'had no money for beggar boys'. On these adventures, when the old ladies were quite staggered by the impudence of the demand, Dickens would explode with laughter and take to his heels.

I met him one Sunday morning shortly after he left the school, and we very piously attended the morning service at Seymour-street chapel. I am sorry to say Master Dickens did not attend in the slightest degree to the service, but incited me to laughter by declaring his dinner was ready and the potatoes would be spoiled, and in fact behaved in such a manner that it was lucky for us we were not ejected from the chapel.[4]

[John W. Bowden, another schoolfriend, sent a letter to the *Daily News* in 1871, recalling that] Dickens tried to learn music, and one day our music-master . . . sent for Mr. Jones, and gave Dickens up as a pupil, declaring it was in vain to try and teach him the piano, as he had no aptitude for music, and it was robbing his parents to continue giving him lessons; and thus abruptly ended Master Dickens's musical education, so far as I know. [Kitton, reprinting this letter in 1890, adds Georgina Hogarth's comment, 'It is quite a mistake that he had "no aptitude" for music. He was *very fond* of it in after-life, and had a most excellent ear and a good voice, but I daresay it would have been useless to have taught him music at school' – whatever she meant by that. Elsewhere Bowden wrote that] Dickens and I occupied adjoining desks, and I remember we jointly used to issue, – written on scraps of copy-book paper – almost weekly, what we called *Our Newspaper*, lending it to read on payment of marbles and pieces of slate pencil. This paper used to contain sundry bits of boyish fun – the following I recollect –

Lost. Out of a gentleman's waistcoat pocket, an acre of land; the finder shall be rewarded on restoring the same.

Lost. By a boy with a long red nose, and grey eyes, a very bad temper. Whoever has found the same may keep it, as the owner is better without it.

The 'Lingo' mentioned by Mr. Forster, as being invented by Dickens, was what we call *gibberish*, and was spoken before Dickens came to the school.[5]

[An anonymous 'School-fellow and Friend' remembered that the Dickenses] appeared to be in rather poor circumstances. . . . My recollection of Dickens is of a rather short, stout, jolly-looking youth, very fresh coloured, and full of fun, and given to laugh immoderately without any apparent sufficient reason.

He was not particularly studious, nor did he show any special signs of ability, although as a boy he would at times indite short tales; as for education, he really received hardly any; Wellington House School in Mornington Place (corner of Granby Street), Hampstead Road, where Dickens was a day scholar and I a boarder, certainly absorbed almost all the respectable youth of that then sparsely inhabited neighbourhood, but the state of proficiency was not very high. . . .

As a slight trait of character, I may cite his appropriation of an old joke; he had on a very much used pair of inexpressibles, and one of us remarking, 'Dickens, those trousers are well worn; it is about time you gave them a rest', he replied good-humouredly, 'Ah, yes! You are right, it *is* a long time since they had a *nap*.'

Referring to the more especially excellent delineations of characters in low life that we find in his writings, I remember being at a juvenile party in Johnson Street, and he, quite a boy, singing the then popular song of 'The Cat's Meat Man', which he delivered with great energy and action, his tone and manner displaying the full zest with which he appreciated and entered into all the vulgarity of the composition.

His well-known liking for theatricals was also early developed. I have no recollection of any performances before the ushers and pupils, and Beverley was not (as has been stated) at the school; but at the age of about 14 Dickens took parts at the small play-house in Catherine Street, of which a Mr. Goodwin was then proprietor, and which was much frequented by amateurs, who would pay 15s. or 20s. for a leading *rôle*, such as Othello, etc., the minor characters being charged proportionately less. . . .

The depressing and melancholy views of school life that pervade his works can scarcely have resulted from his own experiences (at all events with us), for he was one to enter into all the pranks and fun of the place. It is true that Jones, the principal, was what might be termed 'a thrasher', and without much discrimination in the distribution of chastisement; he was a Welshman of irascible temper and very excitable. . . . Sometimes he would charge down the school-room, striking right and left with his cane, and I well remember, as a sample of his cruelty, [the case of] a stoutish boy who had the habit of following with his tongue the strokes of his pen in his copy-book. He wore tight trousers, and in stooping over the desk offered to Jones an irresistible temptation, the latter would fetch his vezoe (?), advance stealthily and administer a swinging cut, and when the poor lad started up in pain would shout out, 'Ah! ah! had you there; you can't rub that off; you can't rub it off.' Dickens, however, was not one who suffered much from his tyranny.[6]

NOTES

1. *Life*, I, iii, 40–2; Robert Langton, *The Childhood and Youth of Charles Dickens* (1912) p. 88.

2. Isaac Pocock's *The Miller and His Men* (1813) was the most famous Gothic melodrama. Dickens retained a nostalgic fondness for it, shattered when he saw a revival of it in the 1860s; see below, II, 230.

3. William Roxby Beverley (1814?–1889) was the best-known scene-painter of his generation, notably at Drury Lane. But another schoolfriend, quoted below, denies that Beverley was a contemporary of Dickens's at Wellington House Academy.

4. *Life*, I, iii, 43–5. For Dickens's appreciation of Danson's 'modest and manly letter', see his reply, 5 May 1864 (*N*, III, 387, or in Forster's footnote).

5. *Pen and Pencil*, p. 128 and note; Langton, *Childhood and Youth*, p. 89.

6. 'A School-fellow and Friend', 'Recollections of Charles Dickens', *Dkn*, VII (1911) 229–30.

A Smart Young Clerk

EDWARD BLACKMORE AND GEORGE LEAR

From their reminiscences in *Pen and Pencil*, pp. 10, 129–33. Dickens's first job (spring 1827 to winter 1828–9) was as a clerk in the office of Ellis and Blackmore, solicitors. Edward Blackmore, the junior partner, knew Dickens's parents, who

asked him to give the boy a post. A briefer version of his reminiscences appears in
Life, I, iii, 46. See W.J.Carlton, 'Mr Blackmore Engages an Office Boy', *Dkn*,
XLVIII (1952) 162–7. George Lear was a fellow clerk.

[Edward Blackmore writes:] Charles, a youth about
fifteen, . . . had just left school and was exceedingly good-looking
and clever . . . and the boy's manners were so prepossessing that I
agreed to take him as a clerk. . . . Why he left [our employment] I
do not remember, but fancy he disliked the drudgery of the office,
and felt, perhaps, equal to a better occupation. . . .

He was very fond of theatricals, and frequently accompanied a
fellow clerk named Potter (with whom he much associated) to a
penny theatre in or near the Strand. This Potter was one of his
characters in the 'Boz' sketch entitled 'Making a Night of it'.

His knowledge of London was wonderful, for he could describe
the position of every shop in any of the West End streets.

After he left me I saw him occasionally in the Lord Chancellor's
Court, taking notes of cases as a reporter. I then lost sight of him
until his *Pickwick* made its appearance. Soon after his marriage I
met him in the green-room in Covent Garden Theatre (it was the
first night Her present Majesty went in state to the theatre); he
passed me two or three times in the room without taking any notice,
and it appeared to me that he had no wish to recognize me.

Some persons have imagined that the character of Mr. Perker in
Pickwick was intended for myself. I do not think so, but I do think it
was for my partner, Mr. Ellis, who was some ten years older and
certainly had some of Mr. Perker's peculiarities, – he was especially
an inveterate snuff-taker. His amusing description of the various
classes of clerks in a solicitor's office in the 30th Chapter of his
Pickwick was taken from life. I can distinctly identify them with the
clerks we then had, two of whom are now living.

I well remember a convivial occasion when I invited all the clerks
to dine with me. Potter was there and guilty of a little excess; he did
not come to the office for a couple of days afterwards, and when he
came Dickens chaffed him with having taken too much wine, but he
insisted upon it that his indisposition did not arise from the wine, but
'*It was the salmon.*' Dickens never forgot this, and has immortalised
the observation in the 7th Chapter of *Pickwick*.

I feel persuaded that the character of Newman Noggs, in *Nicholas
Nickleby*, was taken from a man named Newman Knott, who was in
the habit of coming to the office weekly for an allowance made him

by his friends, and whose eccentricities and personal history were a source of great amusement to the clerks.

With me it is now a matter of great personal regret that I did not take any steps to renew my intimacy with the great novelist in after years. It might have led to the identity of many scenes and characters portrayed in his works which had attracted his early attention while he was with me. He was a universal favourite, and one client in particular, a gentleman (now dead) in extensive practice in Sussex, was especially anxious to take him from me; had I consented, it is more than likely the boy's thoughts and pursuits would have been diverted into a different channel, and the world have lost the benefit of his wonderful genius. Doubtless the varied scenes of life observable in a solicitor's office in London at that time made a great impression on his youthful mind, and constituted the basis of his future success.

[George Lear writes:] His appearance was altogether prepossessing. He was a rather short but stout-built boy, and carried himself very upright – his head well up – and the idea he gave me was that he must have been drilled by a military instructor. His dress, in some measure, perhaps contributed to this impression. He wore a frock-coat (or surtout, as it was then generally called) buttoned up, of dark blue cloth, trousers to match, and (as was the fashion at that time), buttoned with leather straps over the boots; black neckerchief, but no shirt collar showing. His complexion was of a healthy pink, – almost glowing, – rather a round face, fine forehead, beautiful expressive eyes full of animation, a firmly-set mouth, a good-sized rather straight nose, but not at all too large. His hair was a beautiful brown, and worn long, as was then the fashion. His cap was like the undress cap of an officer in the army, of some shining material with a narrow shining leather strap running round the point of the chin. His appearance was altogether decidedly military. I always thought he must have adopted this from his having lived at Chatham. He looked very clean and well fed and cared for. . . .

Dickens took great interest in [the old woman who used to sweep out the offices] and would mimic her manner of speech, her ways, her excuses, etc., to the very life. He could imitate, in a manner that I have never heard equalled, the low population of the streets of London in all their varieties, whether mere loafers or sellers of fruit, vegetables, or anything else. He could also excel in mimicking the popular singers of that day, whether comic or patriotic; as to his acting, he could give us Shakespeare by the ten minutes, and imitate all the leading actors of that time. His father, he said, was intimate with many of them, among whom I particularly recollect Young, Macready, J. P. Harley, etc.[1] He told me he had often taken parts in amateur theatricals before he came to us.

Having been in London two years, I thought I knew something of town, but after a little talk with Dickens I found that I knew nothing. He knew it all from Bow to Brentford.

Dickens describes the clerks in a lawyer's office in his *Pickwick Papers* at the beginning of the 30th Chapter. I am, I have no doubt, the Articled Clerk, and he is the Office Lad in his first surtout. Potter, whom I found in the office when I entered, was the salaried clerk of *Pickwick*. He was a fairly good clerk, and knew all the public offices well, but I doubt if he ever walked about London much with Dickens. He unfortunately became stage-struck, and was thus brought in contact with low, dissolute company. The theatre he became attached to was a poor place called the Minor Theatre, in Catherine Street, Strand. . . . Potter, in my opinion, is decidedly the Jingle of *Pickwick*. . . .

Another character which the novelist made famous is the Little Old Lady of the Court of Chancery, Miss Flite, as described in *Bleak House*. I remember her well; she was always hovering in or about the Chancery Courts, generally in Court. I understood she was the victim of some prolonged Chancery suit which had turned her head.

Our office was what is termed an Agency Office, that is, we were concerned as London agents for solicitors living in the country. Dickens soon became very handy in doing the work at the public offices, and the old clerks who presided over the business in them, both Chancery and Common Law, came in for his imitations and descriptions. . . .

Dickens, probably surmising that I had a great interest in him, used to tell me, when we were alone, about his family. His father, he informed me, was a first-rate shorthand writer on Gurney's system, and a capital reporter. . . . Dickens much resembled his father, whom I saw two or three times, and observed that he had the appearance of an intelligent and clever man. . . .

I cannot close this memoir without stating that during the time young Charley Dickens was in our office, an angry or unkind word never passed between us.

NOTE

1. Either Lear was misremembering here, or Dickens had been 'shooting a line'. There is not the slightest reason to believe that John Dickens was intimate, at this time, with any of these actors.

Prospects Improving

JOHN PAYNE COLLIER

From *An Old Man's Diary: Forty Years Ago* (1872) pt iv, pp. 12–15. Collier (1789–1883), scholar and journalist, was asked (in 1833, he says, but 1834 is more probable) to help Dickens obtain a post on the *Morning Chronicle*, a much superior journal to the *True Sun*, on which he was then working. Dickens's uncle, John Barrow, assured Collier that his 'clever nephew' was not only a good reporter but also 'cheerful company and a good singer of a comic song' – as appeared when they met over a dinner to discuss the matter.

. . . many comic songs were sung . . . two by Dickens, who would not make the attempt until late in the evening, and after a good deal of pressing. One of them was called *The Dandy Dog's-meat Man*, then much in vogue with the lower classes, and the other was an effusion by Dickens himself [beginning 'Sweet Betsy Ogle']. . . . We were all very merry, if not very wise, unless merriment be taken as another sort of wisdom. . . . I may here add, that soon after [his appointment to the *Chronicle*] I observed a great difference in C. D.'s appearance and dress; for he had bought a new hat and a very handsome blue cloak, with black velvet facings, the corner of which he threw over his shoulder *à l' Espagnol*. I overtook him in the Adelphi, and we walked together through Hungerford Market, where we followed a coal-heaver, who carried his little rosy but grimy child looking over his shoulder; and C. D. bought a halfpenny worth of cherries, and, as we went along, he gave them one by one to the little fellow without the knowledge of the father. C. D. seemed quite as much pleased as the child. He informed me, as we walked through it, that he knew *Hunger*ford Market well, laying unusual stress on the two first syllables. He did not affect to conceal the difficulties he and his family had had to contend against.

The Fastest Shorthand Reporter in London

CHARLES MACKAY

From his recollection in *Pen and Pencil*, pp. 133–5, Dickens was a reporter on the *Morning Chronicle* from August 1834 to November 1836. It was the leading Liberal newspaper, its editor John Black being, as J. S. Mill said, the first journalist to carry 'criticism and the spirit of reform into the details of English institutions' and introduce 'Bentham's opinions on legal and judicial reform into newspaper discussion'–*Letters*, ed. H. S. R. Elliott (1910) II, 14–15; *Autobiography* (1873) pp.89–90. On this period of Dickens's career see W. J. Carlton, *Charles Dickens, Shorthand Writer* (1926). Charles Mackay (1814–89), journalist and popular poet, first met Dickens when he (Mackay) joined the *Chronicle* as sub-editor. Some further reminiscences of Dickens appear in his memoirs, *Forty Years' Recollections* (1877) and *Through the Long Day* (1887).

I was then in my twenty-second year, and Mr. Dickens was two years my senior. We were both of us comparatively unknown in literature, but Dickens had acquired some reputation as the author of some lively sketches which he contributed to the *Evening Chronicle* – an offshoot of the *Morning Chronicle* – under the celebrated signature of 'Boz'. He was one of the twelve parliamentary reporters of the *Chronicle*, and had the reputation of being the most rapid, the most accurate, and the most trustworthy reporter then engaged on the London press, and was consequently in high favour with his employers. He earned a salary of five guineas a week in that capacity, supplemented by an extra salary of two guineas for his brilliant sketches of London life and manners, of which he contributed one per week to the *Evening Chronicle*. . . . My remembrance of Charles Dickens at that time is that of a fresh, handsome, genial young man, with a profusion of brown hair, a bright eye, and a hearty manner – rather inclined to what was once called 'dandyism' in his attire, and to a rather exuberant display of jewellery on his vest and on his fingers.

It was part of my duty as sub-editor to confer with Mr. Hogarth and Mr. Black on the employment of the Parliamentary reporters during the recess, when Parliament was not in session, and to utilise their services in the general work of the paper, – such as attendance at public meetings, reviews of books, or notices of new plays at the theatres. Mr. Black desired to spare Mr. Dickens as much as possible from all work of this kind, having the highest opinion of his original genius, and a consequent dislike to employ him on what he considered the very inferior work of criticism. 'Any fool,' he said, in his usual broad Scotch, 'can pass judgement, more or less just or unjust, on a book or a play – but "Boz" can do better things; he can create works for other people to criticize. Besides, he has never been a greater reader of books or plays, and knows but little of them, but has spent his time in studying life. Keep "Boz" in reserve for great occasions. He will *aye* be ready for them.'[1]

The great occasions for reporting speeches in the recess were far rarer in that remote day than they are now, but whenever they occurred, Dickens and his friend Thomas Beard[2] (the two best reporters of the time) were invariably employed by the *Chronicle*, especially if the *Chronicle* desired, as it always did, to beat all competitors, and especially its great and very real rival *The Times*, in the priority of its intelligence and in the fullness and accuracy of its reports. And 'Boz' and Beard were never found lacking in zeal and ability – or success. . . .

[Dickens abandoned journalism as soon as the success of *Pickwick* made this possible.] But the personal intercourse between Mr. Dickens and myself, which commenced in the *Morning Chronicle* office, suffered no abatement until the end of his too short career, and our friendship not only remained unbroken, but grew with the progress of years. Its remembrance remains as one of the pleasantest episodes of my literary life.

NOTES

1. Dickens remained affectionately grateful to John Black (1783–1855). 'Dear old Black!' he wrote in 1870, 'my first hearty out-and-out appreciator' (*Life*, I, iv, 65). Charles Mackay was so impressed by Black's conviction of Dickens's future greatness that he begged and preserved an autograph letter of his (to George Hogarth, 20 Jan 1835, *P*, I, 54–5): see *Forty Years' Recollections* (1877) I, 80.

2. Thomas Beard (1807–91), journalist, had recommended Dickens for appointment to the *Chronicle*. 'There never *was* such a short-hand writter', he often told Forster (*Life*, I, ii, 49). 'Dickens's oldest friend', he has been called; he was best man at Dickens's wedding and godfather to his eldest son, and a friend from 1831–2

until his death. Francis Beard, his brother, became Dickens's family doctor. For family reminiscences of Dickens, see 'Some Recollections of Yesterday' (by Francis Beard's son Nathaniel), *Temple Bar*, CI (1894) 315–39; also W. J. Carlton, ' "Boz" and the Beards', *Dkn*, LVIII (1962) 9–21.

Courtship and Young Marriage

CATHERINE AND MARY HOGARTH

(1), (3) and (4) from L. C. Staples, 'New Letters of Mary Hogarth and Her Sister Catherine', *Dkn*, LXIII (1867) 75–80; (2) from Kathleen Tillotson, 'A Letter from Mary Hogarth', *TLS*, 23 Dec. 1960. Dickens met Catherine Hogarth (1815–79), daughter of the Scottish man-of-letters and journalist George Hogarth, in the winter of 1834–5, and married her on 2 April 1836. Her sister Mary (born 1819) lived with them, on and off, after the marriage, and on 7 May 1837 died–very suddenly – in Dickens's arms, to his enormous distress. All these letters were addressed to a cousin, Mary Scott Hogarth; punctuation, etc., *sic* throughout.

(1) *Catherine Hogarth, 11 Feb 1835*. Speaking of dancing. Papa – Mamma and I were at a Ball on Saturday last and where do you think at Mr Dicken's. It was in honour of his birthday. It was a batchelors party at his own chambers. His Mother and sisters presided. one of them a very pretty girl who sings beautifully – it was a delightful party I enjoyed it very much – Mr Dickens improves very much on acquaintance he is very gentlemanly and pleasant . . . .

(2) *Mary Hogarth, 15 May 1836*. I have just returned home from spending a most delightfully happy month with dearest Catherine in her own house! I only wish you could see her in it, and sincerely hope you may some day or other, not far distant, she makes a most capital housekeeper and is as happy as the day is long – I think they are more devoted than ever since their marriage if that be possible – I am sure you would be delighted with him if you knew him he is such a nice creature and so clever he is courted and made up to by all literary Gentleman, and has more to do in that way than he can well manage . . . .

(3) *Mary Hogarth, 26 Jan. 1837, shortly after Catherine's first confinement.*

Poor Kate! it has been a dreadful trial for her. . . . Every time she sees her Baby she has a fit of crying and keeps constantly saying she is sure he will not care for her now she is not able to nurse him. I think time will be the only effectual cure for her – could she but forget this she has everything in this world to make her comfortable and happy – her husband is kindness itself to her and is constantly studying her comfort in every thing – his literary career gets more and more prosperous every day and he is courted and flattered on every side by all the great folks of this great City – his time is so completely taken up that it is quite a favour for the Literary Gentlemen to get him to write for them.

(4) *Catherine Dickens, 30 May 1837.* Oh dear Mary what pleasure it would give me to see you in my own house, and how proud I shall be to make you acquainted with Charles. The fame of his talents are now known over all the world, but his kind affectionate heart is dearer to me than all. I am sure you would like him . . . .

Boz Emergent; or, the Young Lion

JOHN FORSTER AND OTHERS

Sketches by Boz (first series) appeared in February 1836, and enjoyed considerable success, and *Pickwick Papers* (serialised April 1836 to November 1837) was soon, after a slow start, one of the literary sensations of the century. By the end of 1836 Dickens had also seen two stage works produced, *The Strange Gentleman* and *The Village Coquettes*, had published a second series of *Sketches by Boz*, and had agreed to edit the new monthly *Bentley's Miscellany*, publication of which began in January 1837. Still only twenty-four, he was the literary darling of the nation; and, no recluse, he soon became a familiar figure in society and in literary and artistic circles. These extracts indicate what impression he created in his first years of fame. One of the best-known early descriptions of Dickens – Thomas Carlyle's in 1840 – is quoted, and criticised, by Thomas Adolphus Trollope (below, i, 71–2).

[John Forster (1812–76), journalist, critic and man of letters, soon to become Dickens's most intimate friend and adviser, and later his official biographer, was already well established in literary London when he first met Dickens in late 1836 or early 1837. 'I remember vividly the impression then made upon me', he recalls in the *Life*.]

Very different was his face in those days from that which photography has made familiar to the present generation. A look of youthfulness first attracted you, and then a candour and openness of expression which made you sure of the qualities within. The features were very good. He had a capital forehead, a firm nose with full wide nostrils, eyes wonderfully beaming with intellect and running over with humour and cheerfulness, and a rather prominent mouth strongly marked with sensibility. The head was altogether well formed and symmetrical, and the air and carriage of it were extremely spirited. The hair so scant and grizzled in later days was then of a rich brown and most luxuriant abundance, and the bearded face of his last two decades had hardly a vestige of hair or whisker; but there was that in the face as I first recollect it which no time could change, and which remained implanted on it unalterably to the last. This was the quickness, keenness, and practical power, the eager, restless, energetic outlook on each several feature, that seemed to tell so little of a student or writer of books, and so much of a man of action and business in the world. Light and motion flashed from every part of it. 'It was as if made of steel,' was said of it, four or five years after the time to which I am referring, by a most original and delicate observer, the late Mrs. Carlyle. 'What a face is his to meet in a drawing-room!' wrote Leigh Hunt to me, the morning after I made them known to each other. 'It has the life and soul in it of fifty human beings.' In such sayings are expressed not alone the restless and resistless vivacity and force of which I have spoken, but that also which lay beneath them of steadiness and hard endurance.[1]

[The philosopher and political economist John Stuart Mill (1806–73) was an eminent Victorian whose path rarely crossed Dickens's, but in 1837 he met him at the home of W. C. Macready, on whom see below, 1, 28–32.]

I saw Dickens yesterday; he reminds me of Carlyle's picture of Camille Desmoulins, and his 'face of dingy blackguardism irradiated with genius.' Such a phenomenon does not often appear in a lady's drawing-room.[2]

[Dickens's relations with his publishers were not always easy, for reasons too complex to summarise here: see Robert L. Patten, *Charles Dickens and his Publishers* (1978). Even as a young author he showed a fierce sense of what he regarded as his rights, as the

publisher Richard Bentley (1794–1871) found when he called upon
Dickens to remonstrate with him over his attempt to have a contract
revised in his favour. Dickens, in correspondence on this matter, had
a richly abusive vocabulary for describing Bentley – 'the Robber',
'the Burlington Street Brigand', and, borrowing Bill Sikes's phrase
for Fagin, 'the infernal, rich, plundering, thundering old Jew'. In a
manuscript, 'A Retrospective Sketch of Mr Bentley's Connection
with Mr. Dickens', the aggrieved publisher offers his account of
their encounter.]

On the day appointed (12 August [1837]) I saw Mr. Dickens at
his residence in Doughty St. I approached him in the usual friendly
manner, but was met on his side with an air of coldness and
restraint. In reference to his proposition I observed that although he
must be well aware that the Agreement entered into between us was
a deliberate act & like all contracts mutually binding, & that had
his own popularity declined I could have had no claim whatever for
a reduction in the consideration I had agreed to pay him –
nevertheless I was willing to *present* him with the additional Sums
which he specified for the two novels, but that I could not consent to
take a limited interest in these two novels, the entire copyright of
which I had already agreed for. Moreover I objected to *Oliver Twist*
being considered as his 2nd. novel on the ground that portions of
that work had appeared in the Miscellany and the Copyright had
therefore become my property as far as was already published.
Upon this he exhibited considerable irritability, threatening
amongst other intemperate expressions that he would not write the
novel at all. His object was evidently to provoke me, failing in which
attempt he proposed to refer the matter to the arbitration of
Mr. Serjeant Talfourd.[3]

[Mrs Frances Trollope (1780–1863), novelist, and mother of the
novelists Anthony and Thomas Adolphus, first met Dickens at a
social gathering in March 1838.]
. . . We met *Boz*, who desired to be presented to me. I had a great
deal of talk with him. He is extremely lively and intelligent, has the
appearance of being *very* young, and although called excessively
shy, seemed not at all averse from conversation.[4]

[In August 1838, Dickens made his first visit to Holland House, the
great Whig gathering-place. Its formidable hostess, Lady Holland
(1770–1845), with whom Dickens later became quite friendly, had

condescendingly enquired in advance, of Bulwer Lytton, 'if Boz was presentable' (*P*, 1, 412n.). Her husband, Henry Fox, third Baron Holland (1773–1846), reported to his sister:] We have had the author of *Oliver Twist* here. He is a very young man of 26, very unobtrusive, yet not shy, intelligent in countenance, and altogether prepossessing. It was too large a company of strangers to bring out the fun which must be in him.

[Next year Lord Holland's sister, Caroline Fox, met him there, and] was much struck with him, and liked every thing but the intolerable dandyism of his dress, which is such as he might, and I believe has humorously described himself; but it will probably wear away with his youth. He does not look more than 25 and is undoubtedly under 30. His countenance, I think, beautiful, because blended with its intelligence there is so much expression of goodness.[5]

[The great banking heiress Angela Burdett Coutts, later Baroness Burdett Coutts (1814–1906), who became an intimate friend of Dickens, first met him in 1838 or 1839 (date uncertain: see *P*, 1, 559n.). Years later she told her secretary, C. C. Osborne, that] of her first meeting with Dickens [she] retained a vivid impression. She described to me the impression made upon her by his restlessness, vivacity, impetuosity, generous impulses, earnestness and frank sincerity. He looked more a man of action than a man of letters; alert, eager, and rather overpoweringly energetic. His impetuosity was a failing for which he was often to be taken to task by the two ladies, Miss Burdett Coutts and [her companion] Miss Meredith. . . . I suppose few men have ever had a more expressive and animated face when talking. I cited Leigh Hunt's description of it once to the Baroness: – 'It has the life and soul of fifty human beings' : – and she replied that the phrase was a very true one.[6]

NOTES

1. *Life*, II, i, 84–5, 88.
2. J. S. Mill, letter of 12 July 1837, *Earlier Letters*, ed. Francis E. Mineka (1963), I, 343. Camille Desmoulins is thus described in Carlyle's *The French Revolution*, IV, iv.
3. *P*, 1, 292–3n. Bentley eventually surrendered, and a new agreement was signed the following month. There were further quarrels with Bentley over Dickens's editing of his *Miscellany*, and relations were finally severed in July 1840. Dickens's grievances were real, Robert Patten remarks, but 'One cannot help

feeling that Dickens behaved outrageously at times' during this protracted and acrimonious quarrel (*Charles Dickens and His Publishers*, p. 86).

4. Frances Eleanor Trollope, *Frances Trollope: Her Life and Literary Work* (1895) I, 295.

5. Lord Ilchester, *Chronicles of Holland House* (1937) pp. 240–1.

6. Quoted by Clara Burdett Patterson, *Angela Burdett Coutts and the Victorians* (1953) p. 151. Dickens became an energetic almoner of some of the immense funds which she disbursed to charity: see *Letters from Charles Dickens to Angela Burdett Coutts 1841–1865*, ed. Edgar Johnson (1953).

The Young Novelist at Work and Play

HENRY BURNETT

From his reminiscences in *Pen and Pencil*, pp. 136–43; Supplement, pp: 6–8. Henry Burnett (1811–93), singer and music teacher, played in Dickens's *Village Coquettes*, April 1837, and married his beloved sister Fanny in September 1837; he had known her since 1832. He provides the only substantial family account of Dickens in these early Furnival's Inn and Doughty Street days. A few years later he and Fanny experienced a religious conversion, becoming strict Congregationalists; he abandoned the stage, and never again entered a theatre.

[Discussing the disputed authorship of 'The Loving Ballad of Lord Bateman', Burnett mentions Dickens's proclivity, especially in these earlier years, for singing serio-comic songs to his friends. Dickens's performances were] highly successful, and gave great pleasure even to the most sedate amongst his friends, for it was his habit to give very amusing, droll, and clever sketches of character between the verses, comic and quaint, but never vulgar. He had no vulgarity in his refined nature. If he ever had a double meaning, the half-hidden one, when it floated to the surface, was always transparent and pure, thoughtful and laughable. Yet one never afterwards felt a little sense of shame for having laughed. . . .

I send you his Portrait [by Samuel Laurence; the 'you' is of course Kitton]. Some may doubt the truth of it, and say it is too smooth, the thoughtful markings on the face of such a writer being absent. The strongly-marked tell-tale lines of untiring energy, which announced to the world that he was burning himself out, began to appear unhappily too soon. It was no great length of time after the date of that Portrait [1838], when on one occasion at Devonshire Terrace we were going down to dinner, Dickens first with a lady (whom no doubt he was making happy), when Maclise, following in the rear, called out, 'Why, Dickens, you are becoming quite bald!' 'And no wonder,' Dickens replied, 'for my little ones have contracted a habit of, day by day, feeding on their father's brains, and you are marking the result.' Without hesitancy I affirm of this Portrait that it was, and is, the 'Boz' who wrote *Pickwick*. It is a *facsimile* of the Dickens who married Miss Catherine Hogarth. I can see the same face now helping his young wife out of the carriage after the wedding, and taking her up the steps of the house of quiet, intellectual, unobtrusive Mr. Hogarth in the Fulham Road, then standing opposite orchards and gardens extending as far as the eye could reach. Her sister Fanny thought this Portrait a perfect likeness. . . .

Charles Dickens was brimfull of geniality and sociability. He was reliable and self-reliant. Nothing seemed more pleasurable to him than to be amongst his friends. He never lost an opportunity of doing a kind act, or giving pleasure. One night in Doughty Street, Mrs. Charles Dickens, my wife and myself were sitting round the fire, cosily enjoying a chat, when Dickens, for some purpose, came suddenly from his study into the room. 'What, you here!' he exclaimed; 'I'll bring down my work.' It was his monthly portion of *Oliver Twist* for *Bentley's*. In a few minutes he returned, manuscript in hand, and while he was pleasantly discoursing he employed himself in carrying to a corner of the room a little table, at which he seated.himself and re-commenced his writing. We, at his bidding, went on talking our little nothings – he, every now and then (the feather of his pen still moving rapidly from side to side), put in a cheerful interlude. It was interesting to watch, upon the sly, the mind and the muscles working (or, if you please, *playing*) in company, as new thoughts were being dropped upon the paper. And to note the working brow, the set mouth, with the tongue slightly pressed against the closed lips, as was his habit.[1] . . .

It was natural to Dickens, wheresoever he might be, to aim at making people happy. He was a first-rate 'Master of Ceremonies;' nothing seemed to flag when he was present. Nay! I do recall one evening, when he had been the life of it, that he almost suddenly withdrew within himself. Perhaps he was settling the arrangement of a new chapter. However, the whole party gradually became silent, when after a few minutes he very slowly and gently said, 'Will – somebody – just sniff?' It is a little thing to repeat, but his manner of saying it answered the purpose, broke the silence, and produced a 'babel.'

It always struck me that Dickens was most delightfully companionable and happy in his own home. He was always a true man. Often away from home they tried to make him a 'lion', an intended compliment which he resented and hated. He never left his own social nature in his study with his manuscript, but always brought himself into the family circle. . . .

Soon after this he removed from Doughty Street to Devonshire Terrace, and his house became a general meeting place for men of mark, especially literary men and artists. It was a house for freedom of thought, and – with limitation – for freedom of action. He was always the same. His nature was transparent; you found him to-day as you would find him to-morrow. If he felt the lead within it was sounding his own depth, and the surface was calm. You never saw in him the pride of success; he never affected to be even what he must have known he was. In conversations about other favoured men there often appeared a gleam of pleasure, but none could detect the faintest scowl of jealousy or envy, nor do I believe it was ever felt within. He had a firm gentleness that was attractive, but he was as strong as a lion to hold his own when he had to choose between what he thought right and what he thought doubtful. I have been out with him at night alone when he was out for a purpose, and I look back – I have done so again and again in the past – to aid my memory as to the moral part of his nature, and I fail to remember any act or word that made me hesitate, or that allowed me to nurse the smallest doubt, as to his purity of thought or purity of action. Even so early his aim seemed to be to lift the fallen, to help the unfortunate, and to tussle with every oppressor. . . .

It was a fact not unknown to his friends that he was not always alone in his study, but lived at times, day after day, with his own creations. Himself has said that Little Nell was an object of his love – that he mourned her loss for a month after her death, and felt as if one of his own dear ones had left a vacant chair. I remember a friend once saying, 'Dickens, which of your own productions do you like the best?' To which he replied, 'It is said that if a parent's affection is drawn towards one child more powerfully than towards the rest, it is most likely the one most sickly, the one who has a feeble life. Having said this, I will further state, that I feel drawn most tenderly towards *The Old Curiosity Shop.*' . . .

In the comparatively early days of Charles Dickens his untiring energy became almost a snare, causing many friends to fear he was beginning to burn his candle at both ends. His habit, for a limited time, was to retire to his study after supper – about ten o'clock – and work till one, as a rule; but now and then the rule would be forgotten through the interest taken by him in his work, when the study-door would remain locked on the wrong side for his bed until two, and sometimes three o'clock in the morning, he feeling that the action of his mind – or the essence of it – was impeded in the daytime, that it could be brought with greater ease under control when silence reigned within and without, and there was freedom from noise, light, heat, distraction by a multitude of callers, and other hindrances.[2] A portion of the daytime he would take for what he, laughingly, called his 'daily constitutional', and this he said, when possible, was a ten miles' walk. Once, on returning with him from a tramp over Hampstead Heath, and, after refreshing ourselves at the delightful little inn, back through Highgate, he looked the personification of energy, which seemed to ooze from every pore as from some hidden reservoir; and as we got towards home a watcher looking at him might have said, 'He is seeing written in the air, "Excelsior", at every turn on the way.'

NOTES

1. Neither writing at night, nor writing in company, was his habit after these first years of his career. See next note.

2. Kitton here prints, as a footnote, Georgina Hogarth's comment 'In reference to this paragraph, you must put it "in *very, very* early days",; for within *my* memory (which dates from 1842) of his habits, he rarely wrote in the night. Occasionally, under some very great pressure of work, he would write for *one* night. He was most careful of his health in every way.' For most of his career, the mornings were his normal time for writing.

'Completely outside Philosophy, Science, etc.'

G. H. LEWES

From his 'Dickens in Relation to Criticism', *Fortnightly Review* xvii (1872) 141–54. George Henry Lewes (1817–78), journalist, magazine editor, miscellaneous writer, and (from 1854) consort of the future 'George Eliot', was a man of many parts – 'an *airy* loose-tongued merry-hearted being, with more sail than ballast', in Carlyle's opinion – *New Letters*, ed. Alexander Carlyle (1904), ii, 93. He studied medicine and philosophy in France and Germany, tried professional acting, became a stock-dramatist at the Lyceum, wrote two novels, became a leading reviewer and dramatic critic and intellectual and scientific journalist, published books on the history of philosophy, the physiology of common life, Goethe, animal behaviour, problems of mind and life, and other such topics. Plenty of sail, as Carlyle said. He met Dickens in 1837–8 (see *P*, i, 403n.), later performed in his amateur theatricals, and, though he never became an intimate, Dickens had 'an old and great regard' for him (*Life*, vi, vi, 531). Critically, they crossed swords over the *Bleak House* spontaneous-combustion episode; and the posthumous appraisal from which these reminiscences are cited greatly riled Forster, as references in the *Life* show. See essays by Gordon S. Haight on Dickens and Lewes, *Nineteenth Century Fiction*, x (1955) 53–63, and *PMLA*, lxxi (1956) 166–79. For George Eliot's views on Dickens, see below, i, 100 and 112.

. . . Dickens once declared to me that every word said by his characters was distinctly *heard* by him; I was at first not a little puzzled to account for the fact that he could hear language so utterly unlike the language of real feeling, and not be aware of its preposterousness; but the surprise vanished when I thought of the phenomena of hallucination. . . .

My acquaintance with him began soon after the completion of *Pickwick*. Something I had written on that book pleased him, and caused him to ask me to call on him.[1] . . . He was then living in Doughty Street; and those who remember him at that period will understand the somewhat disturbing effect produced on my enthusiasm for the new author by the sight of his bookshelves, on which were ranged nothing but three-volume novels and books of travel, all obviously the presentation copies from authors and publishers, with none of the treasures of the bookstall, each of which has its history, and all giving the collection its individual physiognomy. A man's library expresses much of his hidden life. I did not expect to find a bookworm, nor even a student, in the marvellous 'Boz'; but nevertheless this collection of books was a shock. He shortly came in, and his sunny presence quickly dispelled all misgivings. He was then, as to the last, a delightful companion, full of sagacity as well as animal spirits; but I came away more impressed with the fulness of life and energy than with any sense of distinction. I believe I only saw him once more before I went to Germany, and two years had elapsed when next we met. While waiting in his library (in Devonshire Terrace) I of course glanced at the books. The well-known paper boards of the three-volume novel no longer vulgarised the place; a goodly array of standard works, well-bound, showed a more respectable and conventional ambition; but there was no physiognomy in the collection. A greater change was visible in Dickens himself. In these two years he had remarkably developed. His conversation turned on graver subjects than theatres and actors, periodicals and London life. His interest in public affairs, especially in social questions, was keener. He still remained completely outside philosophy, science, and the higher literature, and was too unaffected a man to pretend to feel any interest in them. But the vivacity and sagacity which gave a charm to intercourse with him had become weighted with a seriousness which from that time forward became more and more prominent in his conversation and his writings. He had already learned to look upon the world as a scene where it was the duty of each man in his own way to make the lot of the miserable Many a little less miserable; and, having learned that his genius gave him great power, he was bent on using that power effectively. He was sometimes laughed at for the importance he seemed to attach to everything relating to himself, and the solemnity with which he spoke of his aims and affairs; but this belonged to his quality. *Il se prenait au sérieux*, and was admirable because he did so. Whatever faults he may have committed there were none attributable to carelessness. He gave us his best. If the effort were sometimes too strained, and the desire for effect too obtrusive, there was no lazy indulgence, no trading on a great renown, no 'scumbling' in his work. . . .

Since I have been led in the course of argument to touch upon my personal acquaintance with Dickens, I may take advantage of the opening to introduce a point not mentioned in Mr. Forster's memoir, though he most probably is familiar with it. Mr. Forster has narrated Dickens's intense grief at the death of his sister-in-law, Mary – a grief which for two months interrupted the writing of *Pickwick*, and which five years afterwards thus moves him in a letter to Mr. Forster on the death of her grandmother [*Life*, III, i, 198–9; Lewes also quotes another Dickens letter about Mary, *Life*, III, vi, 270.]

Several years afterwards, in the course of a quiet chat over a cigar, we got on a subject which always interested him, and on which he had stored many striking anecdotes – dreams. He then narrated, in his quietest and most impressive manner, that after Mary's death her image not only haunted him by day, but for twelve months visited his dreams every night. At first he had refrained from mentioning it to his wife; and after deferring this some time, felt unable to mention it to her. He had occasion to go to Liverpool, and as he went to bed that night, there was a strong hope that the change of bed might break the spell of his dreams. It was not so however. That night as usual the old dream was dreamt. He resolved to unburthen his mind to his wife, and wrote that very morning a full account of his strange experience.[2] From that time he ceased to dream of her. I forget whether he said he had never dreamt of her since; but I am certain of the fact that the spell had been broken then and there.

Here is another contribution to the subject of dreams, which I had from him shortly before his death. One night after one of his public readings, he dreamt that he was in a room where every one was dressed in scarlet. (The probable origin of this was the mass of scarlet opera-cloaks worn by the ladies among the audience, having left a sort of *afterglow* on his retina). He stumbled against a lady standing with her back towards him. As he apologised she turned her head and said, quite unprovoked, 'My name is Napier.' The face was one perfectly unknown to him, nor did he know any one named Napier. Two days after he had another reading in the same town, and before it began, a lady friend came into the waiting-room accompanied by an unknown lady in a scarlet opera cloak, 'who', said his friend, 'is very desirous of being introduced'. 'Not Miss Napier?' he jokingly inquired. 'Yes; Miss Napier.' Although the face of his dream-lady was not the face of this Miss Napier, the coincidence of the scarlet cloak and the name was striking.[3]

NOTES

1. Probably the review of *Pickwick* and other early works in the *National Magazine and Monthly Critic*, Dec 1837; see *P*, I, 403n.
2. Lewes's, or Dickens's, memory was at fault here. As Dickens told his mother-in-law in 1843, his dreams of Mary ceased after he wrote to his wife about the experience – not from Liverpool but from Greta Bridge, Yorkshire – in February 1838; see *P*, I, 366 and III, 483–4.
3. Other, and somewhat different, accounts of the Miss Napier dream occur in Dickens's letter to Forster, 30 May 1863 (*Life*, XI, iii, 841), and in a footnote to an article in *All the Year Round*, XVII, 620 (22 June 1867), reprinted in *Dkn*, LVI (1960) 95–6.

'Dear Dickens is a Most Extraordinary Man!'

W. C. MACREADY

(1) from *The Diaries of William Charles Macready 1833–1851*, ed. William Toynbee (1912), I, 480, 482; II, 25, 28, 74–6, 153, 178–80, 333, 376, 418, 466. 1862 entry from Gen. the Rt Hon. Sir Nevil Macready, *Annals of an Active Life* (1924) I, 20.
(2) from Lady Pollock, *Macready as I Knew Him* (1884) pp. 59–60, 92–4. Macready (1793–1873), the leading English actor of his generation, met Dickens in 1836 and, though twenty years older than he, became (as Georgina Hogarth said) a 'friend than whom he had none dearer'. *Nickleby* was dedicated to him, and he and Dickens became godfathers to each other's children. 'When I am in town, I see him almost every day', wrote Dickens; 'and when I am away, we are in very frequent correspondence' (*P*, III, 370). His letters to Macready are uncommonly emotional in their expressions of affection, and often they discuss political matters (Macready was a Radical of Dickens's type). 'You are at the head of *my* audience, as you know', Dickens told him (*P*, III, 453), and he was particularly gratified by Macready's approval also of his histrionic efforts – 'undisguisedly sobbing, and crying on the sofa' during the 1844 *Chimes* reading (*P*, IV, 235), and flabbergasted by *Sikes and Nancy*, which he thought equivalent to 'Two Macbeths!' (*N*, III, 704). Macready was highly intelligent and sensitive, moody, cantankerous and irritable, and he usually felt contempt for the acting profession; but for Dickens he was 'Dearest of the Irascibles' (letter of 6 Dec 1854: MS. Morgan). His diary, selections from which were published before the manuscript was burned, contains many references to Dickens, including valuable lists of the guests at dinners, etc., at his and Macready's houses. For information about the suppressed parts of the diary, see Philip Collins, 'W. C. Macready and Dickens: Some Family Recollections', *Dickens Studies*, II (1966) 51–6.

(1) *5 Dec 1838.* Dickens brought me his farce,[1] which he read to me. The dialogue is very good, full of point, but I am not sure about the meagreness of the plot. He reads as well as an experienced actor would – he is a surprising man.

13 Dec 1838. Wrote to . . . Dickens, about his farce, explaining to him my motives for wishing to withdraw it, and my great obligation to him. He returned me an answer which is an honour to him.[2] How truly delightful it is to meet with high-minded and warm-hearted men. Dickens and Bulwer have been certainly to me noble specimens of human nature, and show very strongly the pitiful contrast that a man like Talfourd offers.

5 Oct 1839. [At the '*too* splendid dinner' to celebrate the completion of *Nickleby*] I spoke of him as one who had made the amelioration of his fellow-men the object of all his labours – and whose characteristic was philanthropy. . . . Dickens [replying] stated that the *Nickleby* had been to him a diary of the last two years: the various papers preserving to him the recollection of the events and feelings connected with their production.

25 Aug 1840. Went to Dickens [and then to Katey Dickens's christening, with Macready as godfather. After lunch, he and Dickens went] to Coldbath Fields Prison. Captain Chesterton, the Governor, accompanied us all over the whole prison. Went to dine with Dickens. Met some relations of his, uncles; Miss Ayrton, Mrs. Burnett, Maclise, Jerdan, Forster, Mr. Charlton, etc. Rather a noisy and uproarious day – not so much *comme il faut* as I could have wished.

1 Jan 1842. Dear Dickens called to shake hands with me [before sailing to America]. My heart was quite full; it is much to me to lose the presence of a friend who really loves me. He said there was no one whom he felt so much pain in saying goodbye to. God bless him:

29 June 1842. . . . I was lying on the sofa when a person entered abruptly, whom I glanced at as Forster? – *no*. Jonathan Bucknill? – *no*. Who was it but dear Dickens holding me in his arms in a transport of joy.[3] God bless him!

12 July 1842. . . . Went to Dickens; found Landor, Maclise, and

Forster there. Dickens had been mesmerizing his wife and Miss Hogarth, who had been in violent hysterics. He proposed to make a trial on me; I did not quite like it, but assented; was very nervous . . . .

2 Nov 1845. Forster called and read me Dickens's Prospectus of the new morning paper [the *Daily News*] – or rather I read it over twice attentively. It *increased* my apprehensions. I objected to several parts of it, but my objection is one and all. I feel that he is rushing headlong into an enterprise that demands the utmost foresight, skilful and secret preparation and qualities of a conductor which Dickens has not. Forster agreed in many if not all of my objections, but he did not seem to entertain much hope of moving Dickens.

27 Dec 1845. Called on Forster, with whom I found Dickens; gave them the best directions I could to two unskilled men, how to *manage* their encounter in the play of *The Elder Brother*. Forster spoke, when Dickens had gone, about the *Times*, and the injury it would do.[4] He now *draws in* about the paper, and seems to feel it is a wrong step, and that Dickens is not qualified for the situation of director. *His tone is quite altered now.* He told me that Dickens was so intensely fixed on his own opinions and in his admiration of his own works (who could have believed it?) that he, Forster, was useless to him as a counsel, or for an opinion on anything touching upon them, and that, as he refused to see criticisms on himself, this partial passion would grow upon him, till it became an incurable evil. I grived to hear it.

1 Apr 1846. . . . Went to Richmond – Star and Garter – met Forster, Mr. and Mrs. Dickens, Miss Hogarth, Maclise and Stanfield; we had a very merry – I suppose I must say *jolly* day – rather more tumultuous than I quite like.

4 Nov 1847. Forster dined; was sorry to hear him speak as if the long and intimate friendship between himself and Dickens was likely to terminate or very much relax. They have both faults with their good qualities, but they have been *too* familiar. I hope Dickens is not capricious – not spoiled; he has, however, great excuse.

3 Feb 1849. Finished, with great reluctance, *Vanity Fair.* . . . The book is an extraordinarily clever one, and, differing in its kind, is second to none of the present day, which is an admission I make almost grudgingly for Dickens's sake; but the truth is the truth.

4 June 1850. . . . Maclise . . . told me of a coolness between Thackeray and Dickens – that Thackeray in '49 had been invited to the R[oyal] A[cademy] dinner and Dickens not, that this year Dickens was asked and wrote a very stiff note, *declining*! How weak are the wisest of us!

4 Dec 1850. Read last number of *Copperfield*, which is very, very clever – full of genius. Certainly he, dear Dickens, is a most extraordinary man!

3 Jan 1862. [Macready, in retirement at Cheltenham, attends Dickens's reading of *Nicholas Nickleby at the Yorkshire School* and *Boots at the Holly-Tree Inn*.] His reading was very artistic, giving point and force to every prominent passage. It was a very interesting and satisfactory evening's entertainment. . . . [The next night, Dickens gave his *Copperfield* reading] *admirably*. The humour was delightful, and the pathos of various passages gave me a choking sensation, whilst the account of Emily's flight brought the tears to my eyes. The reading of the story was altogether a truly artistic performance.

(2) [Lady Pollock, a close friend of Macready's – her husband edited his *Reminiscences* (1875) – recalls his enthusiasm for Dickens's genius, 'his irrepressible humour, his force, and his extraordinary powers of perception'. Dickens, he said, did not intrude his opinions so strongly, 'But what a marvellous describer Dickens is! how comprehensive his glance! What a power he has of penetrating his reader with his idea!' Lady Pollock then refers to Macready's great anxiety over his son Harry, who was subject to convulsions, and died young. His first wife, Catherine, was delicate (and died prematurely in 1852), so she could not cope with Harry's illness, the brunt of which fell upon Macready.]

In this trial, as in all others, Macready found in the active sympathy of Charles Dickens, a constant resource. Dickens devised amusements for the child; he wrote to him diverting comical letters suited to his comprehension; he sent him all kinds of tokens of his feeling for him; and the boy, who had a great capacity for love, repaid this care and thought with a most lively affection; his face became all smiles at the very mention of his name; he was next to his father in his breast.

Of all friends, Dickens was the truest; he was enthusiastic, and he was steadfast; no work and no trouble of his own impeded him, if he believed that his friend wanted him; he shared trials which to his sensitive nature were especially painful, and lightened them by his care; he was the last friend (outside the family circle) who saw Catherine in her sinking condition. The last flush of pleasure that passed over her face was caused by the sight of him; and, as he took her hand to say farewell, she, sinking back exhausted in her chair, said feebly and faintly: 'Charles Dickens, I had almost embraced you. What a friend you have been!' He stooped and kissed her forehead; and when he was next one of the family circle the mother was no longer there.

In the latter days of Macready's life, when the weight of time and of sorrow pressed him down, Dickens was his most frequent visitor; he cheered him with narratives of bygone days; he poured some of his own abundant warmth into his heart; he led him into his old channels of thought; he gave readings to rouse his interest; he waked up in him again, by his vivid descriptions, his sense of humour – he conjured back his smile and his laugh. Charles Dickens was and is to me the ideal of friendship.

NOTES

1. Dickens, wishing to help Macready in his efforts 'to bring back to the stage its higher associations of good literature and intellectual enjoyment' (*Life*, II, i, 96), offered him his farce *The Lamplighter*. As the next entry shows, the offer was declined.

2. Dickens's letter (*P*, I, 468) is indeed unruffled and generous. Edward Lytton Bulwer and Thomas Noon Talfourd, mentioned below, were of course offering Macready plays at this time.

3. Dickens had just that evening arrived back in London from America. Forster, Maclise and Macready were the three friends he had most looked forward to meeting again (*P*, III, 244).

4. With their fellow amateurs, they were performing in Beaumont and Fletcher's *The Elder Brother*; Dickens played Eustace, the younger brother. *The Times* had just reviewed *The Cricket on the Hearth* very savagely; Macready, and others, saw this as an attempt to discredit in advance the editor of a rival newspaper. The *Daily News* began publication on 26 January 1846.

Dickens on Holiday (1840) and Afterwards

ELEANOR E. CHRISTIAN

A conflation of passages from E. E. C., 'Reminiscences of Charles Dickens: From a Young Lady's Diary', *Englishwoman's Domestic Magazine*, x (1871) 336–44, and Eleanor E. Christian, 'Recollections of Charles Dickens, his Family and Friends', *Temple Bar*, LXXXII (1888) 481–506. Eleanor Emma Picken (1820/1–1898), minor artist and later an occasional author, was the daughter of the Scottish writer Andrew Picken. In 1842 she married Edward Christian, a relative of Charles Smithson, who, as a partner of Dickens's solicitor Thomas Mitton, was on very friendly terms with Dickens. It was thus that this 'Young Lady' met the novelist. In the summer of 1840 she was with the Smithsons in Broadstairs, where the Dickenses often spent their holidays; after her marriage in September 1842, she and her husband went there again, but Dickens – who had obviously been attracted to her during the previous holiday – was now markedly cooler. Later she lunched with the Dickenses a couple of times, and saw him on several public occasions. These particulars are drawn from William J. Carlton, *Dkn*, LX (1964) 68–77, and *P*, II, 119–20. Carlton traces the relationship between her and the Dickens family, and notes the differences between the 1871 and 1888 essays: 1888, mostly an expansion of 1871, is franker in identifying the people mentioned, but the Pilgrim editors argue that 1871 is generally to be preferred. It predominates in the selections below, though 1888 is substituted where it is fuller or more expressive. Mrs Christian, says Carlton, 'was no mere "seaside acquaintance", as she has been called, and although accused of malice and spite her veracity has never been seriously impugned. . . . The general accuracy of her statements can be confirmed from other sources.' Hers is the most vivid account of Dickens – in an unbuttoned holiday mood – at this period, and her manifest chagrin over not becoming a permanent member of his circle, if not causing 'malice and spite', certainly gave a sharp edge to her recollections. We begin with her first encounter with Dickens, at the Smithsons'.

The first thing that riveted me was the marvellous power of his eyes. Nondescript in colour, though inclining to warm grey in repose; but lighting up suddenly into a luminous depth of hue, they instantly arrested me; and I could see nothing else for the moment. Then I became aware of a rare harmony of features, a combination of strength and delicacy of perception, a breadth and grandeur united to spiritualised refinement, which compelled a prolonged study of the whole countenance. When at last the attention wandered to the costume and style of the man, there was a disappointing mental shock. Everything seemed marred by his 'get up'. Young as I was, I was aware of the vagaries of dress indulged in by authors and artists; but this was something unusual. The general mistake of men who pose as not of the 'common herd' is to attempt the picturesque; but here was merely a perverted idea of what ought to be fashionable costume – utterly unfit for dinner-dress, and only proving a taste for what was 'loud'. The collar and lapels of his *surtout* were very wide and thrown back so as to give full effect to a vast expanse of white waistcoat. He wore drab-coloured trousers, ditto boots, with patent-leather toes, all most inconsistent with the poetic head and its flowing locks, and the genius that glowed in his fine, well-opened eyes.

He talked but little during the evening, seeming rather to allow the lead to be taken by Mr. Forster, who was also one of the guests, and whose greater fluency seemed to interest and impress him. His own speech had a certain thickness – it was a family characteristic – as if the tongue was too large for the mouth, and his tones were low and hurried as though his ideas and words were racing against each other. His humorous remarks were generally delivered in an exaggerated, stilted style, and sometimes with a complete perversion of facts, quite astounding to matter-of-fact minds, and were accompanied by a twinkle in the eyes, and a comic lifting of one eyebrow. I was surprised to find that, instead of the piercing satirical expression one expected, he usually wore a rapt, preoccupied, far-off look which was exceedingly misleading. When I came to know him better I found this was nothing but a trap for the unwary. During these outward semblances of reverie, nothing escaped him; he was quietly and unsuspectedly 'taking in' every incident going on around, and making notes thereon. Many times were we duped by this false appearance of abstraction and were deluded into talking nonsense, arguing illogically, and making silly jokes under the impression that he was miles away in a land of his own peopling, surrounded by characters of his own creation. Then suddenly up would go the curtain from his veiled vision, and he would break forth into most amusing but merciless criticisms of all our conversation; such twisting and distorting of every thoughtless word and unfledged idea that we were covered with confusion, though convulsed with laughter.

When he really did indulge in a reverie or when engaged in any difficulties of composition, he would pull viciously at his mane-like hair, running his fingers through it till his ideas became satisfactorily evolved, at the same time indulging in his habit of sucking his tongue. . . .

A great deal of amusement was excited by Mrs. Charles Dickens perpetrating the most absurd puns, which she did with a charming expression of innocence and deprecation of her husband's wrath; while he tore his hair and writhed as if convulsed with agony. He used to pretend to be utterly disgusted, although he could neither resist laughter at the puns nor at the pretty comic *moue* she made (with eyes turned up till little of the whites were visible) after launching forth one of these absurdities.

Every autumn it was Mr. Dickens's custom to take his family to Broadstairs, and shortly after I became acquainted with him the usual flitting took place. He begged my friends Mr. and Mrs. S[mithson] to take a house there also, and offered to look for one for them. . . . Shortly after this my friends took the house, and I accompanied them as a visitor, to my intense delight, for I hoped to be privileged to daily enjoyment of the presence of this man of genius. And how began a time which I look back to as almost the brightest in my life, as far as enjoyment went. Every day was spent by our family and the Dickens's together, either doing the usual seaside recreations, or at each other's houses. In the familiarity which such friendly association engenders we got up ridiculous relations to each other. He pretended to be engaged in a semi-sentimental, semi-jocular, and wholly nonsensical flirtation with me as well as with Milly T[hompson], one of my friends, a charming woman of a certain age, and we on our side acted mutual jealousy towards each other; and Mrs. Charles Dickens entered into the fun with great gusto and good-humour. My friend Milly he called his 'charmer', 'the beloved of his soul', and I was his 'fair enslaver' and his 'queen'. We generally addressed each other in the old English style of euphuism, and he would ask us to dance in such bombastic nonsense as—

'Wilt tread a measure with me, sweet lady? Fain would I thread the mazes of this saraband with thee.'

'Aye, fair sir, that I will right gladly; in good sooth I'll never say thee nay.'

I need not say that the stately and courtly gravity with which we 'trod our measure' was truly edifying, and the spectators were convulsed at the wonderful 'Turveydrop' deportment of

Mr. Dickens, and the Malvolio-like conceit he contrived to call into his countenance.

'I think I could act a pompous ass to perfection!' he exclaimed, after one of these dances. 'Let us get up some charades, and test our histrionic powers.' [And they did so, in spirited fashion. 'Milly' was Mrs Smithson's sister Amelia, aged twenty-nine. Dickens's holiday party included at various times his mother, his sisters Letitia (Mrs Austin) and Fanny (with her husband Henry Burnett), and his brother Fred.]

It has been said that Mrs. Nickleby and Mr. Micawber were drawn from Charles' parents, and, indeed, he admitted the fact, but I saw no resemblance. She seemed to me to possess a good stock of common sense, and a matter-of-fact manner. I only detected one little weakness—a love of dancing. And though she never indulged in it with any other partner than her son-in-law, or with some relation, Charles always looked as sulky as a bear the whole time.

Her husband appeared younger than she did, and was a plump, good-looking man, rather an 'old buck' in dress, but with no resemblance to Micawber that I could detect; no salient characteristics that could be twisted into anything so grotesque, except that he indulged occasionally in *fine* sentiments, and long-worded sentences, and seemed to take an airy, sunny-sided view of things in general. He avowed himself an optimist, and said he was like a cork— if he was pushed under water in one place, he always bobbed 'up to time' cheerfully in another, and felt none the worse for the dip.

It was wonderful how the whole family had emancipated themselves from their antecedents, and contrived to fit easily into their improved position. They appeared to be less at ease with Charles than with any one else, and seemed in fear of offending him. There was a subdued manner, a kind of restraint in his presence, not merely the result of admiration of his genius, or respect for his opinion, but because his moods were very variable. Sometimes so genial and gay that one became excited and exhilarated (as if champagne had been flowing freely) merely from his contagious spirits: at other times abstracted and even morose—we wondered how we could possibly ever have been so friendly with him. . . .

Like all poetical natures he delighted in gazing at the sea. He would remain for hours as if entranced; with a rapt, immovable, sphinx-like calm on his face, and that far-off look in his magnificent eyes, totally forgetful of everything, and abstracted from us all. We always respected his isolation, and carefully kept aloof. . . .

The next night we were all assembled on the little pier or jetty which ran out into the sea, with an upright spar fixed at the extreme end. At the beginning was a railed-off space with seats, which he called the family pew. Mr. Dickens was in high spirits, and enjoyed the darkness of the evening, because he escaped the curious eyes of the Broadstairs population. We had a quadrille all to ourselves, the music being Frederick Dickens' whistling, and Mr. Dickens' accompaniment on his pocket-comb. . . . Dickens seemed suddenly to be possessed with the demon of mischief; he threw his arm around me and ran me down the inclined plane to the end of the jetty till we reached the tall post. He put his other arm round this, and exclaimed in theatrical tones that he intended to hold me there till 'the sad sea waves' should submerge us.

'Think of the sensation we shall create! Think of the road to celebrity which you are about to tread! No, not exactly to *tread*, but to flounder into!'

Here I implored him to let me go, and struggled hard to release myself.

'Let your mind dwell on the column in *The Times* wherein will be vividly described the pathetic fate of the lovely E[mma] P[icken], drowned by Dickens in a fit of dementia! Don't struggle, poor little bird; you are powerless in the claws of such a kite as this child!'

By this time the gleam of light had faded out, and the water close to us looked uncomfortably black. The tide was coming up rapidly and surged over my feet. I gave a loud shriek and tried to bring him back to common sense by reminding him that 'My dress, my best dress, my *only* silk dress, would be ruined.' Even this climax did not soften him; he still went on with his serio-comic nonsense, shaking with laughter all the time, and panting with his struggles to hold me.

'Mrs. Dickens!' a frantic shriek this time, for now the waves rushed up to my knees; 'help me! make Mr. Dickens let me go – the waves are up to my knees!'

'Charles!' cried Mrs. Dickens, echoing my wild scream, 'how can you be so silly? You will both be carried off by the tide' (tragically, but immediately sinking from pathos to bathos) 'and you'll spoil the poor girl's silk dress!'

'Dress!' cried Dickens, with withering scorn. 'Talk not to me of *dress*! When the pall of night is enshrouding us in Cimmerian darkness, when we already stand on the brink of the great mystery, shall our thoughts be of fleshly vanities? Am I not immolating a brand-new pair of patent leathers still unpaid for? Perish such low-born thoughts! In this hour of abandonment to the voice of destiny shall we be held back by the puerilities of silken raiment? Shall leather or prunella (whatever that may be) stop the bolt of Fate?' with a sudden parenthetical sinking from bombast to familiar accents, and back again.

At this point I succeeded in wrestling myself free, and scampered to my friends, almost crying with vexation, my *only* silk dress clinging clammily round me, and streaming with salt water. . . . During this wrestling match between us, I cannot describe the ridiculous effect produced by his 'mouthing' in the Ercles vein, with now and then a quick descent into comicality–the contrast between the stiltified language, and the gasping struggles caused by my efforts to get free, his suppressed chuckles at my dismay, my wild appeals, and the expostulations of his wife and the rest, who stood by, like the chorus in a Greek play, powerless to help.

I went off, escorted by Frederick Dickens, after hearing Mrs. Charles say –

'It was too bad of you, Charles; remember poor E[mma] cannot afford to have her dress destroyed. Of course you'll give her another?'

'Never!' was the reply. 'I have sacrificed her finery and my boots to the infernal gods. Kismet! It is finished! Eureka! &c., &c.; and now I go to tug myself black in the face getting off my pedal covers.'

Dickens was rather reckless in his fun sometimes, and my wardrobe suffered woefully in consequence. There was a sort of promontory stretching out into the sea, where, in rough weather, the waves used to rush up several feet, and come splashing down like a shower-bath. On two occasions, when I had thoughtlessly ventured near this spot, he seized me and ran me, *nolens volens*, right under the cataract, to the irretrievable ruin of two bonnets of frail fabric, and my slender purse was taxed to the utmost to replace them. . . .

He was not always full of spirits or even-tempered: indeed, I was somewhat puzzled by the variability of his moods. After indulging in the greatest fun and familiarity over-night, we would sometimes meet him walking alone, when he would look at us with lack-lustre eye, and pass on with a hurried 'How d'ye do?'

One day he strolled by our window where Milly and I were standing on the balcony. He turned back, 'struck' an attitude (in actor's phrase); with one hand on his heart, and the other upraised, he began mouthing – ' " '\Tis my lady, 'tis my love. O would I were a glove upon that hand, that I might kiss that cheek." '

'Which of us do you intend to be the Juliet to your Romeo?' asked Milly.

'Whichever you choose, my little dears,' he said nonchalantly, and, touching his hat, sauntered on.

The next morning he came by again, and found us as before, but he only returned a sulky 'How do?' and walked by. Of course we knew he was in the midst of some brain-spinning, and wanted to be alone. I got to understand his face so well that when I saw the pre-occupied look I used to pretend not to see him at all, so as to spare him even the trouble of recognising me, and I found he was all the better pleased. . . .

One morning at his own house Dickens was talking on art to a gentleman present, and they discussed the statue of Venus, which Byron raves about in his *Pilgrimage*. Dickens objected to the expressions used by Byron, 'Dazzled and drunk with beauty,' 'The heart *reels* with its fulness', &c. [*Childe Harold's Pilgrimage*, IV, 443–4], as being an unpoetical metaphor, and said it must have been written tipsily, under the influence of that beverage (gin-and-water) which sometimes inspired this great poet. I defended the verse, and Dickens rose up, pushed his hands through his flowing locks so as to give them their most weird look, turned down his shirt-collar, slapped his brow, and [lampooned Byron] in the Bombastes Furioso style. . . .

My father was a Scottish author of considerable reputation, and had died suddenly at the age of forty-two of apoplexy, when I was only twelve years old. I lent Mrs. Dickens some volumes of his writings about this time, and she expressed to me how delighted she was in their perusal. In my presence she asked Mr. Dickens to read them. He looked his distaste at the idea, and when she pressed him 'just to read one tale, such a beautifully written one, and very short', he turned and walked off abruptly, muttering – 'I hate Scotch stories, and everything else Scotch.' I thought this was very unkind to his wife as well as to me, as she was Scotch too. She coloured up, but laughed it off.

There were times when we gave Mr. Dickens 'a wide berth', and Milly and I have often run round corners to get out of his way, when we thought he was in one of these moods, which we could tell by one glance at his face. His eyes were always like 'danger-lamps', and warned people to clear the line for fear of collision. We felt we had to do with a genius, and in the throes and agonies of bringing forth his conceptions, we did not expect him to submit to be interrupted by triflers like ourselves: at these times I confess I was horribly afraid of him. I told him so, to his great amusement. . . .

I have never met with any one who entered into games with as much spirit and boisterous glee; the simplest of them he contrived to make amusing, and often instructive. His fun was most infectious, and he had three able partisans in his brothers and Mr. Mitton, and under the incentive of his prompting they became irresistibly comic. Under their manipulation 'Vingt-et-un', 'Loc', &c., became so totally altered as to be scarcely recognisable, and generally ended in unblushing cheating and consequent uproar. The stakes were usually thrown into a heap and distributed honestly at the end of the evening. . . .

At last came the sad day when we must leave them, to return to our 'local habitations' in smoky London, and I parted with Mr. and Mrs. Dickens with tears of regret. 'Never mind, dear,' she said, in her sweet caressing way, 'we shall all meet again in London.' Alas! we never met again in the same kindly way. Everything was changed.

When the Dickens's came home we went to luncheon there, and I remarked how pre-occupied he looked, how changed in manner. Mrs. S[mithson], who knew him better than I did, was quite prepared to find him different in London from what he was in Broadstairs, but I was very disappointed. I seldom saw him after this. . . .

[To describe Dickens as always amiable, always just, and always in the right, would be simply false and untrue to nature]. . . . A portrait is incomplete without shadows; witness the unreal representations of Queen Elizabeth, of glorious, but despotic, memory. Dickens was far from being faultless, indeed he was often very disappointing, and the hard edges of his character sometimes required softening with a sweetner, i.e., a brush used to blend tints together. I have no doubt that Dickens was most energetic in doing good, and full of warm sympathy for poverty, but I never, *personally*, saw any instances of his benevolence.

The last time I saw him was at a reading he gave, in Southampton, of the *Christmas Carol* [in 1858]. . . . He was greatly changed – his face lined by deep furrows, hair grizzled and thinned, his expression care-worn and clouded. The nostril was still sensitive and dilated like that of a war-horse, the whole aspect spoke of power, sensibility, and eager restlessness, but overcast with a shadow which blighted its geniality. The open, frank steadiness of eye was gone. He seemed to have withered and dwindled into a smaller man, and his former 'flashy' style of dress had faded into shabbiness. The thickness of utterance was completely conquered by his long course of reading, acting and speaking, his declamation free from all hurry and indistinctness. He identified himself completely with each character, seeming to enjoy the fun and sympathise with the pathos as if all was quite new to him. He held his audience absorbed in the recital, as his sonorous, emphatic tones (alternately ringing with power, or thrilling with tenderness) gave out the heart-stirring *Carol*.

My heart so went out to him that I longed for a touch of his hand, and a kindly word, and I lingered in the entrance of the assembly room, nearly frozen with cold, to wait his coming out; but discovered he had left by means of a window near his platform.

Yankee Inquisitiveness Pays Off

C. EDWARDS LESTER

From his *The Glory and Shame of England* (New York, 1866) II, 504–7. Lester (1815–90), American journalist and author, called on Dickens in July 1840, with a letter of introduction from the poet Thomas Campbell, and published an account of his interview – from a letter to Washington Irving – in the 1841 (New York and London) edition of his book; the 1866 edition contains a rearranged version of this letter, with some later reflections. As the Pilgrim editors remark, his account is 'somewhat naive' (*P*, II, 101 n.); witness Lester's failure to notice Dickens's irony in this exchange: 'I expressed a desire to know something of the history of his authorship, at the same time saying that, of course, I did not expect him to communicate to a stranger anything he would not freely make known to the world. "Oh, sir," he replied, "ask as many questions as you please; as an American, it is one of your inalienable rights to ask questions; and this, I fancy, is the reason why the Yankees are so intelligent"' (1841 edition, II, 6–7). The Pilgrim editors quote the attack on his book in the *Examiner*, 11 Dec 1841, probably by John Forster, reprobating his 'violation of the confidences of social life'. But Dickens had obviously not been offended by Lester's interview; on 19 July 1840 he sent him a scrap of the manuscript of *Oliver Twist* and, on Mrs Lester's request, a lock of his hair (*P*, II, 101–2), Dickens was 'certainly one of the most agreable men I ever saw', Lester stated (1841 edition, II, 15).

. . . I found him sitting in a large arm-chair by his writing table in the library, with a sheet of what he afterwards casually alluded to, of *Master Humphrey's Clock*, before him. Nothing could be more kind or genial than the reception he gave me, and I thought at the time, and perhaps do still, that Dickens is incomparably the finest looking man I ever saw. The portraits of him do him little justice; nor are the artists particularly to blame, for it is not very easy to paint or engrave the expression of his face while he is engaged in an interesting conversation. There is something about his eyes at all times that, in women, we call bewitching; in men we have scarcely any name for it. He is, perhaps, a little above the standard height, but his bearing is free and noble, and he appears taller than he really is. His figure is very graceful, neither too slight, nor too stout; and it is to be hoped he may never get the shape of a burly 'Hinglishman'. His complexion is exquisitely delicate – rather pale generally; but when his feelings are awakened a very rich glow spreads all over his face. I should not blame him if he were somewhat vain of his hair. It reminded me of words in Sidney's *Arcadia*: 'His fair auburn hair, which he wore in great length, gave him at that time a most delightful show.' His head is large, and its phrenological developments indicate a clear and beautiful intellect, in which the organs of perception, mirthfulness, comparison and ideality predominate. I should think the nose had at one time almost determined to be Roman, but hesitated just long enough on the way to make a happy compromise with the classic Greek outline. But the charm of his person is in his full, soft, beaming eyes, which catch, like pure water, an expression from every passing object. You can always see *fun*, as you do in humorous children, sleeping in ambush around those blue eyes, unless they are melted to tenderness, or flashing with indignant fires. . . . Mr. Dickens spoke with the utmost freedom about every body and every thing, with the fullest glow of appreciation of all our well known writers, characterizing in few dashes their most striking traits, and hitting off the strong peculiarities of American character with astonishing familiarity and *bonhomie*. . . .

YANKEE INQUISITIVENESS. I felt very desirous to gratify in asking him a great many questions about his books and his inner intellectual life;

so throwing myself upon Campbell's very strong letter, I thought it would not be absolutely outrageous if I should, and so I did. 'To use one of your own expressive phrases,' he replied, 'go ahead. Aside from other reasons, Mr. Campbell's letter gave you a push into my friendship as far at least as we could both of us have carried it by an acquaintance of years.' Not being an authour myself, and wishing to get the 'hang' of an author's experience, I asked him how far he had in any, or most, instances in portraying his characters, had his eye upon particular persons he had known; for having with all his *dramatis personæ* never painted two characters much alike, I could not well conceive how they could have been to any considerable extent creatures of imagination.

'Allow me to ask, sir,' I said, 'if one-eyed Squeers, coarse but good John Browdie, the charming Sally Brass, clever Dick Swiveller, the demoniac and intriguing Quilp, the good Cheeryble Brothers, the avaricious Fagin, and dear little Nelly, are mere fancies?'

'No, sir, they are not,' he replied; 'they are copies. You will not understand me to say, of course, that they are true histories in all respects, but they are real likenesses; nor have I in any of my works attempted any thing more than to arrange my story as well as I could, and give a true picture of scenes I have witnessed. My past history and pursuits have led me to a familiar acquaintance with numerous instances of extreme wretchedness and deep-laid villainy. In the haunts of squalid poverty I have found many a broken heart too good for this world. Many such persons, now in the most abject condition, have seen better days. Once they moved in circles of friendship and affluence, from which they have been hurled by misfortune to the lowest depths of want and sorrow. This class of persons is very large.

'Then there are thousands in our parish workhouses and in the lanes of London, born into the world without a friend except God and a dying mother. Many, too, who in circumstances of trial have yielded to impulses of passion, and by one fatal step fallen beyond recovery. London is crowded, and, indeed, so is all England, with the poor, the unfortunate, and the guilty. This description of persons has been generally overlooked.by authors. They have had none to care for them, and have fled from the public gaze to some dark habitation of this great city, to curse the cold charities of a selfish world, and die. There are more broken hearts in London than in any other place in the world. The amount of crime, starvation, nakedness, and misery of every sort in the metropolis surpasses all calculation. I thought I could render some service to humanity by bringing these scenes before the minds of those who, from never having witnessed them, suppose they cannot exist. In this effort I have not been wholly unsuccessful; and there is nothing makes me happier than to think that, by some of my representations, I have increased the stock of human cheerfulness, and, by others, the stock of human sympathy. I think it makes the heart better to seek out the suffering and relieve them. I have spent many days and nights in the most wretched districts of the metropolis, studying the history of the human heart. There we must go to find it. In high circles we see every thing but the heart, and learn every thing but the real character. We must go to the hovels of the poor and the unfortunate, where trial brings out the character. I have in these rambles seen many exhibitions of generous affection and heroic endurance, which would do honor to any sphere. Often have I have discovered minds that only wanted a little of the sunshine of prosperity to develop the choicest endowments of Heaven. I think I never return to my home after these adventures without being made a sadder and a better man. In describing these characters I aim no higher than to feel in writing as they seemed to feel themselves. I am persuaded that I have succeeded just in proportion as I have cultivated a familiarity with the trials and sorrows of the poor, and told their story as they would have related it themselves.'

I left Mr. Dickens after a delightful visit of two hours, most deeply impressed with the *essential goodness of his heart*, and the rich, overflowing humanity of his soul. I do not think any other author is doing as much for humanity in the British Empire.

Another Yankee Interviewer, 1841

JOHN D. SHERWOOD

From his 'Visits to the Homes of Authors: The Home of Charles Dickens', *Hours at Home* (New York) v (1867) 239–41. Sherwood, a New York journalist, called to see

Dickens at Devonshire Terrace – 'this neat, cottage-like house', he calls it, 'in a quiet street, near Regent's Park' – late in 1841, and found him preparing for his imminent visit to America, 'cramming himself with all sorts of information to fit himself for observing and for writing the *American Notes*'.

His study was piled high with Maryatt's, [Mrs] Trollope's, Fidler's, Hall's and other Travels in and Descriptions of America, and blazed with highly-coloured maps of the United States, whose staring blues, reds, and yellows, so much in contrast with the colourless maps of Europe, greatly amused him.

'I could light my cigar against the red-hot State of Ohio,' he said.

He was anxiously in quest of knowledge respecting this country; desiring to bring within the compass of his brief stay here, as wide a reach of space, and as great a variety of subjects, as possible. He expressed his inability to go into the Gulf States, as his policy of life insurance forbade it – an interdict which he had, he said, in vain endeavoured to remove.

Speaking of the character of the books which had been written by travelers in America, he remarked the general tendency to draw wide national conclusions from isolated exceptional facts – to charge the nation with the peculiarities of a few individuals met by chance on steamboats and railroad cars.

'There is a great temptation to give all the funny or dramatic incidents one meets in travel – to set out individual grotesqueness – single exaggerations as types—or if not ostentatiously to exhibit them, at least to leave them as types or indices of the average national character. I can go in almost any part of England and find people, scenes, classes, and conversations precisely like these exceptional cases, set down as specimens of American life in general; and yet I know that while these exceptional cases are English, they might just as well and easily be found in Germany, Russia, America, or in any civilized part of the world.' 'No doubt,' he continued, 'there are types of character that take on a national hue and colour. The Sam Slicks – the western jokes and sayings in your newspapers – the large exaggerated expressions, taking the proportions of a continent, even when dealing with neighbourhood or private matters – these are exclusively American – unmistakably belonging to the genus Yankee. Should you search through every variety of English literature you could not match them.'

'What strikes you in London?' he inquired; 'for what impresses a stranger, are the peculiarities – the points that separate it, by contrast, from his own country. One may thus travel, without quitting his own house; for the main object of leaving the comforts of home is to learn the differences between those among whom one lives; the objects, architecture, the social features about you, and those of other nations. The comments of a German on England are the best descriptions of Germany. If you tell me how London strikes you, you but mention wherein New York differs from it. What is common to the two is neither New York nor London.'

The vast masses of London were mentioned as arresting the attention of a visitor from a country then having no cities comparable with the English capital in size; and the stony indifference with which this mass, daily triturated in the same common mortar, regarded its composing atoms, was also remarked. 'Yes, that must be so. In the country every man and horse is observed – the coats of both are known along the whole road. In a village, the appearance of a stranger is discussed at every tea-table. In a city where ninety-nine per cent are strangers to everybody, people would as soon read the Directory as to stop and observe every new face they enountered.'

The sharp contrasts of London life were mentioned; the existence of classes, which, in poverty, personal degradation, and obliteration of all moral features in their foul faces, were wholly unknown in our larger land. On this account, the visitor went on to say, it was difficult for an untraveled American to comprehend that the portraitures drawn in his works were transcripts of actual characters. What he read indoors, life-like and breathing though it was, he never found outdoors in the streets, or under them. The question was then asked whether his characters were drawn from actual life, and whether the places and incidents in his novels were sketched from nature.

'In answering this question, I may say that I have never transferred any character or scene entire; but this I can aver, that there is scarcely a character or description, the nucleus and substantial body of which was not furnished from reality. I was a police reporter – perhaps you know.[1] As such, and pursuing my own vagrant inquiries, I have been over every part – in almost every nook, alley and den in London; I have been through lanes – and such there are – which you could not pass through in broad daylight, with anything safe in your pockets; where I used to put my gloves and handkerchiefs in my hat, and took especial pains to keep my hat from being knocked off, as it certainly would have been had its contents been suspected. From the police-officers, and these various rambles, I got very many outline hints. It is difficult always to tell where a particular character, as it is finally left, comes from. Of course it must be suggested by something seen, met or read of; but in passing through the mental laboratory, its constituents are put together and coloured so subtly and curiously that it is difficult to decompose the various elements.'

Various topics were broached – frank and unrestrained allusions made to persons, living contemporaries on both sides the water; and subjects, still unsettled into history, interplayed through the flitting phases of conversation. To draw these from the sheltering veil of private life, the law which I have prescribed to myself forbids.

Geniality, kindness of heart, and natural humour, which glinted out, just as a brook sings, marked Mr. Dickens' manner and conversation. One easily learned in looking into the depths of his black eyes, emitting a steady light or flashing a sudden glow over his face, then pale and marked in all its lines by deep sensibility, the source of that inspiration which lifts up lowly life, which hates and smites class injustice, and brands so incisively the sleek self-complacency of well-fed social pride.

As he sat, chattily pouring out ready thoughts and shedding a sunny humour over them as these thoughts reached forward and down into philosophic generalization, or shimmered in genial play along topics momentarily started up and pleasantly dismissed, it was manifest that Dickens did not hoard up his mental jewels for his works. He has no need of such frugality. From his quick, prodigal mind he can afford to throw lavishly out the pearls which each new wave brings to the shore.

NOTE

1. Sherwood seems to be romanticising in what follows. The young Dickens's duties as a shorthand reporter in Doctors' Commons and for various newspapers would not have involved such investigatory journalism – which hardly existed, anyway, in British newspapers of this period.

'A Frank Cordiality, and a Friendly Clasp'

W. P. FRITH

From *My Autobiography and Reminiscences*, 8th edn (1890) pp. 68–71, 208–11. William Powell Frith RA (1819–1909) was, as a young artist, greatly encouraged by Dickens's patronage, and became a lifelong friend. His portrait of Dickens in 1859–60 is one of the best-known depictions of him in middle age. In 1841–2 he had produced some very popular pictures of Dolly Varden, the much-liked heroine of *Barnaby Rudge*, and Dickens wrote (15 Nov 1842) to commission 'two little companion pictures' of Dolly Varden and of Kate Nickleby. Having completed them, Frith invited Dickens to his studio.

See me then in hourly and very trembling expectation of a visit from a man whom I thought superhuman. A knock at the door. 'Come in'. Enter a pale young man with long hair, a white hat, a formidable stick in his left hand, and his right extended to me with a frank cordiality, and a friendly clasp, that never relaxed till the day of his untimely death. . . . The reading of Dickens's works has no doubt engendered a love for the writer in thousands of hearts. How that affection would have been increased could his readers have had personal knowledge of the man, can only be known to those who, like myself, had the happiness of his intimate acquaintance. . . .

[In 1859, Forster commissioned Frith to paint a portrait of Dickens.] The change in Dickens's appearance that had taken place during the twenty-five years that had elapsed since Maclise had painted him so admirably was very striking. The sallow skin had become florid, the long hair of 1835 had become shorter and darker, and the expression settled into that of one who had reached the topmost rung of a very high ladder, and was perfectly aware of his position. I find the first entry of Dickens's sittings under date '*Jan.* 21 – Arranged Dickens's portrait till he came at 1.30. He sat delightfully. I drew his head in outline, he talking all the while. The result will be successful.'

Then, next day: 'Dickens again. Miss Hogarth and his daughter came with him, and remained two and a half hours. Got in the head in colours. Dickens most pleasant. No wonder people like him.' . . .

Between Maclise's picture and my own, many portraits of Dickens had been taken, most of them – indeed, according to the sitter himself, all of them – absolute failures. I was curious with regard to one which I knew had been begun, but not finished, by an eminent Academician; and during one of the sittings to me, I inquired the reason of the delay.

'Well, the truth is,' said Dickens, 'I sat a great many times. At first the picture bore a strong resemblance to Ben Caunt' (a prize-fighter of that day); 'then it changed into somebody else; and at last I thought it was time to give it up, for I had sat there and looked at the thing till I felt I was growing like it.'

On our conversation turning on the preconceived idea that people always entertain of celebrities in literature or art, to whose personal appearance they are strangers, he said he had had frequent experience of the dismay which seemed to take possession of persons on their first introduction to him. 'And they occasionally allow their disappointment to take the form of positive objection. For instance,' said he – 'Scheffer, who is a big man, I believe, in your line – said, the moment he saw me, "You are not at all like what I expected to see you; you are like a Dutch skipper." As for the picture he did of me, I can only say that it is neither like me nor a Dutch skipper.'[1]

In my own small way I told him I had had a similar experience, for on being introduced to a North-country art patron, he said: 'You don't look a bit like an artist. I should have put you down for a well-to-do farmer.'

'Yes,' rejoined Dickens, 'and then they look at you as if it was your fault – and one for which you deserve to be kicked – because you fail to realize their ideal of what you ought to be.'

It was at this time that Dickens commenced the public readings of his works, and they became immediately very popular as well as profitable. I availed myself of his offer of tickets of admission to Hanover Square Rooms, and heard him read *The Trial from 'Pickwick'*, and from some other novel, the name of which I forget. It seems a bold thing for me to say, but I felt very strongly that the author had totally misconceived the true character of one of his own creations. In reading the humorous repartees and quaint sayings of Sam Weller, Dickens lowered his voice to the tones of one who was rather ashamed of what he was saying, and afraid of being reproved for the freedom of his utterances. I failed in being able to reconcile myself to such a rendering of a character that of all others seemed to me to call for an exactly opposite treatment. Sam is self-possessed, quick, and never-failing in his illustrations and rejoinders, even to the point of impudence.

When I determined to tell the great author that he had mistaken his own work, I knew I should be treading on dangerous ground. But on the occasion of a sitting, when my victim was more than ever good-tempered, I unburthened my mind, giving reasons for my objections. Dickens listened, smiled faintly, and said not a word. A few days after this my firiend Elmore asked my opinion of the readings, telling me he was going to hear them, and I frankly warned him that he would be disappointed with the character of Sam Weller. A few days more brought a call from Elmore, who roundly abused me for giving him an utterly false account of the Weller episode.

'Why,' he said, 'the sayings come from Dickens like pistol-shots; there was no "sneaking" way of talking, as you described it.'

'Can it be possible,' thought I, 'that this man, who, as it is told of the great Duke of Wellington, never took anybody's opinion but his own, has adopted from my suggestion a rendering of one of the children of his brain diametrically opposed to his own conception of it?'

At the next sitting all was explained, for on my telling Dickens what Elmore had said, with a twinkle in his eye which those who knew him must so well remember, he replied: 'I altered it a little – made it smarter.'

'You can't think how proud I feel,' said I, 'and surprised, too; for from my knowledge of you, and from what I have heard from other people, you are about the last man to take advice about anything, least of all about the way of reading your own books.'

'On the contrary,' was the reply, 'whenever I am wrong I am obliged to anyone who will tell me of it; but up to the present I have never been wrong.'

The portrait had progressed to the time when it was necessary to consider what the background should be, and I thought it best to discard the common curtain and column arrangement, and substitute for these well-worn properties the study in which the writer worked, with whatever accident of surrounding might present itself. Accordingly I betook myself to Tavistock House, and was installed in a corner of the study from whence I had a view of Dickens as he sat writing under the window, his desk and papers, with a framed address to him – from Birmingham, I think – together with a book-case, etc., making both back and fore ground. The first chapter of the *Tale of Two Cities*, or rather a small portion of it, lay on the desk.

After what appeared to me a vast deal of trouble on the part of the writer, muttering to himself, walking about the room, pulling his beard, and making dreadful faces, he still seemed to fail to satisfy himself with his work. I think he seldom if ever wrote after two o'clock; never, at least, when I was at Tavistock House.

NOTE

1. Sir Edwin Landseer's comment on the Frith portrait might be appended: 'I wish he looked less eager, and not so much out of himself, or beyond himself. I should like to catch him asleep and quiet now and then.' Forster bequeathed the portrait (see Plate 9) to the Victoria and Albert Museum.

America 1842

VARIOUS

'How can I give you the faintest notion of my reception here?' Dickens wrote to Forster, a week after his arrival in Boston; as a prominent Bostonian had just told him, 'There never was, and never will be, such a triumph' (*P*, II, 34–5). Later in this four-month tour, the enchantment wore off, on both sides. Dickens offended local susceptibilites by harping on the International Copyright issue – he was entitled to no royalty payments from his huge American public – and he was much offended by the intrusive vulgarity of American newspapers and by much else. No adequate study of his two American trips exists. For 1842, the annotation to the Pilgrim edition of *The Letters of Charles Dickens*, vol. 3, provides the best source. Wilkins's book, cited below, and Edward F. Payne's *Dickens' Days in Boston* (1927) contain useful information, poorly presented. For Dickens's views, see Michael Slater (ed.), *Dickens on America and Americans* (1979) and Philip Collins, 'Charles Dickens', in *Abroad in America: Visitors to the New Nation 1776–1914*, ed. Marc Pachter (1976), pp. 82–91.

[Richard Henry Dana, Jr. (1815–82), author and lawyer, whose *Two Years before the Mast* Dickens greatly admired, recorded his first

meeting with Dickens – who had invited him to call – in his journal,
26 January 1842.] Disappointed in D.'s appearance. We have heard
him called 'the handsomest man in London' &c. He is of the middle
height (under if anything) with a large expressive eye, regular nose,
matted, curling, wet-looking black hair, a dissipated looking mouth
with a vulgar draw to it, a muddy olive complexion, *stubby* fingers &
a hand by no means patrician, a hearty, off-hand manner, far from
well bred, & a rapid, dashing way of talking. He looks 'wide awake',
'up to anything', full of cleverness, with quick feelings & great
ardour. You admire him, & there is a fascination about him which
keeps your eyes on him, yet you cannot get over the impression that
he is a low bred man. . . . He has what I suppose to be the true
Cockney cut. . . . [Dining with him the next evening, Dana was
more impressed.] Like Dickens here very much. The gentlemen are
talking their best, but Dickens is perfectly natural & unpretending.
He could not have behaved better. He did not say a single thing for
display. I should think he had resolved to talk as he would at home,
& let his reputation take care of itself. [Dana was similarly
impressed at the first public dinner given to Dickens in America.]
Dickens spoke excellently. I never heard a speech wh. went off
better. He speaks naturally, with· a good voice, beautiful
intonations, & an ardent, generous manner. It is the speaking of a
man who is no orator, but says what he wishes to say in a manner
natural & unpracticed. [A few days later he offered what the
Pilgrim editors describe as his most acute analysis.] He is the cleverest
man I ever met. I mean he impresses you with the alertness of his
various powers. His forces are all light infantry & light cavalry, &
always in marching order. There are not many heavy pieces, but
few *sappers & miners*, the scientific corps is deficient, & I fear there is
no chaplain in the garrison.[1]

[Elizabeth Wormeley, like Dana on his first encounter, recorded
that Dickens was not refined enough for the best Boston circles. A
young girl, she was staying with the publisher George Ticknor, and
met Dickens at a dinner attended by 'the leading literary characters
of Boston'.] He had brought with him two velvet waistcoats, one of
vivid green, the other of brilliant crimson; these were further
ornamented by a profusion of gold watch-chain. In 1841 a black
satin waistcoat was almost the national costume of gentlemen
in America: so that Mr. Dickens's vivid tints were very conspicuous. Mrs Dickens . . . showed signs of having been born and

bred her husband's social superior. . . . In the course of the entertainment a discussion arose among the gentlemen as to which was the more beautiful woman, the Duchess of Sutherland or Mrs Caroline Norton. 'Well, I don't know,' said Dickens, expanding himself in his green velvet waistcoat: 'Mrs Norton perhaps is the most beautiful; but the duchess, to my mind, is the more kissable person.' Had a bombshell dropped upon Judge Prescott's dinner-table it could hardly have startled the company more than this remark.

I do not think the personality of Mr Dickens was altogether pleasing to the very refined and cultivated literary men and women of Boston at that period, but they did their best to entertain him with consideration and hospitality. They were not sorry, however, to pass him on to New York, where a banquet which had been prepared with great elaboration was awaiting him.[2]

[William Wetmore Story (1819–95), sculptor and writer, found Dickens 'well worth seeing'. He reported from Boston, on 3 February 1842:] Dickens himself is frank and hearty, and with a considerable touch of rowdyism in his manner. But his eyes are fine, and the whole muscular action of the mouth and lower part of the face beautifully free and vibratory. People *eat* him here! never was there such a revolution; Lafayette was nothing to it. But he is too strong and healthy a mind to be spoiled even by the excessive adulation and flattery that he receives[3]

[Richard Henry Dana, Sr. (1787–1879), poet and essayist, was, like his son, initially unimpressed. In letters of February 1842, he reports:] When my eye first fell upon him I was disappointed. But the instant his face was turned towards me, there was a change. He has the finest of eyes; and his whole countenance speaks *life* and *action* – the face seems to flicker with the heart's and mind's activity. You cannot tell how dead the faces near him seemed. . . . He is full of life. And with him life does not appear to be . . . a forced state – but a truly *natural* one. I never saw a face fuller of vivid action, or an eye fuller of light. And he is so freely animated – so unlike *our folk*. He is plainly enough a most hearty man, & a most kind hearted one. People do not seem to crowd about him as to see a lion, but from downright love of him. [To the New York journalist Rufus Wilmot Griswold, he wrote:] We have had great days here with Boz; & a fine fellow he is – you can't help loving him, if you would.[4]

[The poet Henry Wadsworth Longfellow (1807–82), who became a lifelong friend, quickly decided that Dickens was 'a glorious fellow . . . a gay free-and-easy character, with a bright face . . . and withal a slight dash of the Dick Swiveller about him.' His younger brother Samuel, later to become a distinguished divine, was more critical:] I confess I did not find him my ideal Boz. He is very animated and talkative, pleasant but not particularly humorous, with an offhand way, and the slightest possible tincture of rowdyism in his appearance. . . . He has none of that refinement and scholarly look which we are apt to attach to our idea of a literary man; in other words he is just what we ought to expect when we recollect his history instead of his books. His hair is long, combed by his fingers & apparently guiltless of all acquaintance with a brush, in short not neat. His face is agreeable not so handsome as, tho' somewhat resembling the large lithograph which Henry has. His features are in constant play while he talks, particularly his eyebrows, giving him a French aspect. He speaks fast & rather indistinctly. . . . He said that Quilp was entirely a creature of the imagination he had heaped together in him all possible hideousness.[5]

[One of the many newspaper accounts which annoyed Dickens was this, in the *St. Louis People's Organ*, 12 April 1842: see *P*, III, 195.] Dickens stands very straight, is of medium length, and has a good figure. His manner of introduction is free and easy, frank. His head shows large perceptive faculties, a large volume of brain in front of the ears, but not large causality. His eye is, to our perception, *blue, dark blue*, and full; it stands out slightly, and is handsome – very beautiful. It is the *striking* feature of his physiognomy.

His hair has been described as very fine. We did not find it so; it is slightly waxy, and has a glossy, soft texture. It is very long, with unequivocal soap-locks, which to our eye looked badly. We had thought from his portraits that it was thick, but did not find it so. He wore a black dress coat, with collar and facings of velvet, a satin vest with very gay and variegated colours, light colored pantaloons, and boots polished to a fault. . . . One or more rings ornamented his fingers. Dickens is thirty years and one or two months old. He does not look older. No one would suspect from inspection that he is the genius his works prove him to be. . . . His whole appearance is foppish, and partakes of the flash order. To our American taste it

was decidedly so; especially as most gentlemen in the room were
dressed chiefly in black.[6]

[The newspaper description most widely reprinted in other American papers at the time, as Paul B. Davis remarks in an excellent
survey, is this, from the *Aegis* (Worcester, Mass.), 9 February 1842.]
As Mr. Dickens, by this time, is probably beyond the reach of our
remarks, we venture upon a brief description of his person, for the
benefit, exclusively, of those who have had no opportunity to see the
lion of the day.

   In the first place, we must discard all the prints that have been
issued professing to be likenesses of 'Boz'. There is not one of them
that does not give an entirely incorrect impression of his
appearance. Neither his features, nor the tout ensemble of his
expression, are, in our opinion, represented with an approximation
to fidelity. Some of the portraits have a thoughtful and pensive air,
with a dark deep look in the eye, well enough adapted to the
character of a quiet observer and reflective student; others represent
a shorter and rounder visage, with the common countenance of a
good looking, good tempered, and intelligent young man; from all
of them that we have seen, would be received the impression of Ionic
looks, fair smooth forehead and cheeks, and regular outlines of
features; in none are the lines, nerves, or muscles of the face
delineated with any truth to nature. In fact, the lines are deeply
marked, the nerves and muscles strongly developed and active,
arching the eyebrows in conversation, and giving motion and
variety of expression to every part of the countenance. The reality,
therefore, accorded very little with our imagination of his
appearance.

   We found a middle sized person, in a brown frock coat, a red
figured vest, somewhat of the flash order, and a fancy scarf cravat,
that concealed the dickey, and was fastened to the bosom in rather
voluminous folds by a double pin and chain. His proportions were
well rounded, and filled the dress he wore. His hair, which was long
and dark, grew low upon the brow, had a wavy kink where it started
from the head, and was naturally or artificially corkscrewed as it fell
on either side of his face. His forehead retreated gradually from the
eyes, without any marked protuberance, save at the outer angle, the
upper portion of which formed a prominent ridge a little within the
assigned position of the organ of ideality. The skin on that portion of

the brow which was not concealed by the hair, instead of being light and smooth, flushed as readily as any part of the face, and partook of its general character of flexibility. The whole region about the eyes was prominent, with a noticeable development of nerves and vessels, indicating, say the phrenologists, great vigor in the intellectual organs with which they are connected. The eyeballs completely filled their sockets. The aperture of the lids was not large, nor the eye uncommonly clear or bright, but quick, moist, and expressive. The nose was slightly aquiline – the mouth of moderate dimensions, making no great display of the teeth, the facial muscles occasionally drawing the upper lip most strongly on the left side, as the mouth opened in speaking. His features, taken together were well proportioned, of glowing and cordial aspect, with more animation than grace, and more intelligence than beauty.

We will close this off-hand description without going more minutely into the anatomy of Mr. Dickens, by saying that he wears a gold watch guard over his vest and a shaggy coat of bear or buffalo skin that would excite the admiration of a Kentucky huntsman. In short, you frequently meet with similar looking young men, at theatres, and other public plces, and you would infer that he found his enjoyments in the scenes of actual life, rather than in the retirement of study; and that he would be likely to be about town and to witness those scenes which he describes, with such unrivalled precision and power.[7]

'NOTES'

1. R. H. Dana, Jr, *Journal 1841–60*, ed. R. F. Lucid (1968) I, 57–61, quoted in *P*, III, 39n, 67n.

2. Mrs Elizabeth Wormeley Latimer, 'A Girl's Recollections of Dickens', *Lippincott's Magazine*, Sep 1893, pp. 338–9.

3. Henry James, *William Wetmore Story and His Friends* (1903) I, 58–9.

4. Quoted from manuscripts, in *P*, III, 32n.

5. Quoted by Edward Wagenknecht, 'Dickens in Longfellow's Letters and Journals', *Dickens and the Scandalmongers* (Norman, Oklahoma, 1965) pp. 72–3.

6. William Glyde Wilkins, *Charles Dickens in America* (1911) p. 224, corrected and amplified from *P*, III, 195n.

7. Reprinted by Paul B. Davis, 'Dickens and the American Press, 1842', *Dickens Studies* (1968) IV, 59–60.

His American Secretary in 1842

GEORGE WASHINGTON PUTNAM

From 'Four Months with Charles Dickens, during his First Visit to America (in 1842): By His Secretary', *Atlantic Monthly*, XXVI (1870) 476–82, 591–9. Putnam (1812–96) was at this time a pupil of the Boston artist Francis Alexander, who was painting Dickens's portrait soon after his arrival in America. He thus met Dickens, who on Alexander's recommendation appointed him to deal with the masses of correspondence that had descended on him. Putnam proved so useful that Dickens retained his services for the whole tour. Towards Dickens, Putnam felt 'an ardent attachment, which has its origin not alone in the splendor of his genius, but in the daily and hourly exhibition of the finest and noblest feelings of the human heart' (letter of March 1842, quoted in *P*, III, 27n.). For further particulars see N.C. Peyrouton, 'Mr. "Q": Dickens's American Secretary', *Dkn*, LIX (1963) 156–9.

The doorway and stairs leading to [Francis Alexander's] studio were thronged with ladies and gentlemen, eagerly awaiting [Dickens's] appearance, and as he passed they were to the last degree silent and respectful. It was no vulgar curiosity to see a great and famous man, but an earnest, intelligent, and commendable desire to look upon the author whose writings – already enlisted in the great cause of humanity – had won their dear respect, and endeared him to their hearts. He pleasantly acknowledged the compliment their presence paid him, bowing slightly as he passed, his bright, dark eyes glancing through and through the crowd, searching every face, and reading character with wonderful quickness, while the arch smiles played over his handsome face. . . .

The crowd waited till the sitting was over, and saw him back again to the Tremont; and this was repeated every morning while he was sitting for his picture.

The engravings in his books which had then been issued either in England or America were *very little* like him. Alexander chose an attitude highly original, but very characteristic. Dickens is represented at his table writing. His left hand rests upon the paper. The pen in his right hand seems to have been stopped for a moment, while he looks up at you as if you had just addressed him. His long brown hair, slightly curling, sweeps his shoulder, the bright eyes glance, and that inexpressible look of kindly mirth plays round his mouth and shows itself in the arched brow. Alexander caught much of that singular *lighting up of the face* which Dickens had, beyond any one I ever saw, and the picture is very like the original, and will convey to those who wish to know how 'Boz' looked at thirty years of age an excellent idea of the man. . . .

In one corner of the room, [Henry] Dexter the sculptor was earnestly at work modelling a bust of Mr. Dickens. . . . The whole soul of the artist was engaged in his task, and the result was a splendid bust of the great author. Mr. Dickens was highly pleased with it, and repeatedly alluded to it, during his stay, as a very successful work of art.

Alexander's picture and Dexter's bust of Dickens should be exhibited at this time [1870, shortly after his death], that those who never saw him in his young days may know *exactly how he looked*. The bust by Dexter has the rare merit of *action*, and in every respect faithfully represents the features, attitude, and look of Charles Dickens. . . .

A day or two after his arrival in Philadelphia an individual somewhat prominent in city politics came with others and obtained an introduction. On taking his leave, he asked Mr. Dickens if he would grant him the favor to receive a few personal friends the next day; and Mr. Dickens assented. The next morning it was announced through the papers that Mr. Dickens would 'receive the *public*' at a certain hour! At the time specified the street in front was crowded with people, and the offices and halls of the hotel filled. Mr. Dickens asked the cause of the assembling, and was astonished and indignant when he learned that all this came of his permission to the individual above mentioned to 'bring a few personal friends for an introduction', and he positively refused to hold a 'levee'. But the landlord of the house and others came and represented to him that his refusal would doubtless create a riot, and that great injury would be done to the house by the enraged populace; and so at last Mr. Dickens consented, and, taking his place in one of the large parlors up stairs, prepared himself for the ordeal. Up the people came, and soon the humorous smiles played over his face, for, tedious and annoying as it was, the thing had its *comic* side, and, while he shook ·hands incessantly, he as usual studied human character. For two mortal hours or more the crowd poured in, and he shook hands and exchanged words with all, while the dapper little author of the scene stood smiling by, giving hundreds and thousands of introductions, and making, no doubt, much social and political capital out of his supposed intimacy with the great English author. This scene is substantially repeated in *Martin Chuzzlewit* [ch. 22], when his new-made American friends insisted upon Martin's 'holding a levee', having announced without his authority, as in the case of Mr. Dickens, that he would 'receive the public'. . . .

At last, in Mr. Dickens's case, the 'levee' was over, and, tired to the last degree, he went to his room.

Mr. Dickens maintained throughout his travels a constant and large correspondence with friends at home; and often, while writing, his face would be convulsed with laughter at his own fun; and on his showing the letters to Mrs. Dickens she would join heartily in the mirth.

Whenever the boat [down the Ohio] reached a town on the river, word would be passed by the passengers to the people on the landing that 'Boz was on board', and there would be a gathering of persons earnestly looking for him, and many gentlemen would hasten on board to get a glimpse of the great author. . . .

One day [in St Louis] a well-known literary gentleman called and was cordially received by Mr. Dickens. After conversing for some time he began to speak of the condition of society in America, and at last in a most bland and conciliating manner asked: 'Mr. Dickens, how do you like our domestic institution, sir?' 'Like what, sir?' said Mr. Dickens, rousing up and looking sharply at his visitor. 'Our domestic institution, sir,—slavery!' said the gentleman. Dickens's eyes blazed as he answered promptly, 'Not at all, sir! I don't like it at all, sir!' 'Ah!' said his visitor, considerably abashed by the prompt and manly answer he had received, 'you probably have not seen it in its *true* character, and are prejudiced against it'. 'Yes, sir!' was the answer, 'I have seen it, sir! all I ever wish to see of it, and I detest it, sir!'

The gentleman looked mortified, abashed, and offended, and, taking his hat, bade Mr. Dickens 'Good morning', which greeting was returned with promptness, and he left the room. Mr. Dickens then, in a towering passion, turned to me. 'Damn their impudence, Mr. P.! If they will not thrust their accursed "domestic institution" in my face, I will not attack it, for I did not come here for that purpose. But to tell me that a man is better off as a slave than as a freeman is an insult, and I will not endure it from any one! I will not bear it!'

It was not uncommon, in the various places at which we stayed, for persons of unsettled minds persistently to seek an interview with the novelist. It was impossible, of course, for him to see them, for he had not half time enough to devote to the *sane* people who thronged his rooms. But to these unfortunates he always sent a kind word, expressing his regret that he could not see them personally. . . .

At Columbus we hired a stage-coach exclusively for our party, and the stage company sent an agent with the driver to go through with us. The upper portion of Ohio was largely at that time an unbroken forest, and the accommodations for travellers were very poor. Nothing but corn-bread and bacon could be obtained at the log-cabins on the road, and so our good landlord of the Neil House had a basket of provisions put up for us to dine upon. . . . Soon after noon we came to a pleasant nook in the woods, not far from a log-cabin, and our basket of provisions was opened and the cloth spread upon the grass. I obtained a pitcher of cool water at the cabin near by, and dinner was ready. I trust I shall be excused if I mention here a little instance of the kindness of heart always shown by Charles Dickens. The driver and his friend, who were now waiting with the coach at a little distance, had dined at the log-tavern which we passed a half-hour before. But before *we* dined Mr. Dickens, heaping up a large quantity of oranges, apples, nuts, and raisins, which we had brought for dessert, and a quantity of wine added, requested me to take them to the driver and his companion, which I did. It was a little incident; but it was characteristic of that man throughout life to *remember others*. . . .

Only those whose opportunities brought them in close contact with Charles Dickens can know the full beauty and purity of his nature, and how intensely he loathed all that was coarse and low. An incident occurred during our journey which illustrated this. On one occasion, at a public dinner given him – many ladies being present as spectators – some persons, entirely mistaking the character of their guest, had secured the presence of a certain 'Doctor', famous it would appear for story-telling. After the speeches commenced, there were frequent calls for the 'Doctor', and at last he rose and said that he 'must be excused from saying anything while the ladies were present'. There was instantly a movement among the ladies to go. Mr. Dickens beckoned to me and said earnestly, 'Please ask the ladies to stay, say I wish them to say!' I spoke to Mrs. Dickens, and she said a few words to those around her, and the ladies remained. The rebuke was gentle but efficient, and there were no more calls for the 'Doctor' during the rest of the evening.

Many kind letters of remembrance came to me from Mr. Dickens during the long interval which has passed since his memorable visit in 1842, and it scarcely need be said that on the occasion of his last coming he received the writer of these recollections with both hands outstretched and with a most cordial greeting.

Maddest Nonsense and Tragic Depths

THOMAS AND JANE WELSH CARLYLE

For references, see Notes. Dickens greatly admired Carlyle (1795–1881) and his wife Jane (1801–66), dedicating *Hard Times* to him and acknowledging a debt to his ideas, and saying of her that 'None of the writing women come near her at all' (*Life*, VIII, vii, 702). For Carlyle's first impressions of Dickens, in 1840, see Thomas Adolphus Trollope, below, I, 71–2; and for particulars of their relationship, see Michael Goldberg, *Carlyle and Dickens* (1972), and William Oddie, *Dickens and Carlyle* (1972). Carlyle was a close friend of Forster; and his biographer J. A. Froude, writing of the 1860s, remarks that Carlyle was by then 'dining nowhere save now and then with Forster, to meet only Dickens, who loved him with all his heart' (*Life in London*, II, 243). In the first extract, Jane Welsh Carlyle is describing a Boxing Day party at the Macreadys' house; Macready was away on an American tour.

Jane Welsh Carlyle, to Jeannie Welsh, Dec 1843. . . . it was the *very* most agreeable party that ever I was at in London – everybody there seemed animated with one purpose to make up to Mrs. Macready and her children for the absence of 'The Tragic Actor', and so amiable a purpose produced the most joyous results. Dickens and Forster above all exerted themselves till the perspiration was pouring down and they seemed *drunk* with their efforts! Only think of that excellent Dickens playing the *conjuror* for one whole hour – the *best* conjuror I ever saw – (and I have paid money to see several) – and Forster acting as his servant. This part of the entertainment concluded with a plum pudding made out of raw flour, raw eggs – all the usual raw ingredients – boiled in a gentleman's hat – and tumbled out reeking – all in one minute before the eyes of the astonished children and astonished grown

people! That trick – and his other of changing ladies' pocket
handkerchiefs into comfits – and a box full of bran into a box full of –
a live guinea-pig! would enable him to make a handsome sub-
sistence, let the bookseller trade go as it please – ! Then the dancing . . . !! Dickens did all but go down on his knees to make *me* –
waltz with him! . . . In fact the thing was rising into something not
unlike the rape of the Sabines! . . . when somebody looked at her watch
and exclaimed 'twelve o' clock!' Whereupon we all rushed to the cloak-
room – and there and in the lobby and up to the last moment the
mirth raged on. Dickens took home Thackeray and Forster with
him and his wife '*to finish the night there*' and a *royal* night they would
have of it I fancy! – ending perhaps with a visit to the watch-house.

After all – the pleasantest company, as Burns thought, *are* the
blackguards! – that is, those who have just a sufficient dash of
blackguardism in them to make them snap their fingers at *ceremony*
and 'all that sort of thing'.[1]

Carlyle to Forster, 6 June 1844. I truly love Dickens; and discern in the
inner man of him a tone of real Music, which struggles to express
itself as it may, in these bewildered stupefied and indeed very empty
and distracted days, – better or worse! This, which makes him in my
estimation one of a thousand, I could with great joy and freedom
testify to all persons, to himself first of all, in any good way.[2]

Jane Welsh Carlyle to Jeannie Welsh, 'Holy Thursday, 1849'. I have been
to several parties – a dinner at Dickens's last Saturday where I never
went before. 'A great fact!' Forster might have called it. Such
getting up of the steam is unbecoming to a literary man, who *ought* to
have his basis elsewhere than on what the old Annandale woman
called 'ornament and grandeur'. The dinner was served up in the
new fashion – not placed on the table at all – but handed round –
only the dessert on the table and quantities of *artificial* flowers – but
such an overloaded dessert! pyramids of figs, raisins, oranges – ach!
At the Ashburton dinner served on those principles there were just
four cowslips in china pots – four silver shells containing sweets, and a
silver filigree temple in the middle! but here the very candles rose
each out of an artificial rose! Good God![3]

Carlyle to John Carlyle, 29 Apr 1863. I had to go yesterday to Dickens's
Reading, 8 p.m., Hanover Rooms, to the complete upsetting of my
evening habitudes and spiritual composure. Dickens does do it

capitally, such as *it* is; acts better than any Macready in the world; a whole tragic, comic, heroic *theatre* visible, performing under one *hat*, and keeping us laughing – in a sorry way, some of us thought – the whole night. He is a good creature, too, and makes fifty or sixty pounds by each of these readings.[4]

Carlyle to the Dickens family, 4 July 1870. It is almost thirty years since my acquaintance with him began: and on my side, I may say, every new meeting ripened it into more and more clear discernment of his rare and great worth as a brother man; a most cordial, sincere, clear-sighted, quietly decisive, just and loving man: till at length he had grown to such recognition with me as I have rarely had for any man of my time.[5]

Carlyle to Forster, 11 June 1870. I am profoundly sorry for *you*, and indeed for myself and for us all. It is an event world-wide; a *unique* of talents suddenly extinct; and has 'eclipsed', we too may say, 'the harmless gaiety of nations'. No death since 1866 has fallen on me with such a stroke. No literary man's hitherto ever did. The good, the gentle, high-gifted, ever-friendly, noble Dickens, – every inch of him an Honest Man.[6]

Carlyle to John Forster, 16 Feb 1874. This Third Volume [of the *Life*] throws a new light and character to me over the Work at large. . . . So long as Dickens is interesting to his fellow-men, here will be seen, face to face, what Dickens's manner of existing was; his steady practicality, withal; the singularly solid business talent he continually had; and deeper than all if one had the eye to see deep enough, dark, fateful silent elements, tragical to look upon, and hiding amid dazzling radiances as of the sun, the elements of death itself. Those two American Journies especially transcend in tragic interest to a thinking reader most things one has seen in writing.[7]

Dickens [Carlyle told Charles Gavan Duffy] was a good little fellow, and one of the most cheery, innocent natures he had ever encountered. But he lived among a set of admirers who did him no good – Maclise the painter, Douglas Jerrold, John Forster, and the like; and he spent his entire income in their society. He was seldom seen in fashionable drawing-rooms, however, and maintained, one could see, something of his old reporter independence. His theory of life was entirely wrong. He thought men ought to be buttered up, and the world made soft and accommodating for them, and all sorts of fellows have turkey for their Christmas dinner. Commanding and controlling and punishing them he would give up without any misgivings in order to coax and soothe and delude them into doing right. But it was not in this manner the eternal laws operated, but quite otherwise. . . .

Carlyle said of Dickens that his chief faculty was that of a comic actor. He would have made a successful one if he had taken to that sort of life. His public readings, which were a pitiful pursuit after all, were in fact acting, and very good acting too. He had a remarkable faculty for business; he managed his periodical skilfully, and made good bargains with his booksellers. Set him to do any work, and if he undertook it, it was altogether certain that it would be done effectually.[8]

NOTES

1. *Jane Welsh Carlyle: A Selection of her Letters*, ed. Trudy Bliss (1959 edn) pp. 140–1.

2. Charles Richard Saunders, 'Carlyle's Letters', *Bulletin of the John Rylands Library*, xxx (1956–6) 199–224.

3. *Jane Welsh Carlyle*, p. 184. The 'Ashburton' referred to is Lady Ashburton (Lady Harriet Baring), the celebrated and highly aristocratic hostess, who lived in grand style. Carlyle was an intimate friend of hers.

4. J. A. Froude, *Thomas Carlyle: A History of His Life in London 1834–1881* (1884) II, 270.

5. *Life*, XI, iii, 836.

6. *Life*, XI, iii, 836. ' . . . we too . . . ' because this was what Johnson had said on Garrick's death; Jane Welsh Carlyle had died in 1866.

7. Saunders, in *Bulletin of the John Rylands Library*, xxx, 199–224.

8. Charles Gavan Duffy, *Conversations with Carlyle* (1892) pp. 75, 77.

A French View in 1843

PAUL FORGUES

From his 'Souvenirs de Londres', *L'Illustration*, 1844, trs. William J. Carlton in his ' "Old Nick" at Devonshire Terrace: Dickens through French Eyes in 1843', *Dkn*, LIX (1963) 138–44. Paul Émile Daurand Forgues (1813–83), literary and dramatic critic on various Paris journals under the pseudonym of 'Old Nick', called on Dickens in June 1843, with Amedée Pichot and another French journalistic colleague (see *P*, III, 501–2). All three of them published accounts of the interview, which are cited by Carlton and the Pilgrim editors. Pichot (1795–1877), editor of the *Revue britannique*, had translated, and was further to translate, Dickens into French; his recollections of Dickens in 1843 appear in a preface to *Le Neveu de ma tante*, his translation of *David Copperfield*. 'Pichot found it unexpected that an Englishman should make so much use of gesture (though "without going beyond the limits of British dignity") and was not surprised at learning later of his talent in private theatricals. . . . Dickens was more ready to speak of his children [Charley entered the room at one point] than of his works, but discussed translations of his books' (*P*, III, 502n.). The annotation to this item is mainly from Carlton.

My friend and I had an appointment—a necessary precaution in the case of a man so sought after, or for that matter of anyone in England where strangers are not welcome. . . . The famous novelist greeted us on the threshold of his study: an oval room, simply furnished, the walls screened by books, having an air of quiet restfulness. The portrait of Dickens published in this paper[1] gives but a vague idea of his face, one of the most intelligent and vivacious I have seen. He is young; long, brown, rather untidy hair falls over the forehead of an unhealthy pallor. The bright, restless eyes testify to an unusual sagacity and quick intelligence. My uneasy curiosity, nevertheless, did not find there all that I expected, and I wondered what I would have thought of Dickens had I met him by chance, not knowing him, in a theatre, at a ball, in a public vehicle or on a steamboat. I felt that I might well have taken the most popular novelist of the day for the head clerk of a big banking house, a smart reporter at an assize court, the secret agent of a diplomatic intrigue, an astute and wily barrister, a lucky gambler, or simply the manager of a troupe of strolling players.

But most of these hypotheses were ruled out by his conversation, for Dickens talks modestly and frankly, with an open countenance, unflinching gaze and honest smile. He spoke chiefly to my fellow traveller, under whose auspices I had come to see him and whose ear was more attuned to the terrible ellipses of English pronunciation. This arrangement pleased me as it left me free to study the man by his accent, the inflexions of his voice, and the hundred and one details of his surroundings. . . .

And the conversation? It flowed unceasingly, but I did not follow it well, listening only by fits and starts. Dickens spoke to us of a journey to France he was to make shortly and expressed doubts as to the value that might be placed on his works, though far from disdaining any success he might achieve outside his own country. He had there a few translations of his novels and had few complaints to make about the translators, from which I concluded that Dickens was either very indulgent or very polite. Then, as he excluded from this benevolent approval a certain German version of *Nicholas Nickleby* and *Oliver Twist*, I could not help reflecting that we came neither from Weimar nor Berlin.

He seemed to be much preoccupied with certain physiological studies. His enquiring and subtle mind was clearly exercised by magnetism, the systems of Gall and Mesmer,[2] everything relating to the phenomenal existence of man, all those unexplained miracles the analysis of which will eventually throw light on the great question raised by Cabanis.[3] So I was not at all surprised when he recommended a visit to a penitentiary as one of the curiosities which should be included in our stay in London.[4]

NOTES

1. A poorly executed woodcut of Maclise's '*Nickleby*' portrait of Dickens had appeared in *L'Illustration*, 9 Sep 1843.

2. Franz Joseph Gall (1758–1828) was the founder of phrenology; Friedrich Anton Mesmer (1733–1815) was the founder of the theory of animal magnetism ('mesmerism').

3. Pierre Jean George Cabanis (1757–1808), French physician and philosophical writer, author of *Rapports du physique et du moral de l'homme* (1802).

4. Dickens gave them an introduction to his friend George Laval Chesterton, governor of the Middlesex House of Correction, Coldbath Fields; see Philip Collins, 'Dickens and the Prison Governor', *Dkn*, LVII (1961) 11–26. He had discussed with his French visitors the famous penitentiary at Philadelphia, described in his *American Notes* (1842) ch. 7.

'Abominably Vulgar', but 'at the Top of the Tree'

W. M. THACKERAY

From *The Letters and Private Papers of William Makepeace Thackeray*, ed. Gordon N. Ray (1945–6) II, 110, 304, 333, 569, and IV, 86, 122; and Gordon N. Ray, *Thackeray: The Age of Wisdom 1847–1863* (1958) pp. 288–9. Though Thackeray often wrote about Dickens's writings (and usually with notable warmth and generosity: see below, II, 293), he recorded much less about Dickens the man, except for repeated, and dubiously founded, accusations that Dickens hated and was jealous of him, expressed during the recurrent feuds between their supporters and sometimes themselves. Thackeray (1811–63), a few months older than Dickens but a decade later in achieving eminence, was of much more genteel birth (and was educated at Charterhouse and Cambridge), and as Gordon Ray remarks 'could not rid himself of the conviction that there was a taint of vulgarity in Dickens' (*Letters*, I, cxxi). *Vanity Fair* (1847–8) established him as a leading novelist, and thenceforth he was always measuring himself for size against the acknowledged leader of the profession. As a friend said, he often suffered from 'Dickens-on-the-brain'; or, as Dickens's daughter Katey put it, she had 'countless conversations' with Thackeray about her father, whose 'way of life, his daily habits of writing, his likes and dislikes – his friends – and, above everything else, his written books, all held for Thackeray a singular fascination, and he never seemed to tire of what I had to tell him. Sometimes, but that was later on, he would criticise my father's work. . . . But there were times when he said things about my father that satisfied even my craving for appreciation of his genius' – 'Thackeray and my Father', *Pall Mall Magazine*, n.s. XIV (1911) 213–14). Thackeray was never one of Dickens's intimates, but was well acquainted with him throughout his career. The 'Garrick Club affair' of 1858 – a prolonged squabble between the two novelists and their parties – resulted in a frosty cessation of the friendship, but they were reconciled shortly before Thackeray's death. Dickens greatly admired *Vanity Fair* but otherwise has little to say about Thackeray's novels. Thackeray, who did a lot of reviewing, found more occasions to discuss Dickens's work in public; and in private, while expressing major reservations about Dickens's art and method, he consistently recognised his genius. He also much admired Dickens's histrionic powers, exclaiming after his performance in *The Frozen Deep*, 'If that man would go upon the stage, he would make his £10,000 a-year!' – Carl Ray Woodring, *Victorian Samplers: William and Mary Howitt* (1952) p. 184.

To his wife, May 1843. Did I write to tell you about Mrs. Procter's grand ball, and how splendid Mrs. Dickens was in pink satin and Mr. Dickens in geranium & ringlets?

To Mrs Macready, 15 June 1847. Dickens has just written begging me to dine with him and meet Forster, and make up Quarrels and be Friends.

To his mother, 7 Jan 1848. There is no use denying the matter or blinking it now. [With the serialisation of *Vanity Fair*] I am become a sort of great man in my way – all but at the top of the tree: indeed there if the truth were known and having a great fight up there with Dickens.

To Mrs Brookfield, 24 July 1849. I met on the pier [at Ryde, Isle of Wight] as I was running for the dear life, the great Dickens with his wife his children his Miss Hogarth all looking abominably coarse vulgar and happy and bound for Bonchurch where they have taken one of White's houses for the summer.

To his mother, May 1858. Here is sad news in the literary world – no less than a separation between Mr. & Mrs. Dickens – with all sorts of horrible stories buzzing about. The worst is that Im in a manner dragged in for one – Last week going into the Garrick I heard that D is separated from his wife on account of an intrigue with his sister in law. No says I no such thing – its with an actress – and the other story has not got to Dickens's ears but this has – and he fancies that I am going about abusing him! We shall never be allowed to be friends that's clear. I had mine from a man at Epsom the first I ever heard of the matter, and should have said nothing about it but that I heard the other much worse story whereupon I told mine to counteract it. There is some row about an actress in the case, & he denies with the utmost infuriation any charge against her or himself – but says that it has been known to any one intimate with his family that his and his wifes tempers were horribly incompatible & now that the children are grown up – it is agreed they are to part – the eldest son living with her the daughters &c remaining under the care of Miss Hogarth who has always been mother governess housekeeper everything to the family. I havent seen the statement[1] but this is what is brought to me on my bed of sickness, and I'd give 100£ (if it weren't true.) To think of the poor matron after 22 years of marriage going away out of her house! O dear me its a fatal story for our trade.

To his daughters, 4 Dec 1858. Dined at Forster's with Elwin. Forster was admirably grotesque and absurd. I was glad to get out of the house without touching on the Dickens affair. John Brown[2] writes from Edinburgh today, that CD is a miscreant. He is $\frac{1}{2}$ mad about his domestic affairs, and tother $\frac{1}{2}$ mad with arrogance and vanity.

To William Webb Synge, winter 1858–9. I'm not even angry with Dickens now for being the mover in the whole [Garrick Club] affair. He can't help hating me; and he can't help being a – you know what I daresay. His quarrel with his wife has driven him almost frantic. He is now quarrelling with his son; and has just made himself friends of the whole Garrick Club, by withdrawing his lad's name, just as it was coming up for ballot[3] . . . and the poor boy is very much cast down at his father's proceedings.

NOTES

1. The 'statement' Thackeray means is what Dickens called his 'violated letter'. He had given his readings manager, Arthur Smith, a statement about the unhappiness of his marriage and the 'peculiarity' of his wife's character; Smith was to show it 'to any one who wishes to do me right'. An American journalist printed the complete text, which was then copied by some English newspapers. Dickens was greatly 'shocked and distressed' by this 'violation' (predictable though it was).

2. Dr John Brown (1810–82), Scottish physician and man of letters, was a close friend of Thackeray's.

3. Dickens's eldest son, Charley, had contributed to *Punch*, 11 Dec 1858, an attack on Edmund Yates, whom Dickens was supporting against Thackeray in the Garrick Club row. Dickens retaliated by removing the lad's name from the Club's proposal list. Gossip at the *Punch* table, as recorded in Henry Silver's diary, was very snide about Dickens. Shirley Brooks even defended Yates, on the ground that 'he was merely acting for Dickens – who never spoke well of Thackeray or anybody else: which Mark Lemon confirms'. Lemon remarked that 'the applause when he acted turned Dickens's head and caused his bad conduct to his wife – Professor Owen foretold a catastrophe' (quoted by Ray, *Thackeray: The Age of Wisdom*, pp. 476–7). 'Dickens has grown so arrogant', Owen had said in 1858, and Percival Leigh, a member of the *Punch* table, had agreed: it would not surprise him if Dickens proclaimed himself to be God Almighty. 'Thinks himself God now', Shirley Brooks replied. 'If he is we are atheists, for I don't believe in him' – A. A. Adrian, *Mark Lemon, First Editor of 'Punch'* (1966) p. 134. Pleasantly, Dickens was returning good for evil during the final weeks of his life – visiting Brooks, who

was ill, and urging Gladstone to grant a pension to the widow of Mark Lemon, who died less than three weeks before himself.

'No Nonsense' about Him

R. H. HORNE

From his *The New Spirit of the Age* (1844) 1, 72 – 6. Richard Hengist Horne (1803–84), poet, journalist and miscellaneous writer, was friendly with Dickens and later worked on the *Daily News* and *Household Words*. The passage here reprinted comes at the end of his chapter on Dickens in his compilation of essays modelled on Hazlitt's *The Spirit of the Age* (1825). The Dickens chapter is the first, and much the longest. See also his 'Bygone Celebrities: The Guild of Literature and Art at Chatsworth', and 'Mr. Nightingale's Diary', *Gentleman's Magazine*, n.s. VI (1871) 247–62, 660–72; 'John Forster: His Early Life and Friendships', *Temple Bar*, XLVI (1876) 491–505; and K. J. Fielding, 'Charles Dickens and R. H. Horne', *English*, IX (1952) 17–19.

Mr. Dickens is manifestly the product of his age. He is a genuine emanation from its aggregate and entire spirit. He is not an imitator of any one. He mixes extensively in society, and continually. Few public meetings in a benevolent cause are without him. He speaks effectively – humorously, at first, and then seriously to the point. His reputation, and all the works we have discussed, are the extraordinary product of only eight years. Popularity and success, which injure so many men in head and heart, have improved him in all respects. His influence upon his age is extensive – pleasurable, instructive, healthy, reformatory. . . .

Mr. Dickens is, in private, very much what might be expected from his works, – by no means an invariable coincidence. He talks much or little according to his sympathies. His conversation is genial. He hates argument; in fact, he is unable to argue – a common case with impulsive characters who see the whole truth, and feel it crowding and struggling at once for immediate utterance. He never talks for effect, but for the truth or for the fun of the thing. He tells a story admirably, and generally with humorous exaggerations. His sympathies are of the broadest, and his literary tastes appreciate all excellence. He is a great admirer of the poetry of Tennyson. Mr. Dickens has singular personal activity, and is fond of games of practical skill. He is also a great walker, and very much given to dancing Sir Roger de Coverley. In private, the general impression of him is that of a first-rate practical intellect, with 'no nonsense' about him. Seldom, if ever, has any man been more beloved by contemporary authors, and by the public of his time.

A 'Manly Man', a 'Hearty Man'

THOMAS ADOLPHUS TROLLOPE

From *What I Remember* (1887) II, 110–17. Thomas Adolphus Trollope (1810–92), elder son of the novelist Mrs Frances Trollope (see above, I, 19) and brother of Anthony Trollope, was also a novelist. He lived in Italy, 1843–90, and contributed to *All the Year Round* (not *Household Words*, as he states), mainly on Italian topics. He first met Dickens in 1845, at his mother's villa in Florence. They became more intimate in Dickens's later years, because Trollope's second wife, whom he married in 1866, was Frances Eleanor Ternan, elder sister of Dickens's actress friend Ellen Ternan (on whom see below, I, 154); indeed, he met her through Dickens. She too wrote novels, and Dickens was rumoured to have over-paid for those she serialised in *All the Year Round*, because of his partiality for the family: see Ada Nisbet, *Dickens and Ellen Ternan* (1952).

[It was in 1845] that I saw Dickens for the first time. One morning in Casa Berti my mother was most agreeably surprised by a card brought in to her with 'Mr. and Mrs. Charles Dickens' on it. We had been among his heartiest admirers from the early days of *Pickwick.* . . . And it was with the greatest curiosity and interest that we saw the creator of all this enjoyment enter in the flesh.

We were at first disappointed, and disposed to imagine there must be some mistake! No! *that* is not the man who wrote *Pickwick*! What we saw was a dandified, pretty-boy-looking sort of figure, singularly young looking, I thought, with a slight flavour of the whipper-snapper genus of humanity.

Here is Carlyle's description of his appearance at about that period of his life, quoted from Froude's *History of Carlyle's Life in London*: 'He is a fine little fellow – Boz – I think. Clear blue, intelligent eyes, eyebrows that he arches amazingly, large, protrusive, rather loose mouth, a face of most extreme *mobility*, which he shuttles about – eyebrows, eyes, mouth and all – in a very singular manner when speaking. Surmount this with a loose coil of common-coloured hair, and set it on a small compact figure, very small, and dressed à la D'Orsay rather than well – this is Pickwick. For the rest, a quiet, shrewd-looking little fellow, who seems to guess pretty well what he is and what others are.'[1]

One may perhaps venture to suppose that had the second of these guesses been less accurate, the description might have been a less kindly one. But there are two errors to be noted in this sketch, graphic as it is. Firstly, Dickens's eyes were not blue, but of a very distinct and brilliant hazel – the colour traditionally assigned to Shakspeare's eyes.[2] Secondly, Dickens, although truly of a slight, compact figure, was *not a very* small man. I do not think he was below the average middle height. I speak from my remembrance of him at a later day, when I had become intimate with him; but curiously enough, I find on looking back into my memory, that if I had been asked to describe him, as I first saw him, I too should have said that he was very small. Carlyle's words refer to Dickens's youth soon after he had published *Pickwick*; and no doubt at this period he had a look of delicacy, almost of effeminacy, if one may accept Maclise's well-known portrait as a truthful record, which might give those who saw him the impression of his being smaller and more fragile in build than was the fact. In later life he lost this D'Orsay look completely, and was bronzed and reddened by wind and weather like a seaman.

In fact, when I saw him subsequently in London, I think I should have passed him in the street without recognising him. I never saw a man so changed. . . .

Dickens was only thirty-three when I first saw him, being just two years my junior. I have said what he appeared to me then. As I knew him afterwards, and to the end of his days, he was a strikingly manly man, not only in appearance but in bearing. The lustrous brilliancy of his eyes was very striking. And I do not think that I have ever seen it noticed, that those wonderful eyes which saw so much and so keenly, were appreciably, though to a very slight degree, near-sighted eyes. Very few persons, even among those who knew him well, were aware of this, for Dickens never used a glass.[3] But he continually exercised his vision by looking at distant objects, and making them out as well as he could without any artificial assistance. It was an instance of that force of will in him, which compelled a naturally somewhat delicate frame to comport itself like that of an athlete. Mr. Forster somewhere says of him,

'Dickens's habits were robust, but his health was not.' This is entirely true as far as my observation extends.

Of the general charm of his manner I despair of giving any idea to those who have not seen or known him. This was a charm by no means dependent on his genius. He might have been the great writer he was and yet not have warmed the social atmosphere wherever he appeared with that summer glow which seemed to attend him. His laugh was brimful of enjoyment. There was a peculiar humorous protest in it when recounting or hearing anything specially absurd, as who should say "Pon my soul this is *too* ridiculous! This passes all bounds!' and bursting out afresh as though the sense of the ridiculous overwhelmed him like a tide, which carried all hearers away with it, and which I well remember. His enthusiasm was boundless. It entered into everything he said or did. It belonged doubtless to that amazing fertility and wealth of ideas and feeling that distinguished his genius. . . .

But it is impossible for one who knew him as I did to confine what he remembers of him either to traits of outward appearance or to appreciations of his genius. I must say a few, a very few words of what Dickens appeared to me as a man. I think that an epithet, which, much and senselessly as it has been misapplied and degraded, is yet, when rightly used, perhaps the grandest that can be applied to a human being, was especially applicable to him. He was a *hearty* man, a large-hearted man that is to say. He was perhaps the largest-hearted man I ever knew. I think he made a nearer approach to obeying the divine precept, 'Love thy neighbour as thyself', than one man in a hundred thousand. His benevolence, his active, energising desire for good to all God's creatures, and restless anxiety to be in some way active for the achieving of it, were unceasing and busy in his heart ever and always.

But he had a sufficient capacity for a virtue, which, I think, seems to be moribund among us – the virtue of moral indignation. Men and their actions were not all much of a muchness to him. There was none of the indifferentism of that pseudo-philosophic moderation, which, when a scoundrel or a scoundrelly action is on the *tapis*, hints that there is much to be said on both sides. Dickens hated a mean action or a mean sentiment as one hates something that is physically loathsome to the sight and touch. And he could be angry, as those with whom he had been angry did not very readily forget.

And there was one other aspect of his moral nature, of which I am reminded by an observation which Mr. Forster records as having been made by Mrs. Carlyle. 'Light and motion flashed from every part of it [his face]. It was as if made of steel.'⁴ The first part of the phrase is true and graphic enough, but the image offered by the last words appears to me a singularly infelicitous one. There was nothing of the hardness or of the (moral) sharpness of steel about the expression of Dickens's face and features. Kindling mirth and genial fun were the expressions which those who casually met him in society were habituated to find there, but those who knew him well knew also well that a tenderness, gentle and sympathetic as that of a woman, was a mood that his surely never 'steely' face could express exquisitely, and did express frequently.

NOTES

1. J. A. Froude, *Thomas Carlyle: A History of His Life in London 1834–1881* (1884) I, 177–8. Carlyle's famous description occurs in a letter dated 17 March 1840. The encounter took place at Lord Stanley's, with various other members of the peerage present (Lords Holland, Normanby, Morpeth, Lansdowne). Carlyle remarks, of Dickens's presence at this dinner party, that 'they do not seem to heed him over-much'.

2. As readers will have noticed, many observers remark upon the intensity of Dickens's eyes, but differ about their colour: 'black' according to John D. Sherwood, or 'nondescript in colour, though inclining to warm grey in repose' according to Eleanor E. Christian (both above), and now 'blue' or 'hazel', according to Carlyle and Trollope. 'You ask me, what was the real colour of my Father's eyes?' Mamie Dickens wrote to Kitton. 'Well, the question so "staggered" me – as he would have said – for when I began to think of the actual colour, I really was at a loss to define it. I never saw eyes so constantly changing in expression and in colour as his did. But I have it, on true artistic authority, from one who knew him *intimately*, that his eyes were undoubtedly "dark *slatey* blue, looking black at night – not in the least brown – only as the little orange line round the pupil was very strongly marked it gave a warm look to the eye. The pupils also were large and sometimes much dilated – that also made the eyes look darker than they really were – *a dark slatey blue.*" I have never seen any other eyes at all like them, as to expression, or variableness of expression, nor have I ever seen any other eyes altogether *so* beautiful' (*Pen and Pencil*, Supplement, p. 49). See also below, Marcus Stone, who reports them as being 'of a colour rarely met with, a sort of green hazel grey' (II, 183). The topic is well surveyed, with sundry descriptions by Dickens's friends and acquaintances, by Arthur S. Hearn, 'These Wonderful Eyes', *Dkn*, XXII (1926) 25–9.

3. But see Percy Fitzgerald's account of his 'peering through the gold-rimmed glasses, always of strong power' (quoted above, I, xxiii). To my knowledge, only one portrait of him shows him wearing spectacles – a sketch by Leslie Ward ('Spy') made in 1870 (copy in Dickens House, file C849).

4. Trollope is quoting from memory. The 'made of steel' phrase is Jane Welsh Carlyle's; the 'light and motion' one is Forster's own (*Life*, II, i, 84, for both).

Editor of the *Daily News*

W. H. RUSSELL AND OTHERS

(1) John Black Atkins, *The Life of Sir William Howard Russell* (1911) I, 58; (2) and (3) from K. J. Fielding, 'Dickens as J. T. Danson Knew Him', *Dkn*, LXVIII (1972) 151–61; (4) from C. Wilkins, 'The Machinist who Knew Dickens', *Dkn*, II (1906) 99.

W. H. Russell (1820–1907), knighted 1895, became famous as the *Times* war correspondent covering the Crimean War. He admired Dickens's novels – he read *Pickwick* in 1836, he said, and 'In five minutes a new world was open to me. I have been living in it ever since' (*Life of Russell*, I, 14) – and was on very friendly terms with him. He records an amusing anecdote, from April 1852, illustrating Dickens's special status. He, Thackeray, Jerrold, and various others were expected at a shooting party, but at the last moment Dickens sent a letter excusing himself, whereupon their hostess 'fled along the hall, and the guests heard her calling to the cook, "Martin, don't roast the ortolans; Mr. Dickens isn't coming." Thackeray said he never felt so small. "There's a test of popularity for you! No ortolans for Pendennis!" ' (ibid., I, 113–14).

John Towne Danson (1817–98), journalist and statistician, was engaged by Dickens for the *Daily News* staff, and wrote these two accounts of Dickens's brief tenure as founder-editor in 1895 Obviously a severe commentary, as K. J. Fielding remarks, but 'We have to take into account that he was writing a quarter of a century after Dickens's death with the dubious help of hindsight and the benefit of various biographies' (*Dkn*, LXVIII, 161). Dickens's editing this newspaper was the only major mistake of his career; he recognised this quickly, and resigned within three weeks of the paper's beginning.

(1) 'The 21st of January, 1846, came at last,' writes Russell, 'and there was a wild rush for the first number. At the sight of the outer sheet, hope at once lighted up the gloom of Printing House Square, the Strand, and Shoe Lane. The *Daily News*, No. 1, was ill-printed on bad paper, and "badly made up", and, despite the brilliant picture from Italy by Dickens, was a fiasco. There were reports that there had been a Saturnalia among the printers. I am not sure that there were not social rejoicings that night in the editorial chambers which had been so long beset by dread. Dickens had gathered round him newspaper celebrities, critics in art, music and literature, correspondents, politicians, statists. Yea, even the miscalled penny-a-liner was there. But Dickens was not a good editor; he was the best

reporter in London, and as a journalist he was nothing more. He had no political instincts or knowledge, and was ignorant of and indifferent to what are called "Foreign Affairs"; indeed, he told me himself that he never thought about them till the Revolution of 1848. He had appointed as manager his father, whom he is said to have immortalised in Micawber, and if his father was not really a Micawber, he was at all events destitute of the energy and experience of Delane, senior.[1] Dickens having all the tools at his hand to turn out a splendid newspaper, failed to exhibit even moderate carpentry. What he did was to shake the old confidence in established relations, break up old associations and raise the cost of the *personnel* in all departments.'

(2) *J. T. D., '"Daily News"—Starting off in 1846'*. Dickens was thrust by his admirers, and by some who thought they saw in him the makings of a new London Morning paper, into a position, which, I believe, he never quite thought himself fit for. He had no business faculty or training. His father (sd. to have been the original of 'Micawber') had himself no such quality – nor would it appear had his mother. And except at home he had no such training during the years in wh. he might have profited by it.

In the autumn of 1845 I received from him an offer of an engagement to write leaders for the newspaper, on financial and commercial topics. . . . We met, and agreed; and I took an engagement for 12 months, from the starting of the paper.

I found that the capital was being supplied mainly, by, or through, the printers, Bradbury & Evans, who had already secured a notable success in the starting of *Punch*. Two or three old Houses in a narrow street, near their printing works, were gutted and converted into offices for their paper. The building was ill-lighted, ill-ventilated, & very inconvenient: the old staircases remaining: & being intersected by cross passages above.

I found Mr. Dickens had appointed his father chief, or Superintendt. of the Reporting Staff. Leading articles for a morning paper being often based mainly on accurate reports, and my articles often dealing with dates and sums, I found in this department a notable deficiency of the care which should be given to this matter. But in fact the paper suffered in every department, from the first, from this sort of deficiency. . . .

Mr. Dickens went on as he began, doing his best but with no experience, and no clear conception, of the duties of the post he held. . . . From the first, the paper seemed to me to have little chance of success; and I soon noticed signs of a similar opinion among others connected with it. Within three months it was in difficulties; and had it not soon been taken up by Mr. Dilke, of the *Athenaeum*, it would have come down, altogether.

(3) *J.T.D.*, *'Charles Dickens as I Knew Him'*. I saw a good deal of Charles Dickens for a time. When the *Dy. News* started, I was one of the staff of Leader Writers retained on it. I had to write about 4 articles a week, & did so. Of course I had to see Dickens, as the Editor, frequently. Had he been fit for, & had he done, his duty fully, I shd. have seen more of him. But my department was the Economic & financial; and of political Economy, or of political finance, he knew nothing. It was with me that lay the part of his duty he liked least. For he had a sincere desire to be effective in all he did; and a great pleasure in feeling that he was so. But in any attempt to aid, & still more in any effort [to] guide, or to correct me, he was, & felt himself to be, very weak. He thought with the 'humane public'; & with the tax-hating public; and with the 'good government and anti-corruption' public; but of how he was to serve them, except by giving way to their chief popular tendencies, as touching such matters he was really ignorant, & felt himself so. But he had already got into a class in the estimation of the public, to which the public will attribute ability in such matters. He had been selected for, and put into a position, arming him with much power to act in such matters. He was even largely and personally responsible for acting in them, & for taking an intelligent & well considered course upon every public question within their range which the news of the day brought to his knowledge. And he was, in a vague sort of way, conscious of this power, & of the correlative responsibility. But he could not act upon his convictions with any sort of satisfaction, because he could not see clearly, what he was about. This was a source, to him, occasionally of much uneasiness; and my presence always roused and intensified this uneasiness. Hence our interviews were, sometimes, not, for either of us, satisfactory. He was always friendly & acquiescent. But, unless when wandering from the matter which brought us together, he was absent-minded, & indisposed to say anything definite; and never would *discuss* any topic properly within the lines of my department.

From my observation of him & his position and actions at that time, and of his gradually developed unfitness for the post he had taken, and of his relations to myself, and to others, about him, I learned much that enabled me to understand how it was that he became (as he undoubtedly was) a decidedly unhappy man.

His success was sudden. It was based on a power to interest & amuse a large number of readers. He could draw laughter, and tears, from almost everybody who read him, as no one else of his time could. It brought him money, and fame – & took him into any society he chose to enter. He was admired, adulated, fêted, made much of, for a time. And when the lionizing period ceased, his constantly appearing works were still in vogue, and eagerly read, & quite unrivalled. He was surrounded with flatterers. He was strongly disposed to social enjoyment, and well fitted, personally, to promote it. He was an excellent after-dinner speaker, and fully shared the tendency to make much of good eating and drinking which prevailed when he entered the world. For a time, he was intoxicated with this. As it palled upon him, & he came to 'take stock' of what he had achieved, and began to adjust himself to the place he had to fill in Socy., he began to perceive what it was, exactly that made him a favourite in Socy., and how narrow & feeble, tho' almost universal, was the hold he had upon the attention, and admiration, of his fellow-men. It was better than that of a mere mountebank, yet he was of that order of men, – a man who can amuse only. He could perceive that the sound of his name, 'Mr. Dickens', tho' it roused the pleased attention of every social assembly, gave him a place rather 'notorious' than 'famous', in any elevated sense. Of course he could no more talk 'Pickwick' than Stephenson could talk Railway-making, or Rowland Hill postal Economy, or Peel Free trade. And when dealt with as abstracted from his peculiar *métier*, he found himself by no means a very important person. It was true that every social assembly, in every class, equally welcomed and fêted him. The 'mob' he interested was, for a long time, larger than the 'mob' interested in any other social celebrity of his time, excepting, perhaps, the Duke of Wellington. But though the quantity of his popularity was great, the quality of it was not high. Every body contributed to it; but it was its volume, and not its intrinsic worth, that was extraordinary. He soon found that esteem, or respect, for him, as a man, had, and could have, but a small share in it. It did not at all imply that he was preeminently, either a great man or a good one. And he honestly to himself, tho' not avowedly, set it down accordingly, as a thing not to be very proud of. He also measured himself, in the literary world, with others; and saw and accepted, though not with pleasure, the evidence he found that his absolute personal merit was not great. He had an extraordinary natural gift; and, as soon as he discovered it, he had set himself to work to develop, shape and improve it. But, when all was said and done, he had, somehow, rather inherited than achieved the means of his Greatness. So has it been, no doubt, with most of our great writers. But to find this out, and to face it, was, after the first great outburst of his literary success, not pleasing to Dickens. It could not be; and the consequent revulsion of feeling marked him to the end of his life.

I trace his disagreement with his wife to one of the incidents of this severe trial. She, a commonplace, but not an ill-disposed woman, or one incompetent to the ordinary duties of life, or of a wife and mother, regarded his success much as would the wife of any very popular *artiste* that of her husband. She had married a newspaper reporter. – He suddenly became a very popular Author, – popular, in some respects, beyond all previous experience. . . . But though everyone sought to meet him, nobody wanted to meet her, and in fact she got little or none of this. Nobody wished to entertain her or to converse with her, and when he was invited, she was not. Her appearance & Conversation were in no way distinguished in themselves. One rather wondered how such a man as Dickens could have married her. She was one of the daughters of a theatrical musician, a Mr. Hogarth, who had made friends with Dickens when he was yet unknown. The Socy. he cultivated – (that of his literary followers & parasites) – quite rejected her; & would have done so whatever her social rank or accomplishments. Where Dickens was great, *she* was small, or her presence was hardly tolerated. She did not analyse the cause of this; she only felt and resented it. His fame had, in fact, severed him from her; & had even acted upon upon her so as to make her seem no fit companion for him; – and to leave her worse off than before.

Few women could have borne this; and she could not. Nor could Dickens make it welcome, or otherwise than disgusting, to her. Her dissatisfaction was incurable; and her mode of expressing it induced great & constant vexation to him; and produced a constant sense of incompatibility in the daily lives of husband & wife, which resulted, as all the world came to know, in alienation, & separation.

(4) [C. Wilkins, working on a Swansea newspaper in the 1860s,

heard that one of the machinists had 'known Dickens intimately', so he sought him out.]

'Knew him?' he said. 'Yes, I knew him well. No stand-offishness about him. He would drop in sometimes at "The Corner", and when he knew we were all on the same paper as he wrote in, he passed a kind word, yes, and more, and not a few pewters have Charles and I looked down into, he standing treat one time and I another.'

NOTE

1. The father of John Thadeus Delane, editor of *The Times* 1841–77, was the paper's financial manager until 1846.

Views from the Castle

RICHARD AND LAVINIA WATSON

(1) from L. C. Staples, 'Sidelight on a Great Friendship', *Dkn*, XLVII (1951) 16–21; (2) 'Recollections of the Late Hon. Mrs. Watson', in *Pen and Pencil*, pp. 144–5. Dickens met the Watsons in Lausanne in 1846, at the home of an English expatriate, William Haldimand, and they became very close friends; his later letters to Mrs. Watson are among his most intimate and revealing. *David Copperfield* is dedicated to the Watsons, and the Chesney Wold of *Bleak House* was confessedly based on their seat, Rockingham Castle: see Philip Collins, 'Charles Dickens and Rockingham Castle', *Northamptonshire Past and Present*, 1980, pp. 133–40. The castle had belonged to this family for over three hundred years; the Watsons were the closest of Dickens's few blue-blooded friends. The Hon. Richard Watson (1800–52), son of the 2nd Lord Sondes, had been a cavalry officer and an MP; his wife Lavinia (1816–88) was the daughter of Lord George Quin and grand-daughter of the 1st Marquis of Headfort and of the 2nd Earl Spencer. Watson's 1846 diary records many other meetings than the excerpts below mention. Mrs. Watson sent her 'Recollections' to Kitton in 1886.

(1) *29 June 1846.* Dined with Mr Haldimand. Met Boz. . . . Liked him altogether very much as well as his wife. He appears unaffected. . . .

16 July. Dined with the Dickenses and passed an evening very much as one would expect in the home of Boz. He was in extraordinary spirits and was very amusing: Tricks, Characters, etc.

12 Sept. A Soiree at Mr. Dickens' to hear him read the first number of his new work *Dombey and Son*. He reads remarkably well and we are all of opinion that the beginning of this work is more interesting than the commencement of any of his other works. He has great expectations of it himself. . . .

12 Nov. This evening we dined with Boz and after dinner he read his new Christmas Book called *The Battle of Life*. We are all inclined to think it the most poetical and refined of all his works. He read it with wonderful charm and spirit.

15 Nov. Dined at Denantou [the Haldimands' house] to meet the Dickenses who leave tomorrow to our great grief. It is impossible to describe the feelings of regard and friendship with which he has inspired us. He certainly is the most unaffected distinguished man I ever met.

(2) Dickens was so essentially an original and individual character, that he leaves on the minds of his friends, I think, a more vivid impression, and indelible beyond that of any one I have ever known, so that the lapse of time does not seem in any way to weaken one's recollection of him in the smallest degree.

As to telling you anything more about the man himself than you already know, I am doubtful at succeeding, but I will let my recollections of him, first of all, endorse Mr. Forster's *very* clever pen-portrait, but I should like to add, as very characteristic, the extraordinary, yet perfectly natural, sudden change of brightness and light to deep pathos in look, voice, and manner, according to the subject just in hand. I purposely say natural, because I want to emphasize the unusual absence of all affectation or conceit in him. His expression in repose was *observant*, never *absent*, but also never conscious of self. Some have remarked to me their wonder that he could praise and approve of his writing as he occasionally does in his letters to his friends, when he had been talking of some work at the time. Those who knew him well, saw how entirely he judged himself as he would have done another person's performance. I think that the greatest artists do that also. They love the art – not themselves;

and he was so *perfectly true* that he could simply express himself as he felt, without reflecting on his powers.

Another characteristic was his marvellous quickness of vision, taking in everything at a passing glance. Thus, driving through a town with tall houses, he described, with all the details of a weird portrait, the appearance of an old woman looking out of a top-storey window. Though he had seen her but for a moment, the impression was complete and indelible. Nothing escaped him, and one understands the power of detail in his books.

He was comically aware himself of the gay style of dress he liked – cheerful, bright colours. He liked to cheer the world – yet, at the same time, he has told me that he preferred the power of making the world cry, rather than laugh. So, he did not care for *Pickwick*!

His face used to *blaze* with indignation at any injustice or cruelty, and be awful, almost, over horrors. I remember well the intense feeling of horror over the only execution he ever saw – *Never again* would he go to one.[1]

His delightfully comic descriptions of people, ways, or things, used to break out in beaming fun all over his face, as it were – but I *never* – speaking seriously – heard him say an unkind word of any one; hot – fiery – feeling *intensely*, but all seemed to be open – honest – generous – and most genuine.

Frith's portrait,[2] I think is the one which always reminded me most of him as I first knew him in '46, – barring a little theatrical pose which is not quite natural to the subject. Afterwards his beard changed him much, added years to his age – and we lost for good seeing the joke coming before it was spoken, which had such a specially humorous effect.

I should lastly (tho' not exactly belonging to a portrait) mention his extraordinary love of order in all arrangements to be made – into every particular did he go, with the strongest *will*, as being the only thing to be done – and no one could resist the wonderful (so to call it) tyranny he exerted, not for himself, but for the carrying out of the object in hand! His face expressed all this in a most amusing way.

I would sum up all these very slight details by saying that intensity of feeling – absolute truth – energy and power of action – were about the most characteristic points of his being; and I suppose, according to their unusual force, made him very different from others.

To strangers he was somewhat reserved, but a warm reception

1b. Miniature by Rose Emma Drummond (1835)

1a. Miniature by Janet Barrow (1830)

2. Drawings by Samuel Laurence (1837), with Dickens's signature

'Without hesitancy I affirm of this Portrait that it was, and is, the "Boz" who wrote *Pickwick*. It is a *facsimile* of the Dickens who married Miss Catherine Hogarth. . . . His sister Fanny thought this Portrait a perfect likeness' – Henry Burnett (Fanny Dickens's husband)

3. Portrait by Daniel Maclise (1839)

The *Nickleby* portrait, commissioned by its publishers and reproduced, in Finden's engraving, as frontispiece to that novel. A 'face of me', Dickens wrote, 'which all people say is astonishing'. Thackeray agreed: 'As a likeness perfectly amazing; a looking glass could not render a better facsimile. Here we have the real identical man Dickens: the artist must have understood the inward Boz as well as the outward before he made this admirable representation of him'. George Eliot later called it 'that keepsakey impossible face . . . engraved for [Forster's] *Life* in all its odious beautification' – but, of course, she never saw Dickens at this period.

4. Pencil drawing, touched with chalk, by Alfred, Comte D'Orsay (1842)

Dated 28 December 1842 and endorsed by D'Orsay 'the better of the two'. D'Orsay, a friend of Dickens at this time, had been dissatisfied with an earlier sketch (for which see *Dickensian,* 1951). Of the second attempt, Dickens wrote to the artist: 'Mrs Dickens thinks the portrait "capital", and so do divers other domestic authorities who have seen it – though some protest that the lower part of the face is susceptible of improvement.'

5. Dickens, his wife and Georgina Hogarth (1843), by Daniel Maclise

A pencil sketch, made while on holiday. 'Never did a touch so light carry with it more truth of observation,' commented Forster. 'The likenesses of all are excellent; and nothing ever done of Dickens himself has conveyed more vividly his look and bearing at this yet youthful time. He is in his most pleasing aspect; flattered, perhaps; but nothing that is known to me gives a general impression so lifelike and true of the then frank, eager, handsome face.'

6. Reading *The Chimes* to friends (1844), sketch by Daniel Maclise

The two pre-publication readings of his Christmas book, *The Chimes*, in December 1844 were, wrote Forster 'the germ of those readings to large audiences by which, as much as by his books, the world knew him in his later life'. Guests seen here include John Forster, Thomas Carlyle, the artists Maclise and Clarkson Stanfield, and the journalists W. J. Fox, Douglas Jerrold and Laman Blanchard.

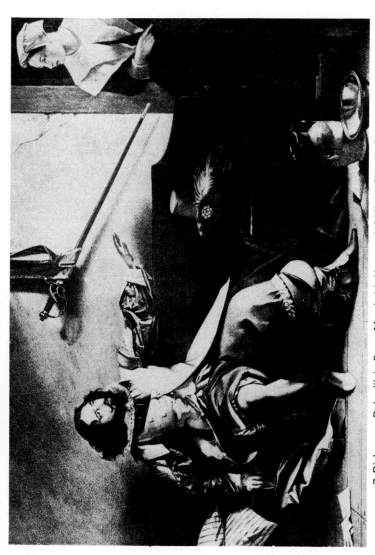

7. Dickens as Bobadil, in *Every Man in his Humour* (1846), by Charles R. Leslie, R.A.

Dickens's son Charley regarded this, and Maclise's painting of 1838, as the 'only really satisfactory portraits of him that were ever painted'. Mamie Dickens, too, thought Leslie's depiction 'an excellent likeness'. On the right is Miss Bew as Tib.

8. Daguerreotype by Henri Claudet (c.1850)

ever met those who made the slightest advance, and once a friend, he *never* varied in the slightest degree.

NOTES

1. Maybe Mrs Watson is here recalling an early conversation. Executions Dickens is known to have witnessed are Courvoisier's (1840), the Mannings' (1849), one in Rome (1845) and possibly one in Switzerland. See Philip Collins, *Dickens and Crime* (1962) ch. 10, 'The Punishment of Death'.
2. A slip of her pen: clearly she means Maclise's portrait of 1839, not Frith's of 1859–60 (in which Dickens is bearded).

Dickens's 'Dearest Meery' Remembers

MARY BOYLE

(1) from 'Miss Mary Boyle's Recollections', in *Pen and Pencil*, pp. 146–7; (2) from *Mary Boyle: Her Book*, ed. Sir Courtenay Boyle (1901) pp. 231–40. The Hon. Mary Boyle (1810–90), daughter of Vice-Admiral the Hon. Sir Courtenay Boyle, was a relative of Mrs Lavinia Watson (see previous item) and met Dickens at the Watsons' seat, Rockingham Castle, in 1849. A vivacious and well-connected spinster, she was confessedly 'ever a flirt'; Dickens greatly took to her, and a close and semi-flirtatious relationship with 'My dearest Meery' (as he called her) continued for the rest of his life. He regarded her as 'the very best actress I ever saw off the stage, and immeasurably better than a great many I have seen on it' (*N*, II, 230), and this was a further bond; she became 'Dickens's Prima Donna'. Also she was an occasional author, and contributed to his weeklies. She joined the Dickenses on holidays in Boulogne, and was a regular visitor to Gad's Hill; she rushed there, on 9 June 1870, the moment that she heard of Dickens's fatal collapse.

(1) You ask my opinion of the different Portraits which exist of Charles Dickens. When I say that none of them thoroughly satisfy me as likenesses, I trust you will believe that I do not mean to disparage the works of those who have been anxious to represent to future generations the features of the great Novelist. On the contrary, I am desirous of adding my lowly tribute of admiration, more especially to the two admirable paintings by Messrs. Maclise and Frith, men not only distinguished in the highest degree as

artists, but between whom and their subject there existed that sympathy and understanding without which, I feel convinced, no fine portrait can be produced.

But at all periods of his life I feel sure that his was a countenance most difficult to arrest (if I may so express myself), from its extreme mobility, and constant change, – characteristics which, combined with a sweet and powerful voice and remarkable grace of movement, made him the consummate actor he undoubtedly was. I speak advisedly, having had the honour of playing in his company on several occasions.

We know by the letters lately published in Mr. Frith's delightful volume of Reminiscences that the portrait of Charles Dickens by that eminent artist gave complete satisfaction to Mr. Forster, for whom it was painted. Could there be a better judge of the production, either as a work of Art, or a resemblance of his dearest friend?

Respecting the Portraits of Charles Dickens, I find that I have spoken of paintings only, and have made no mention of photographs. Mr. Mason, a most excellent photographic artist who came down frequently to Gadshill, executed (if I remember right) the last portrait that formed the frontispiece to *Edwin Drood*, a very good likeness; but there was one in a family group taken some time before, in the front porch at Gadshill with Dickens, his two daughters and their aunt, Mr. Charles Collins, and Mr. Chorley, which I consider admirable, and often wished it had been enlarged – I mean the single figure of Dickens himself. It is very animated, and gives a good impression of his countenance.

There is a theory I have often heard adduced, to which I myself thoroughly subscribe, and in which perhaps lies the secret of my never being fully satisfied with any likeness I have ever seen of him. It is this – that, in recalling the features of the friends we have lost, there is almost invariably one expression that predominates over every other in the memory of each individual. And so it is with me as regards my beloved friend. That look is the one he cast around him before commencing a public Reading. As I write, the whole picture rises vividly before me After acknowledging the enthusiastic welcome which always awaited him, he stood for a few moments in silence, beside the little table on the platform, paper-cutter in hand, a bright flower in his button-hole sent him that evening by one of his numerous admirers. Then he cast a glance round the Hall, and, if ever a look spoke, it was at that moment, when (as a neighbour whispered to me one evening) 'he made friends with us all'. His wonderful eyes seemed to have the power of meeting those of every separate individual in the audience, while a smile as eloquent as the words he was about to utter played round his lips. This is the look (beyond the power of painting to reproduce) which I best remember, which I best love to remember, though, as regards that dear friend, the prayer he himself taught us has in my case been strictly fulfilled, for the Lord has kept 'my memory green'.

You desire me to send you any recollection by which I can convey to you an idea of what our French neighbours so expressively term his *manière d'être*. One especial characteristic I may mention which, in my opinion, added greatly to the charm of his society, I mean the remarkable gift he had of setting others at ease when in his company.

(2) In November 1851, Charles Dickens and his family went to live in Tavistock House, Tavistock Square, where they remained until the year 1857. The very sound of the name is replete to me with memories of innumerable evenings passed in the most congenial and delightful intercourse; dinners, where the guests vied with each other in brilliant conversation, whether intellectual, witty, or sparkling – evenings devoted to music or theatricals. First and foremost of that magic circle was the host himself, always 'one of us', who invariably drew out what was best and most characteristic in others, who used the monosyllable 'we' much more frequently than that of 'I', and who made use of his superiority to charm and quicken the society around him, but never to crush or overpower it with a sense of their inferiority. The most diffident girl was encouraged to express her modest opinion to the great man, and in him the youngest child ever found a ready playfellow.

I can never forget one evening, shortly after the arrival at Tavistock House, when we danced in the New Year. It seemed like a page cut out of the *Christmas Carol*, as far, at least, as fun and frolic went: authors, actors, friends from near and far, formed the avenues of two long English country dances, in one of which I had the honour of going up and down the middle, almost 'interminably' as it seemed, with Charles Dickens for my partner. . . .

[At Gad's Hill in the mornings] Boz was left to his work, in what I called his 'lair', for few of us would have risked disturbing him, when he had taken up his position for the morning's labour, in the *châlet*, which his friend Fechter, the tragedian, had brought him from

Paris. In the setting-up of the said *châlet*, after the manner of a child's architectural toy, Charles had found the greatest amusement, for he was indeed one of those who find 'A child's keen delight in little things', and the hanging of his pictures, the arranging his furniture, the annexation of a tiny conservatory, and the construction of an underground tunnel, which connected the area round the house with a small plantation of lofty cedars, under the shade of which he had erected his *châlet*, were all sources to him of intense interest.

In the afternoon he sought relaxation, and then the other inmates of the house came in for their share of his enviable society, and the basket-carriage was brought to the door, drawn by the 'sober Newman Noggs', the harness adorned with musical bells, which his friend Mr Lehmann had brought him from Norway, and we would take long drives all around this picturesque neighbourhood. Sometimes we would alight at a distant point, to return home on foot; sometimes we would wend our way through green hop-gardens on one side, and golden cornfields on the other for a distance of many miles; yet we were never wearied. I remember once Georgina Hogarth and I had accompanied him to a new spot of interest which he had lately discovered. He walked at his usual swinging rate, and we had proudly kept up with him. Only five minutes had been allowed for refreshment, as he called it, otherwise rest, between reaching the goal and arriving at home. How pleased his fellow-pedestrians were to receive the following tribute: 'Well done! – ten miles in two hours and a half!' I sit in my armchair now, and look back on that feat as almost miraculous.

Charles Dickens, himself a hero, was a hero-worshipper, and in all of my experience I never knew a man so utterly exempt from the slightest tinge of professional jealousy.

One day I went with his two daughters, Mary and Katie (Mrs Charles Collins, who, with her husband, spent most of the summer under the paternal roof) and their aunt to meet him at the station. Lifting up the hand-bag which he always carried he exclaimed. 'Here girls, I have a treat for you – Tennyson's magnificent poem of *The Idylls of the King*. Is it not glorious to think, that after having written for so many years, a man should now bring forth, perhaps, the noblest of his works.'

Beaming Eye, Bank Balance, and Babies

FRANCIS JEFFREY

From Lord Cockburn [Henry Thomas Cockburn], *Life of Lord Jeffrey, with a Selection of his Correspondence* (1852) II, 338, 390, 408–10, 462–3. Dickens was 'very very deeply grieved' when Jeffrey died in 1850: 'I believe I have lost as affectionate a friend as I ever had, or ever shall have, in this world' (*N*, II, 201, 204). His friendship with Jeffrey, dating from 1841, was the most intimate and touching of his friendships with illustrious members of an older generation. Jeffrey (1773–1850), a leading Whig, was a lawyer, judge, politician, critic, and editor of the *Edinburgh Review*, 1803–29, where his severely dismissive 'giant-killer' critiques were notorious. He loved Dickens, and warmly admired his writings: see selections in *Dickens: The Critical Heritage*, ed. Philip Collins (1971), and recall the famous incident of his being found prostrate with grief over the death of 'Boz's little Nelly' (in *The Old Curiosity Shop*). He proclaimed himself Dickens's 'Critic Laureate', 'father confessor' and 'elder brother'. Greatly moved by Jeffrey's admiration and affection, Dickens made him godfather to his third son, Francis Jeffrey Dickens (born 1844), and dedicated to him *The Cricket on the Hearth*, (1845). On their friendship, see J. W. T. Ley, *The Dickens Circle* (1918) ch. 16. Jeffrey's letters to Dickens constitute one of the few runs of the novelist's incoming correspondence. In later years Dickens burned almost all the letters he had received, being distressed by some recent biographers' use of intimate correspondence; but in 1850–2 he had given Lord Cockburn access to Jeffrey's letters to him – the more surprisingly, because they contained very frank admonitions from Jeffrey about limiting his expenditure, and the number of his children, etc. The first extract here given is from a letter to Lord Colburn, from London; the others were written to Dickens, from Scotland.

8 May 1841. I have seen a good deal of [various friends] and, above all, of Charles Dickens, with whom I have struck up what I mean to be an eternal and intimate friendship. He lives very near us here, and I often run over and sit an hour *tête à tête*, or take a long walk in the park with him – the only way really to know or be known by either man or woman. Taken in this way I think him very amiable and agreeable. In mixed company, where he is now much sought after as a lion, he is rather reserved, &c. He has dined here (for Charlotte has taken to giving quiet parties), and we with him, at rather too sumptuous a dinner for a man with a family, and only beginning to be rich, though selling 44,000 copies of his weekly issues, &c.

12 Dec 1844. Blessings on your kind heart, my dearest Dickens, for *that*, after all, is your great talisman, and the gift for which you will be not only most loved, but longest remembered.

31 Jan 1847. But I forget to thank you for your most kind and interesting letter of December 27th.[1] I certainly did not mean to ask you for the full and clear, if not every way satisfactory, statement you have trusted me with. But I do feel the full value of that confidence, and wish I had any better return to make to it than mere thanks, and idle, because general, advice. I am rather disappointed, I must own, at finding your *embankment* still so small. But it is a great thing to have made a beginning, and laid a foundation; and you are young enough to reckon on living many years under the proud roof of the completed structure, which even I expect to see ascending in its splendour. But when I consider that the public has, upon a moderate computation, paid at least £100,000 for your works (and had a good bargain too at the money), it is rather provoking to think that the author should not now have —— in bank, and have never received, I suspect, above ——. There must have been some mismanagement, I think, as well as ill-luck, to have occasioned this result – not extravagance on your part, my dear Dickens – nor even excessive beneficence – but improvident arrangements with publishers – and too careless a control of their proceedings. But you are wiser now; and, with Forster's kind and judicious help, will soon redeem the effects of your not ungenerous errors. I am as far as possible from grudging you the elegances and indulgences which are suitable to your tasteful and liberal nature, and which you have so fully earned; and should indeed be grieved not to see you surrounded, and your children growing up, in the midst of the refinements, which not only gratify the relishes, but improve the capacities, of a cultivated mind. All I venture to press on you is the infinite importance, and unspeakable comfort, of an achieved and secure *independence*; taking away all anxiety about decay of health or mental alacrity, or even that impatience of task work which is apt to steal upon free spirits who would work harder and better, if redeemed from the yoke of necessity. But this is twaddle enough, and must be charitably set down to the score of my paternal anxiety and senile caution.

27 July 1849. My ever dear Dickens – I have been very near dead; and am by no means sure that I shall *ever* recover from the malady which has confined me mostly to bed for the last five weeks, and which has only, within the last three days, allowed me to leave my room for a few hours in the morning. But I must tell you, that, living or dying, I retain for you, unabated and unimpaired, the same cordial feelings of love, gratitude, and admiration, which have been part of my nature, and no small part of my pride and happiness, for the last twenty years.[2] . . . I am better, however, within these last days; and hope still to see your bright eye, and clasp your open hand, once more at least before the hour of final separation. . . .

With kindest and most affectionate remembrances to your true-hearted and affectionate Kate, and all your blooming progeny, ever and ever, my dear Dickens, affectionately yours.

6 Jan 1850. It is like looking forward to spring to think of seeing your beaming eye again! Come, then, to see us when you can, and bring that true-hearted Kate with you – but not as you did last time, to frighten us, and imperil her. Let that job be well over first, and consider whether it had not better be the last?[3] There can never be too many Dickenses in the world; but these *overbearings* exhaust the parent tree, and those who cannot hope to repose in the shade of the saplings, must shrink from the risk of its decay.

I daresay you do right to send one boy to Eton; but what is most surely learned there is the habit of wasteful expense, and, in ordinary natures, a shame and contempt for plebeian parents.[4] But I have faith in races, and feel that *your* blood will resist such attaints.[5] You do not think it impertinent in me to refer to them? I speak to you as I would to a younger brother. And so God bless you again, and ever yours.

NOTES

1. This letter – unpublished and presumably not extant – had obviously dealt with Dickens's financial solvency, his 'embankment' as Jeffrey called it.

2. Affection or the lightheadedness consequent upon illness here induced Jeffrey to more than double the span of his friendship with Dickens.

3. Catherine Dickens was now in her eleventh pregnancy; the baby, born seven months later, died in infancy. Two of her pregnancies had terminated in a miscarriage, and the more recent of these had come on during a railway journey from Edinburgh to Glasgow, in December 1847 (*N*, II, 64, 69).

4. Charley, the eldest child, had just entered Eton, where his fees were paid by Dickens's very rich friend Angela Burdett Coutts, who took a quasi-godmotherly interest in him.

5. Jeffrey's faith in the Dickens blood was misplaced. See Philip Collins, *Dickens and Education* (1963) ch. 2, on the indifferent careers of Charley and most of his brothers.

Splendid Strolling

MARY COWDEN CLARKE

(1) from Charles and Mary Cowden Clarke, *Recollections of Writers* (1878) pp. 296–333; (2) from her letter to Kitton, 13 Dec 1886, in *Pen and Pencil*, p. 171. Mary Cowden Clarke (1809–98) collaborated on this and other works with her husband Charles (1787–1877); it was she that wrote this chapter on Dickens. They were both prolific miscellaneous authors, and friends of many authors, but she did not meet Dickens until 1848. Long an admirer of his work, her days with him were 'one of the most peculiarly bright episodes of my life. . . . Genial, kind, most sympathetic and fascinating was his companionship, and very precious to me was his friendship.' Knowing her reputation as an amateur actress, Dickens immediately invited her to play Mistress Quickly in his production of *The Merry Wives of Windsor*; she did so, and performed in this and other plays with his amateur troupe, both in London and on its 'Splendid Strolling' provincial tours. He was, in her judgement, 'supreme as manager [and] super-excellent as actor' – *My Long Life* (1896) pp. 127, 133, 132. From 1856 the Clarkes were living abroad, so they dropped out of the Dickens circle, but she contributed to *All the Year Round*.

(1) At length came that never-to-be-forgotten day – or rather, evening – when we met him at a party, and were introduced to him by Leigh Hunt, who, after a cordial word or two, left us to make acquaintance together. At once, with his own inexpressible charm of graceful ease and animation, Charles Dickens fell into delightful chat and riveted for ever the chain of fascination that his mere distant image and enchanting writings had cast about M. C. C., drawing her towards him with a perfect spell of prepossession. The prepossession was confirmed into affectionate admiration and attachment that lasted faithfully strong throughout the happy friendship that ensued, and was not even destroyed by death; for she cherishes his memory still with as fond an idolatry as she felt during

that joyous period of her life when in privileged holiday companionship with him.

Charles Dickens – beaming in look, alert in manner, radiant with
good humour, genial-voiced, gay, the very soul of enjoyment, fun,
good taste and good spirits, admirable in organizing details and
suggesting novelty of entertainment – was of all beings the very man
for a holiday season; and in singularly exceptional holiday fashion
was it my fortunate hap to pass every hour that I spent in his society.
First, at an evening party; secondly, during one of the most
unusually festive series of theatrical performances ever given;
thirdly, in delightful journeys to various places where we were to
act; fourthly, in hilarious suppers after acting (notedly among the
most jubilant of all meal-meetings!); fifthly, in one or two choice
little dinner-parties at his own house; sixthly, in a few brilliant
assemblages there, when artistic, musical, and literary talent were
represented by some of the most eminent among artists, musicians,
and people of letters of the day; seventhly, in a dress rehearsal at
Devonshire House of Lytton Bulwer's drama of *Not so bad as we seem*,
played by Charles Dickens and some of his friends; and, eighthly, in
a performance at Tavistock House (where he then lived) of a piece
called *The Lighthouse*, expressly written for the due display of Charles
Dickens' and his friend Mark Lemon's supremely good powers of
acting.[1] . . .

[The] rehearsals [were] delightful in the extreme; Charles
Dickens ever present, superintending, directing, suggesting, with
sleepless activity and vigilance: the essence of punctuality and
methodical precision himself, he kept incessant watch that others
should be unfailingly attentive and careful throughout. Unlike most
professional rehearsals, where waiting about, dawdling, and losing
time, seem to be the order of the day, the rehearsals under Charles
Dickens' stage-managership were strictly devoted to work – serious,
earnest, work; the consequence was, that when the evening of
performance came, the pieces went off with a smoothness and polish
that belong only to finished stage-business and practised
performers. He was always there among the first arrivers at
rehearsals, and remained in a conspicuous position during their
progress till the very last moment of conclusion. He had a small
table placed rather to one side of the stage, at which he generally sat,
as the scenes went on in which he himself took no part. On this table
rested a moderate-sized box; its interior divided into convenient

compartments for holding papers, letters, etc. and this interior was always the very pink of neatness and orderly arrangement. Occasionally he would leave his seat at the managerial table, and stand with his back to the foot-lights, in the very centre of the front of the stage, and view the whole effect of the rehearsed performance as it proceeded, observing the attitudes and positions of those engaged in the dialogue, their mode of entrance, exit, etc., etc. He never seemed to overlook anything; but to note the very slightest point that conduced to the 'going well' of the whole performance. With all this supervision, however, it was pleasant to remark the utter absence of dictatorialness or arrogation of superiority that distinguished his mode of ruling his troop: he exerted his authority firmly and perpetually; but in such a manner as to make it universally felt to be for no purpose of self-assertion or self-importance; on the contrary, to be for the sole purpose of ensuring general success to their united efforts. . . .

The date of our first night at the Haymarket Theatre was the 15th of May 1848; when the entertainment consisted of *The Merry Wives of Windsor* and *Animal Magnetism*. The 'make up' of Charles Dickens as Justice Shallow was so complete, that his own identity was almost unrecognizable, when he came on to the stage, as the curtain rose, in company with Sir Hugh and Master Slender; but after a moment's breathless pause, the whole house burst forth into a roar of applausive reception, which testified to the boundless delight of the assembled audience on beholding the literary idol of the day, actually before them. His impersonation was perfect: the old, stiff limbs, the senile stoop of the shoulders, the head bent with age, the feeble step, with a certain attempted smartness of carriage characteristic of the conceited Justice of the Peace – were all assumed and maintained with wonderful accuracy; while the articulation – part lisp, part thickness of utterance, part a kind of impeded sibillation, like that of a voice that 'pipes and whistles in the sound' through loss of teeth – gave consummate effect to his mode of speech. . . .

The way in which Charles Dickens impersonated that arch braggart, Captain Bobadil [in Jonson's *Every Man in His Humour*], was a veritable piece of genius: from the moment when he is discovered lolling at full length on a bench in his lodging, calling for a 'cup o' small beer' to cool down the remnants of excitement from last night's carouse with a set of roaring gallants, till his final boast of having 'not so much as once offered to resist' the 'coarse fellow' who set upon him in the open streets, he was capital. [She instances details from his performance – 'all the very height of fun' – and describes the rapturous reception of Dickens and his company on their provincial tour, June 1848.]

Moreover, what enchanting journeys those were! The coming on to the platform at the station, where Charles Dickens' alert form and beaming look met one with pleasurable greeting; the interest and polite attention of the officials; the being always seated with my sister Emma in the same railway carriage occupied by Mr. and Mrs. Charles Dickens and Mark Lemon; the delightful gaiety and sprightliness of our manager's talk; the endless stories he told us; the games he mentioned and explained how they were played; the bright amenity of his manner at various stations, where he showed to persons in authority the free-pass ticket which had been previously given in homage to 'Charles Dickens and his party'; the courteous alacrity with which he jumped out at one refreshment-room to procure food for somebody who had complained of hunger towards the end of the journey, and reappeared bearing a plate of buns which no one seemed inclined to eat, but which he held out, saying, 'For Heaven's sake, somebody eat some of these buns; I was in hopes I saw Miss Novello[2] eye them with a greedy joy': his indefatigable vivacity, cheeriness, and good humour from morning till night – all were delightful. . . .

Before the month of June concluded, a second performance was arranged for Birmingham; and as, in addition to *Merry Wives* and *Love, Law, and Physic*, it was proposed to give the screaming after-piece of *Two o'Clock in the Morning* (or *A Good Night's Rest*, as it was sometimes called), Charles Dickens asked me to dine at his house, that we might cut the farce to proper dimensions. A charming little dinner of four it was, – Mr. and Mrs. Dickens, Mark Lemon, and myself; followed by adjournment to the library to go through our scenes in the farce together. Charles Dickens showed to particular advantage in his own quiet home life; and infinitely more I enjoyed this simple little meeting than a brilliant dinner-party to which I was invited at his house, a day or two afterwards, when a large company were assembled, and all was in superb style, with a bouquet of flowers beside the plate of each lady present. On one of these more quiet occasions, when Mr. and Mrs. Dickens, their children, and their few guests were sitting out of doors in the small garden in front of their Devonshire Terrace house, enjoying the fine warm evening, I recollect seeing one of his little sons draw Charles Dickens apart, and stand in eager talk with him, the setting sun full upon the child's upturned face and lighting up the father's, which looked smilingly down into it; and when the important conference was over, the father returned to us, saying 'The little fellow gave me so many excellent reasons why he should not go to bed so soon, that I yielded the point, and let him sit up half an hour later.'

On our journey down to Birmingham I enjoyed a very special treat. Charles Dickens – in his usual way of sparing no pains that could ensure success – asked me to hear him repeat his part in *Two o' Clock in the Morning*, which, he and Mark Lemon being the only two persons acting therein, was a long one. He repeated throughout with such wonderful verbal accuracy that I could scarcely believe what I saw and heard as I listened to him, and kept my eyes fixed upon the page. Not only every word of the incessant speaking part, but the stage directions – which in that piece are very numerous and elaborate – he repeated verbatim. He evidently committed to memory all he had to *do* as well as all he had to *say* in this extremely comic trifle of one act and one scene. . . .

On our last night at Glasgow, after a climax of successful performance at the theatre – the pieces being *Used up, Love, Law, and Physic*, and *Two o' Clock in the Morning* – we had a champagne supper in honour of its being the Amateur Company's last assemblage together. Charles Dickens, observing that I took no wine, said, 'Do as I do: have a little champagne put into your glass and fill it up with water; you'll find it a refreshing draught. I tell you this as a useful secret for keeping cool on such festive occasions, and speak to you as *man to man*.' He was in wildest spirits at the brilliant reception and uproarious enthusiasm of the audience that evening, and said in his mad-cap mood, 'Blow Domestic Hearth! I should like to be going on all over the kingdom, with Mark Lemon, Mrs. Cowden Clarke, and John [his manservant], and acting everywhere. There's nothing in the world equal to seeing the house rise at you, one sea of delighted faces, one hurrah of applause!'

We travelled up to town next day: he showing us how to play the game of 'Twenty Questions', and interesting me much by the extreme ingenuity of those he put to us with a view of eliciting the object of our thought. He was very expert at these pastimes, and liked to set them going. I remember one evening at his own house, his playing several games of apparently magical divination, – of course, by means of accomplices and preconcerted signals. Once, while he was explaining to Augustus Egg[3] and myself the mode of procedure in a certain game of guessing, he said, 'Well, I begin by thinking of a man, a woman, or an inanimate object; and we'll suppose that I think of Egg.' 'Ay, an inanimate object', I replied. He gave his usual quick glance up at me, and looked at Augustus Egg, and then we all three laughed, though I protested – with truth – my innocence of any intended quip.

During our journey homeward from Glasgow, Charles Dickens exerted himself to make us all as cheery as might be, insensibly communicating the effect of his own animation to those around him. . . .

In the summer of 1855 my husband and I received an invitation to witness the performance of Mr. Wilkie Collins's piece called *The Lighthouse*, and of Charles Dickens's and Mark Lemon's farce entitled *Mr. Nightingale's Diary*. The play-bill – which, as I write, lies before me – is headed, 'The smallest Theatre in the World! Tavistock House' (where Dickens then resided); and is dated 'Tuesday Evening, June 19th, 1855'. The chief characters were enacted by himself, some members of his own family, and his friends, Mark Lemon, Augustus Egg, Frank Stone, and Wilkie Collins; while the scenery was painted by another of his friends, the eminent Clarkson Stanfield.[4] Choicely picturesque and full of artistic taste was the effect of the lighthouse interior, where Mark Lemon's handsomely chiselled features, surrounded by a head of grizzled hair that looked as though it had been blown into careless dishevelment by many a tempestuous gale, his weather-beaten general appearance, and his rugged mariner garments, formed the fine central figure as the curtain drew up and discovered him seated at a rough table, with his younger lighthouse mate, Wilkie Collins, stretched on the floor as if just awakened from sleep, in talk together. Later on in the scene a low planked recess in the wall is opened, where Charles Dickens – as the first lighthouse keeper, an old man with half-dazed wits and a bewildered sense of some wrong committed in bygone years – is discovered asleep in his berth. A wonderful impersonation was this; very imaginative, very original, very wild, very striking; his grandly intelligent eyes were made to assume a wandering look, – a sad, sacred, lost gaze, as of one whose spirit was away from present objects, and wholly occupied with absent and long-past images.

(2) So handsome, so engaging, so entirely fascinating was he, that I recollect once, when I was standing at a little distance from him while he was speaking with his usual animation to some one near,

and I was expressing my enthusiastic impression of his personal attractiveness to a lively clever writer of the day who was looking at him with me, my interlocutor said: – 'He makes one almost wish oneself a woman, to fall in love with him!'

Certainly, a more complete beauty of manliness than was in the fine eyes and frank accost of Charles Dickens, or a more bewitching winningness than the one with which he was gifted, it would be difficult to imagine. Their full charm and grace were appreciated and are still vividly remembered by

Yours faithfully, ...

NOTES

1. Mark Lemon (1809–70), editor of *Punch*, was a notable amateur actor. He played Falstaff in this *Merry Wives* production, and often partnered or collaborated with Dickens until their friendship ceased over the breakup of his marriage in 1858.

2. Mary Cowden Clarke's sister Emma. Their father was the musician Vincent Novello.

3. Augustus Egg (1816–1863), subject-painter, and close friend of the Dickens family; Dickens hoped that Georgina Hogarth might marry him, but she refused him.

4. Frank Stone ARA (1800–59) and Clarkson Stanfield RA (1793–1867) were other artist friends of Dickens. The novelist Wilkie Collins (1824–89) was among his closest intimates and collaborators.

In the Chair

GEORGE ELIOT AND OTHERS

In this composite item, the authorship and circumstances will be given at the beginning of every extract, and sources will be given in the Notes. *The Times* in its obituary of Dickens (10 June 1870, p. 9) remarked that, 'even irrespective of his literary genius, he was an able and strong-minded man, who would have succeeded in almost any profession to which he devoted himself'. One evidence of this was his skill as a chairman, whether of a committee or of a large public meeting. Not only was he an eloquent and charming platform speaker but also he had a thoroughly business-like grasp of the relevant facts and commanded respect and confidence as a leader of any enterprise. When asked whether he ever felt nervous while speaking in public, he replied: 'Not in the least' – adding that 'when first he took the chair he felt as much confidence as though he had already done the like a hundred times!' – Charles Kent, *Dickens as a Reader* (1872) p. 45. Cocky, it might well be said: but his self-confidence was thoroughly justified.

[Dickens's presiding at the first Annual Soirée of the Manchester Athenæum in the Manchester Free Trade Hall, 5 October 1843, was the largest public occasion he had chaired, to date. The Athenæum was one of the most prominent adult-education establishments in the country, but was running short of funds; this and subsequent soirées mended the situation. The following account of the occasion is by Sir Edward Watkin, Bart., MP (1819–1901), Director of the Athenæum at the time, who writes:] The Soirée of 1843 was stamped with success by the presidency of Charles Dickens. . . . We were indebted for the presence of Charles Dickens to the kind influence of his elder sister – Mrs. Burnett [who was then living in Manchester] – a self-denying saint, if ever one existed. . . . [Watkin quotes from his diary of the time:] Mr. Dickens wrote to us, desiring an interview for Wednesday night, October 4, to arrange for the meeting. . . . [So Watkin, with two colleagues, called upon him at the Burnetts' house.] He cordially welcomed us, and . . . commenced the business conversation by asking as to the programme of the meeting. This I briefly gave him. We then spoke of the speakers, and talked of their several qualities in a free and laughing manner – Dickens elevating his eyebrows and nodding his head forward as the remarks struck him. An interjection as to the doubt he had in *Pickwick* cast upon 'swarries', provoked a quick, funny glance, which preluded an immediate turn of the talk to something else. 'Whom do you intend to place beside me?' said Dickens. 'We thought Mr. and Mrs. Burnett', I replied, 'as we imagined you would like better to have them with you, than to be environed by perfect strangers. Of course we wish to put off, if possible, the customary stiffness and stateliness of such meetings on this occasion. We wish to consult your comfort and wishes.' 'No, I should not wish that,' he rejoined, 'by any means. I am obliged, but I could not allow that. You must look at the result upon your object in choosing my supporters.' 'Then,' we replied, 'we might place Mr. Cobden on one side and the Mayor on the other.'[1] 'That would do very well – excellently.' 'Or we might place a better mixture of parties. Perhaps we could place Mr. Cobden and Mr. James Crossley side by side, and thus make violent political opponents for once put aside their differences for the good of the Athenæum.' 'That would be beautiful. If you can get them to sit together, it will be excellent indeed. . . . Then this meeting, I see, is to be held in the Free Trade Hall.' (Then followed inquiries as to the size of the room, &c., &c.) 'You had 10,000 in it at the Education meeting, had you not?' said Dickens, addressing Giles.[2]

Then we went into the history of the Athenæum – spoke of the class to be benefited by it – of their sufferings and wants. In all this Dickens appeared to take great interest. . . .

Speaking of the bazaar and its proceeds, he displayed a complete knowledge of all the history of the undertaking. . . . Mr. Giles happened to hint about the utility of appealing to the audience from the chair for money. To this I objected that it would be unfair to Dickens, and too much like making a marketable commodity of him. He said, 'Yes, I should not like to do that; but I will try to excite their liberality in another and equally or more useful way.' [They further discussed the aims and benefits of the Athenæum – which, Dickens added, included two balls and two concerts a year, as well as the educational provision.] We arranged that he should come into the hall immediately after tea. He talked of the *effect*. 'Get the tea all over – I must confess to a sort of horror of tea-things (or tea on a grand scale), and I think the best way to excite and keep up the interest would be to appear immediately after tea, *and go to work at once.*'

[The next morning, he was introduced to the Mayor and other local dignitaries, and continued his investigations.] We then all walked round the institution, talked about it in all ways, dived into its cellars, and mounted to its top. . . . Then we went to the Free Trade Hall, amid sundry jokes about Crossley and Cobden, political parties, &c., &c. Dickens was much pleased with the hall; immediately on entering it he said he *felt* he could make himself exceedingly well heard in it. . . .

I noticed that Dickens occasionally said, when interested in conversation, 'Oh, lord (or law)!' 'Oh, law, no!' – a cockneyism.

Dickens is in appearance about thirty-five or thirty-six years of age,[3] about 5 feet 8 inches high, elegantly, compactly, but slightly, made; his face is not, strictly speaking, *handsome*; the features are not *very* good, as some people say they are. His eyes are very dark and full of fire, and, when turned upon you, give a light to his rather dark countenance, such as I have seldom before seen beaming upon any face. He has a good deal of the eyebrow-elevating, shoulder-shrugging, and head-nodding peculiar to people who have travelled a great deal. His voice is well regulated and strong, but there is an occasional slight peculiarity, of which the defect of 'maw-mouthed' people would be the extreme caricature. He can look very expressively. When he looks 'droll', he looks *very* droll; when interested, deeply so. His hair is dark brown and abundant.[4]

[Watkin gives no account of the Soirée itself, but Henry Burnett's may be quoted:] The meeting at the old Free Trade Hall proved a great success; all the best families in the neighbourhood were there, and some of every class that could pay for a ticket. Dickens was at his best, and was received like a King. The platform was crowded with ladies, and at the close of the meeting one lady was bold enough to ask the Chairman for his autograph. A gentleman of the Committee – I think it was the present Sir Edward Watkin – pleasantly interfered, and proposed that if Mr. Dickens would still further assist the fund, each lady or gentleman desiring his autograph should drop a sovereign on the table. Dickens, with a smile of good nature and acquiescence, and with a supply of paper, began his work and continued until the table began to look golden.[5]

[At this time, Dickens was very active as chairman of a more private concern, the Elton Fund. The popular actor Edward Elton had been drowned at sea in July 1843, leaving his children in poor circumstances. George Hodder, who became secretary of the Fund, recalls:] A committee was therefore formed, with Mr. Charles Dickens at the head, for the purpose of promoting a public subscription in aid of the orphan children, and the members of that committee included, as may well be supposed, many men of distinction in art, literature and the drama. . . . Mr. Charles Dickens was, as may be supposed, elected chairman by general acclamation, and under his practical and business-like direction the subjoined resolutions were prepared and agreed to at the first meeting (which took place at the Freemasons' Tavern, as was the case with all subsequent ones), the mighty author of *Pickwick* drafting them in his own hand-writing, with a view to their being copied afterwards by whomsoever should chance to be employed as amanuensis. [Hodder gives the text. When he became secretary, Dickens] treated me with such friendly consideration, and gave me all my instructions so clearly and succinctly, that I soon felt perfectly at ease by his side; and it was not unusual for me to write upwards of twenty letters in the course of an evening, showing how vigorously and determinedly the committee pursued their philanthropic mission.

It is quite unnecessary for me to weary the reader with details of the sayings and doings at the several meetings of the 'Elton Committee'; but as I had never before seen Mr. Dickens under similar circumstances – or indeed under any circumstances at all – I may here take leave to observe that he displayed at that period the same remarkable tact and dominating power, without any undue assumption, which he has been known to manifest on many subsequent occasions, when called upon to discharge a duty requiring the exercise of judgment and decision.[6]

[George Eliot, as she later became known, was living in 1852 at the house of John Chapman, with whom she edited the *Westminster Review*. A meeting was held there, in opposition to the Booksellers' Association's price-fixing policy. She writes:] The meeting last night went off triumphantly. . . . Dickens in the chair – a position he fills remarkably well, preserving a courteous neutrality of eyebrow, and speaking with clearness and decision. His appearance is certainly disappointing – no benevolence in the face and I think little in the head – the anterior lobe not by any means remarkable. In fact he is not distinguished looking in any way – neither handsome nor ugly, neither fat nor thin, neither tall nor short.[7]

[From late 1850, Dickens had been the leading spirit in establishing the Guild of Literature and Art, intended to provide homes for retired or indigent artists. Bulwer Lytton was its President. John R. Robinson (1828–1903), journalist and newspaper editor, knighted 1893, whose recollections follow, was not among the original members or planners of the Guild, but from 1854 was 'the most regular attendant at its meetings'.]

At our meetings Charles Dickens, if present, was always in the chair. We held a Council meeting first and followed with a 'General' Meeting. But it will be understood, after what has been said, that the latter mettings were not at all crowded. Almost immediately after I had joined I had one day a trying time in this respect. When I arrived at the office of *All the Year Round* where we met, I was told that the Council were sitting but would not be many minutes. Then came the intimation that the General Meeting was on. I went upstairs and entered the room, in which I found several gentlemen talking and laughing together. There were Robert

Chambers, Charles Knight, Augustus Egg, Dudley Costello, Mark Lemon, and a few more. 'Here's the General Meeting!' said [W. H.] Wills [the Honorary Secretary], and everybody laughed. 'Shall we read the Minutes of the last meeting?' he said, addressing me, and there was another laugh. I was nervous enough, but not too nervous to resolve to be even with my friend if I could. 'If you please', I replied, and I chuckle even now to think of the gravity with which I listened to him, and how Charles Dickens, who was in the chair, showed his amusement. In the minute book, the entry is 'General Meeting, Monday, June 3, '61, only Mr. Robinson attended', and this is signed 'Charles Dickens'. Charles Dickens, it was often said, was above all things an actor. He was indeed an actor and a consummate one. He was never when in public what in the ordinary sense of the word is termed 'natural'. I saw him again and again at these Guild meetings. I heard him address various public assemblages, and I listened I think, to each of his Public Readings; and in all he had consciously an ideal in his mind, up to which he may be said to have acted. His characters have been counted, and they run into hundreds and hundreds. He must have created them as he walked and rode and conversed or mused. The situation in which he found himself for the time became an ideal one forthwith and his part a part with the rest. I once saw him hurry forward in St James's Square to help a policeman who was struggling with a desperate fellow whom he had arrested for stealing lead. My friend Mr. J. C. Parkinson, well known to and much liked by Dickens, was with me, and we hastened to assist. I really trembled, for the man looked savagely at Mr. Dickens, and in another moment a blow might have fallen. 'I'll go with you to the station', said Mr. Dickens to the policeman, and he did. Even then, his voice, his air, his walk made me think of some accomplished artist called upon to represent all this upon the stage.

As chairman he was as precise and accurate as possible in carrying out the traditions of the post. Before business began, his happy laugh rang through the room; he had a word for every friend and generally they were his associates as well as friends. Voices were high in merriment, and it looked as though business would never begin; but when Mr. Dickens did take his seat, 'Now, gentlemen; Wills will read us the Minutes of the last meeting. Attention, please. Order!' – it might have been the most experienced chairman of Guildhall, purpled by a hundred public dinners. At the time of my election to the Council, a sanguine spirit was abroad, and the chairman specially partook of it, but when disappointment followed disappointment everybody was more serious. There was little laughter, and Mr. Dickens showed that the matter was worrying him. Among the early troubles was the occupancy of the houses. The right people would not turn up, or they backed out if they did say they would come. [But at last Dickens delighted the Council by announcing that a very eligible tenant had applied for a house.] We were not supposed to be allowed by the rules to find any kind of furniture with a house, but to-day Dickens, who all his life long was always looking to do a kind thing for somebody, said in his most winning way (and those who never witnessed it can scarcely understand what an adorable sort of way it was): 'And now, what do you say about finding carpets? Can't we let him have carpets? House very chilly when he comes to it without carpets. What do you say, Lemon? Carpets, my boy.' He addressed Mark Lemon as by instinct, suggesting as he did everything that was comfortable. We tried to look grave. The joke was to pretend we were concerned about the letter of the law. Then came the laughter, and the carpets carried the day. Alas! at the next meeting our chairman, in an amusingly melancholy voice, told us the carpets had not been ordered. They would not be wanted. ——had altered his mind. . . .

On reaching Wellington Street, one day, to attend a Council meeting, I found Mr. Dickens alone. Though he was always most kind to me and liked to talk of the *Daily News*, for instance, I felt rather alarmed, for I knew he would insist upon business being done. The Minute Book records three resolutions as having been passed at that meeting. We waited a while, talking about things in the papers, and then Mr. Dickens in an inimitably funny way, remarked: 'Will you move me in the chair?' 'I will,' I answered, 'I know you can be trusted to keep order in a large gathering.' Then came resolutions, carried after discussions, little speeches in the imitated voice of absent members, the appropriate gravity never departed from. My share was insignificant, but it served to supply Mr. Dickens with hints and texts and to keep the fun going. I have often wished a reporter had been in hiding.

Mr Dickens signed the Minutes in the most methodical way. I fancied in after days he shook hands with me with a merrier expression.[8]

[In 1858, Dickens was in the Manchester Free Trade Hall again for another adult-educational occasion – chairing the annual distribution of prizes and certificates by the Institutional Association of Lancashire and Cheshire. This organisation was a grouping of Mechanics' Institutes and other such bodies. The *Manchester Guardian* commented on his speech:] It . . . is in itself an admirable reproof of the folly of those persons who accuse the public of false taste of giving so much encouragement to novelists who attempt to do more than make us laugh. Noble Lords and Members of Parliament in dozens have tried their hands at lecturing this autumn, yet even on the platform, when the subject is one that Legislators are supposed to be peculiarly qualified to deal with, Mr. Dickens shows how superior genius always is to mediocrity. Presiding over the meeting last night, he was emphatically the right man in the right place. Of all the men and women there assembled, there was not one, probably, whose mind had not been influenced, more than many of them would like to own, by the writings of the gifted Chairman. This strong hold on the sympathies of an audience is the chief thing necessary to command their respectful and docile attention; and the want of this can be atoned for by no amount of condescending familiarity on the part of peripatetic lecturers who have the good fortune to be members of our aristocracy. Nor did the Chairman, as might have been expected, display any repugnance to grapple with the dry details of his subject. Instead of wandering off into vague, meaningless platitudes about education, and seasoning a vapid speech with jocose anecdotes that had no bearing at all upon what he was saying, after the fashion of autumnal orators, Mr. Dickens kept himself strictly to the matter he had in hand, and gave so clear and interesting a statement of the objects, the work and the prospects of the Association, that all who were present could understand for what purpose the meeting had been called.[9]

[Maltus Questell Holyoake recalls a meeting held on 11 May 1864 to promote the establishment of the Shakespeare Foundation Schools, in connection with the Royal Dramatic College:] Another occasion on which I saw Dickens was at a meeting at the Adelphi Theatre in connection with the Royal Dramatic College. Charles Dickens, whose interest in theatrical matters needs no enlarging upon, was in the chair. At that time I was assisting my father at his Fleet Street publishing house, and being so near the Adelphi Theatre, I seized the opportunity of running down to hear what Dickens might have to say. The meeting was held in the afternoon, and it comes back to me after all the long years that have passed, how dull and dingy the theatre looked in the daytime. Dickens, to my disappointment, gave a thoroughly business-like address, unrelieved by brilliancies of thought or touches of Dickensian humour as I had hoped. He, however, made a model chairman, and dealt with several interruptions in a manner which showed intimate acquaintance with the procedure of public assemblies.[10]

NOTES

1. Richard Cobden (1804–65), the Liberal politician and Free-Trader, was an alderman in Manchester at this time. James Crossley (1800–83), mentioned below, was a Manchester solicitor and a Tory, whom Dickens had met during a visit in 1838.

2. Samuel Giles, brother of Dickens's old schoolmaster, the Rev. William Giles.

3. He was thirty-one, but he aged rapidly.

4. Sir E. W. Watkin, *Alderman Cobden of Manchester* (1891) pp.123–30.

5. Burnett's reminiscences in *Pen and Pencil*, p. 143.

6. George Hodder, *Memories of My Time* (1870) pp. 142–6. For Dickens's activities on behalf of the Elton Fund, see *P*, III, 527–37 and *passim*. George Hodder (1819–70), journalist, first met Dickens over this affair. Later Dickens was to help him in various ways.

7. Letter of 5 May 1852, from *The George Eliot Letters*, ed. Gordon S. Haight (1954), II, 23. The phraseology of George Eliot's letter reflects her belief, at that time, in phrenology. The 'anterior lobe' governed the intellectual faculties such as Casuality and Comparison.

8. Sir John R. Robinson, 'Charles Dickens and the Guild of Literature and Art', *Cornhill Magazine*, n.s. XVI (1904) 28–33. As Robinson's reminiscences suggest, the Guild met with many difficulties, accomplished little, and was later wound up. For his other reminiscences of Dickens see Justin H. McCarthy and Sir John Robinson, *The Daily News Jubilee* (1896) and *Fifty Years of Fleet Street: Being the Life and Recollections of Sir John R. Robinson*, ed. Frederick Moy Thomas (1904).

9. Leading article, *Manchester Guardian*, 4 Dec 1858, repr. in *Dkn*, XXXIV (1938) 140–1. For Dickens's speech, see *Speeches*, pp. 278–85.

10. Maltus Questell Holyoake, 'Memories of Charles Dickens', *Chambers's Journal*, 5th ser., XIV (1897) 723. The author was the son of George Jacob Holyoake, the rationalist and publicist, who has some notes on Dickens in his autobiography, *Sixty Years of an Agitator's Life* (1892). For Dickens's 1864 speech, see *Speeches*, pp. 333–7.

The Company He Kept

JOHN FORSTER AND ELIZABETH GASKELL

Life, IV, iii, 327; VI, vi, 529, 531, 540; VIII, vi, 685; *Letters of Mrs Gaskell*, ed. J. A. V. Chapple and Arthur Pollard (Manchester, 1966) pp. 828–9. Several times in the *Life*, Forster lists the people Dickens was seeing at that period, thus usefully indicating the range of his social contacts. As was noted in the Introduction, most (though not all) of his friends were well-known personages, and it would be otiose – besides grossly overloading this item – to annotate all these names, many of which are very familiar. Collectively they witness both to his sociability and to his being in regular contact with a good sample of the Establishment. For a survey of some three hundred of the people he knew more than casually, see J. W. T. Ley, *The Dickens Circle: a Narrative of the Novelist's Friendships* (1918).

That dinner [the guests at which included Samuel Rogers, Jules Benedict, Albany Fonblanque, Dr Frederic Quin, Edwin Landseer and Lord Strangford] was in the April of 1849, and among others present were Mrs. Procter and Mrs. Macready, dear and familiar names always in his house. No swifter or surer perception than Dickens's for what was solid and beautiful in character; he rated it higher than intellectual effort; and the same lofty place, first in his affection and respect, would have been Macready's and Procter's, if the one had not been the greatest of actors, and the other a poet as genuine as old Fletcher or Beaumont. There were present at this dinner also the American minister and Mrs. Bancroft (it was the year of that visit of Macready to America, which ended in the disastrous Forrest riots); and it had among its guests Lady Graham, the wife of Sir James Graham, and sister of Tom Sheridan's wife, than whom not even the wit and beauty of her nieces, Mrs. Norton and Lady Dufferin, did greater justice to the brilliant family of the Sheridans; so many of whose members, and these three above all, Dickens prized among his friends. The table that day will be 'full' if I add the celebrated singer Miss Catherine Hayes. . . .

Others familiar to Devonshire-terrace in these years will be indicated if I name an earlier dinner (3rd of January), for the 'christening' of the *Haunted Man*, when, besides Lemons, Evanses,

Leeches, Bradburys, and Stanfields, there were present Tenniel, Topham, Stone, Robert Bell, and Thomas Beard. Next month (24th of March) I met at his table, Lord and Lady Lovelace; Milner Gibson, Mowbray Morris, Horace Twiss, and their wives; Lady Molesworth and her daughter (Mrs. Ford); John Hardwick, Charles Babbage, and Doctor Locock[, the] distinguished physician. . . . The Lovelaces were frequent guests after the return from Italy, Sir George Crawford, so friendly in Genoa, having married Lord Lovelace's sister; and few had a greater warmth of admiration for Dickens than Lord Byron's 'Ada', on whom Paul Dombey's death laid a strange fascination. They were again at a dinner got up in the following year for Scribe and the composer Halévy, who had come over to bring out the *Tempest* at Her Majesty's theatre, then managed by Mr. Lumley, who with M. Van de Weyer, Mrs. Gore and her daughter, the Hogarths, and I think the fine French comedian, Samson, were also amongst those present. Earlier that year there were gathered at his dinner-table the John Delanes, Isambard Brunels, Thomas Longmans (friends since the earliest Broadstairs days, and special favourites always), Lord Mulgrave, and Lord Carlisle, with all of whom his intercourse was intimate and frequent, and became especially so with Delane in later years. . . .

The preceding month was that of the start of *David Copperfield*, and to one more dinner (on the 12th) I may especially refer for those who were present at it. Carlyle and Mrs. Carlyle came, Thackeray and Rogers, Mrs. Gaskell and Kenyon, Jerrold and Hablot Browne, with Mr. and Mrs. Tagart; and it was a delight to see the enjoyment of Dickens at Carlyle's laughing reply to questions about his health, that he was, in the language of Mr. Peggoty's housekeeper, a lorn lone creature and everything went contrairy with him. . . .

[Captain Marryat's] name would have stood first among those I have been recalling, as he was among the first in Dickens's liking; but in the autumn of 1848 he had unexpectedly passed away. Other names however still reproach me for omission as my memory goes back. With Marryat's on a former page of this book stands that of Monckton Milnes, familiar with Dickens over all the period since, and still more prominent in Tavistock-house days when with Lady Houghton he brought fresh claims to my friend's admiration and regard. Of Bulwer Lytton's frequent presence in all his houses, and of Dickens's admiration for him as one of the supreme masters in his art, so unswerving and so often publicly declared, it would be needless again to speak. Nor shall I dwell upon his interchange of hospitalities with distinguished men in the two great professions so closely allied to literature and its followers; Denmans, Pollocks, Campbells, and Chittys; Watsons, Southwood Smiths, Lococks, and Elliotsons. To Alfred Tennyson, through all the friendly and familiar days I am describing, he gave full allegiance and honoured welcome. Tom Taylor was often with him; and there was a charm for him I should find it difficult to exaggerate in Lord Dudley Stuart's gentle yet noble character. . . . Incomplete indeed would be the list if I did not add to it the frank and hearty Lord Nugent. . . . Nor should I forget occasional days with dear old Charles Kemble and one or other of his daughters; with Alexander Dyce; and with Harness and his sister, or his niece and her husband, Mr. and Mrs. Archdale; made especially pleasant by talk about great days of the stage. . . .

There are yet some other names that should have place in these rambling recollections, though I by no means affect to remember all. One Sunday evening Mazzini made memorable by taking us to see the school he had established in Clerkenwell for the Italian organ-boys. This was after dining with Dickens, who had been brought into personal intercourse with the great Italian by having given·money to a begging impostor who made unauthorized use of his name. Edinburgh friends made him regular visits in the spring time: not Jeffrey and his family alone, but Sheriff Gordon and his, with whom he was not less intimate, Lord Murray and his wife, Sir William Allan and his niece, Lord Robertson with his wonderful Scotch mimicries, and Peter Fraser with his enchanting Scotch songs; our excellent friend Liston the surgeon, until his fatal illness came in December 1848, being seldom absent from those assembled to bid such visitors welcome. Allan's name may remind me of other artists often at his house, Eastlakes, Leslies, Friths, and Wards, besides those who have had frequent mention, and among whom I should have included Charles as well as Edwin Landseer, and William Boxall. Nor should I drop from this section of his friends, than whom none were more attractive to him, such celebrated names in the sister arts as those of Miss Helen Faucit, an actress worthily associated with the brightest days of our friend Macready's managements, Mr. Sims Reeves, Mr. John Parry, Mr. Phelps, Mr. Webster, Mr. Harley, Mr. and Mrs. Keeley, Mr. Whitworth, and Miss Dolby. Mr. George Henry Lewes he had an old and great regard for; among other men of letters should not be forgotten the cordial Thomas Ingoldsby, and many-sided true-hearted Charles Knight; Mr. R. H. Horne and his wife were frequent visitors both in London and at seaside holidays; and I have met at his table Mr. and Mrs. S. C. Hall. There were the Duff Gordons too, the Lyells, and, very old friends of us both, the Emerson Tennents; there was the good George Raymond; Mr. Frank Beard and his wife; the Porter Smiths, valued for Macready's sake as well as their own; Mr. and Mrs. Charles Black, near connections by marriage of George Cattermole, with whom there was intimate intercourse both before and during the residence in Italy; Mr. T. J. Thompson, brother of Mrs. Smithson formerly named, and his wife, whose sister Frederick Dickens married; Mr. Mitton, his own early companion; and Mrs. Torrens, who had played with the amateurs in Canada. These are all in my memory so connected with Devonshire-terrace, as friends or familiar acquaintance, that they claim this word before leaving it; and visitors from America, I may remark, had always a grateful reception. Of the Bancrofts mention has been made, and with them should be coupled the Abbot Lawrences, Prescott, Hillard, George Curtis, and Felton's brother. Felton himself did not visit England until the Tavistock-house time. In 1847 there was a delightful day with the Coldens and the Wilkses, relatives by marriage of Jeffrey; in the following year, I think at my rooms because of some accident that closed Devonshire-terrace that day (25th of April), Dickens, Carlyle, and myself, foregathered with the admirable Emerson. . . . Lord Shaftesbury first dined with him in the following year. . . .

To name the principal persons present [at the wedding of Kate Dickens and Charles Collins in 1860] will indicate the faces that (with addition of Miss Mary Boyle, Miss Marguerite Power, Mr. Fechter, Mr. Charles Kent, Mr. Edmund Yates, Mr. Percy Fitzgerald, and members of the family of Mr. Frank Stone, whose sudden death in the preceding year had been a great grief to Dickens) were most familiar at Gadshill in these later years. Mr. Frederic Lehmann was there with his wife, whose sister, Miss Chambers, was one of the bridesmaids; Mr. and Mrs. [W. H.] Wills were there, and Dickens's old fast friend Mr. Thomas Beard; the two nearest country neighbours with whom the family had become very intimate, Mr. Hulkes and Mr. Malleson, with their wives, joined the party; among the others were Henry Chorley, Chauncy Hare Townshend, and Wilkie Collins; and, for friend special to the occasion, the bridegroom had brought his old fellow-student in art, Mr. Holman Hunt.

[Elizabeth Gaskell (1810–65), enjoying her new fame as a novelist, dined at Devonshire Terrrace in May 1849.] We were shown into Mr Dickens' study . . . where he writes all his books. . . . There are books all round, up to the ceiling, and down to the ground; a standing-desk at which he writes; and all manner of comfortable easy chairs. There were numbers of people in the room. Mr Rogers (the old poet, who is 86, and looked very unfit to be in such a large party,) Douglas Jerrold, Mr & Mrs Carlyle, Hablot Browne, who illustrated Dickens' works, Mr Forster, Mr and Mrs Tagart, a Mr Kenyon. We waited dinner a long time for Lady Dufferin; (*the* Hon. Mrs Blackwood who wrote the Irish Emigrant's lament,) but she did not come till after dinner. . . . In the evening quantities of other people came in. We were by this time up in the drawing-room, which is not nearly so pretty or so home-like as the study. Frank Stone the artist, Leech & his wife, Benedict the great piano-forte player, Sims Reeves the singer, Thackeray, Lord Dudley Stuart, Lord Headfort, Lady Yonge, Lady Lovelace, Lady Dufferin, and a quantity of others whose names I did not hear. We heard some beautiful music. Mr Tom Taylor was there too, who writes those comical ballads in Punch; and Anne said we had the whole Punch-bowl, which I believe we had. I kept trying to learn people's faces off by heart, that I might remember them; but it was rather confusing there were so *very* many. There were some nice little Dickens' children in the room, – who were so polite, and well-trained.[1]

NOTE

1. One of these guests, Douglas Jerrold (1803–57), the radically-minded *Punch* contributor, and a close friend of Dickens, was dining, together with Charles Mackay (1814–89), the radical poet and journalist, with Nathaniel Hawthorne (then U.S. Consul in Liverpool) in 1856, and Hawthorne recorded from their conversation: 'They spoke approvingly of Bulwer, as valuing his literary position, and holding himself one of the brotherhood of authors, and not so approvingly of Dickens, who, born a plebeian, aspires to aristocratic society.' This, I think, is as dubious a generalisation as Hawthorne's report, in 1855, that 'Dickens evidently is not liked nor thought well of by his literary brethren – at least, the more eminent of them, whose reputation might interfere with his. Thackeray is much more to their taste' – *The English Notebooks by Nathaniel Hawthorne*, ed. Randall Stewart (New York, 1941) pp. 315, 118. Had such judgments been common, I would expect to

have found more evidence of them. But the incidence of titled guests – as well as of colleagues from 'the brotherhood of authors' – in Forster's and Gaskell's lists gives some colour to Jerrold's accusation.

Dickens in Conversation: 'A Demon of Delightfulness'

HENRY CRABB ROBINSON AND OTHERS

Many other items mention Dickens's conversational interests and talents (see Index). Outstanding as a platform speaker, he was surprisingly self-effacing and unspectacular in private conversation, though few witnesses went so far as the poet Longfellow, who reported that 'Dickens saved himself for his books, there was nothing to be learned in private – he never talked!' (Dickens equally astounded their friends by remarking that Longfellow 'had not a word to say for himself'.) Nor did many acquaintances go so far in the opposite direction as 'Cuthbert Bede', who asserted that 'His conversation was as sparkling as his writing; his vivacity was unflagging; and there was a special fascination in his manner.'[1] Most people reported Dickens as being courteous, charming and sensible in conversation, delightful but not in an epigrammatic or quotable manner, and as good a listener as a talker. The topic is surveyed by Philip Collins, *Dkn*, LIX (1963) 145–55.

[Henry Crabb Robinson (1775–1867), veteran diarist and lawyer, first met Dickens in 1839 ('an interesting face, but rather a disagreeable expression') and occasionally thereafter. In April 1848 they were fellow guests at the Rev. Edward Tagart's, where] Dickens himself had the post of honour. He did not affect the *bel esprit*, but talked like a man of judgment on the news of the day.[2]

[Robert Shelton Mackenzie (1809–80), journalist and author, saw a little of Dickens before emigrating to America in 1852. Dickens publicly denounced Mackenzie's brief biographical sketch of him in 1838 (*P*, 1, 367), and Mackenzie's *Life of Charles Dickens* (Philadelphia, 1870) is inaccurate though knowledgeable. Among his observations is this:] Mr. Dickens was not a conversationalist, although he told a story well, and with humorous exaggeration. He hated argument, – indeed, he would not, and could not, go into it. He used to observe, 'No man but a fool was ever talked *out* of his own opinion and *into* your state of mind. Arguments are only cannonballs, fired at a sandbank, or water poured into a sieve – a sheer waste of time and trouble. I won't argue with a man: it is going down, on all-fours, to an obstinate dog. In emphatic cases the only argument is a punch on the head. That's a stunner!' In general Mr. Dickens was not happy in retort. . . .[3]

[Sir Frederick Pollock, 2nd Baronet (1815–88), lawyer, Queen's Remembrancer, and author, 'had the great pleasure of becoming personally acquainted with Dickens and his family' when they met in Broadstairs in 1850.] The first impression of his delightful manner and conversation was only confirmed by much subsequent friendly intercourse. No one could be more free from egotism than Dickens was. He never talked about himself or his books, and was thus in great contrast with Thackeray, who, after he became famous, liked no subject so well.[4]

[Lord John Russell (1792–1878), Whig/Liberal statesman and Prime Minister, was the only leading politician with whom Dickens was on familiar and affectionate terms. *A Tale of Two Cities* was dedicated to him. He and his wife wept over *David Copperfield* 'till we were ashamed', she records; and in her 1852 journal she writes, 'Dickens came to luncheon and stayed to dinner. He is very agreeable – and more than agreeable – made us feel how much he is to be liked.' Her husband concurs: 'Very agreeable and amiable'.[5] Their daughter Georgiana recalls:] Mr. Dickens was a very great friend, and was always very welcome at any time. These two great novelists [Dickens and Thackeray] often lunched and dined with us, both at Chesham Place and Pembroke Lodge. Mr. Dickens had such a very evident respect and love for my father, both as a statesman and in private life, that few things gave him more pleasure than a day at Pembroke Lodge. In the evening, I remember, he was conspicuous, owing to wearing a pink shirt-front embroidered with white, but a genius can always wear whatever he chooses. Sometimes he would be seized with a fit of shyness or modesty, for he would suddenly slip away directly after dinner, and people who had come in later, having been asked to meet him, would all be saying: 'But where is Mr. Charles Dickens?'[6]

[One of Russell's grandchildren recalls spending three days à *trois* with him and Dickens (Lady Russell being ill at the time) – a good fortune which caused great 'delight and astonishment' except that] I cannot remember Mr. Dickens saying anything to me. Indeed, he was not nearly so polite and agreeable as Lord Clarendon, nor, strange to say, do I remember his talking much to Lord John. My grandfather did all the talking. Dickens, I imagine, was apt to be a little florid where, as in this case, he greatly admired; and Lord John Russell, from shyness and naturalness, was not a responsive altar to praise and oblations of any kind. The first evening, I recollect that two or three tributes – tributes of the kind which gave little opportunity for rejoinder – were coldly received. However, these two evenings were most agreeable, Lord John at his best and Mr. Dickens an admiring audience – upon the whole, of the House of Lords type. He listened like a Red Indian, with an occasional grunt of assent, like the 'Wah' of that interesting people, according to Fenimore Cooper. . . .

At dinner he ate and drank very little. Champagne did not circulate at Pembroke Lodge, nor was it the fashion of those days to have whisky-and-sodas; but there was port and madeira, and we sat for some time over the wine. Mr. Dickens drank madeira sparingly. I remember noticing that, with the warmth of the room and food, a vein in the centre of his forehead became very prominent. His evening-clothes were extremely well cut; the shirt frilled, with bright, perhaps diamond, studs. Although his hair was white, he gave me no sense of age in movements or appearance. With a lesser man, I should have described the whole look and character as dapper, but Dickens was one of my heroes, and I was charmed by everything about him.[7]

[Dickens had long known George Eliot's consort, G. H. Lewes (see above, 1, 25–8), but did not meet her until November 1859, by which time he was 'an intense admirer' of her *Scenes of Clerical Life* and *Adam Bede*. 'We had a delightful talk about all sorts of things', Lewes noted in his journal; and George Eliot wrote to a friend:] Yesterday Mr. Dickens dined with us. . . . That was a great pleasure to me: he is a man one can thoroughly enjoy talking to – there is a strain of real seriousness along with his keenness and humour.[8]

[John Lothrop Motley (1814–77), the distinguished American historian and diplomat, first met Dickens in 1861, at a dinner at John Forster's. He wrote to his mother:] I had never even seen him before, for he never goes now into fashionable company. He looks about the age of Longfellow. His hair is not much grizzled and is thick, although the crown of his head is getting bald. His features are good, the nose rather high, the eyes largish, greyish and very expressive. He wears a moustache and beard, and dresses at dinner in exactly the same uniform which every man in London or the civilised world is bound to wear, as much as the inmates of a penitentiary are restricted to theirs. I mention this because I had heard that he was odd and extravagant in his costume. I liked him exceedingly. We sat next each other at table, and I found him genial, sympathetic, agreeable, unaffected, with plenty of light easy talk and touch-and-go fun without any effort or humbug of any kind. He spoke with great interest of many of his Boston friends, particularly of Longfellow, Wendell Holmes, Felton, Sumner, and Tom Appleton.[9]

[Frederic Chapman (1823–95), cousin of Edward Hall (of Chapman and Hall, first publishers of Dickens's novels) and later head of the firm himself, first met Dickens in 1845, 'and from then onward until his death', he told the journalist James Milne, 'I constantly saw him. When he went to stay at Gad's Hill I used to go down there and visit him, and so we were really personal friends, not merely publisher and author.' Milne got Chapman to tell him more.] Dickens, he began, had charm, always an indefinable quality, always a gift from the gods of good-fortune or the gods of chance. Where did his charm lie? In his conversation, or in his disposition, or was it in all-round, all-over charm? It was difficult to say what was the most pleasing thing about him, but behind everything was the magic of personality. For a time after he sprang into fame, he went a good deal into society, whereas in his later years it saw little of him. He hardly, perhaps, at any period, cared to be 'lionised', for, by nature, he was essentially simple.

At Gad's Hill, his Kent home, he lived in good style, and he had many notable people visiting him, yet his tastes remained simple. His talk, which ran naturally, easily, was fascinating and full of anecdotes and incidents about folk he had met and places he had seen. And, please, at Gad's Hill there was no sitting by the men at the dinner-table after the ladies had left. Within a few minutes Dickens would be on his feet, leading the way to the drawing-room. He was chivalrous and kind-hearted, and therefore thoughtful of his guests, whoever they might be.[10]

[The Rev. Whitwell Elwin (1816–1900), critic and scholar, editor of the Quarterly Review, 1853–60, and of a notable edition of Pope, was a distinguished figure in literary circles. He knew Dickens from at least 1855, meeting him chiefly at Forster's, who was a close friend. His son remarks that Elwin, a great admirer of Thackeray, rather undervalued Dickens as a novelist but, 'personally and socially, he was very fond of him'. In 1861 he went to two of the public readings, which he greatly admired, and afterwards he chatted with Dickens, and recorded the conversation in his commonplace-book.] Fanny Kemble's reading of Shakespeare was mentioned. I said it was hateful, because it was coarse and masculine; that the first quality in a woman was to be feminine, and that without this charm there was no charm in any gift of mind or person she might possess. Dickens acquiesced with marked emphasis. He said, 'The people who write books on the rights of women beg the question. They assume that if women usurped the functions of men it would be a clear gain, – so much added to their present merits. It never occurs to them that it would be destructive of what they have, – a total overthrow of everything in them which is winning and lovable. A male female is repulsive.' To which it may be added that their mimicry of qualities which Providence has denied them is in general only a bad imitation, so that, in throwing off womanly grace, they do not attain to manly attributes.

Dickens began life as a reporter. He said that Brougham in his prime was by far the greatest speaker he ever heard. Nobody rivalled him in sarcasm, in invective, and in spirit-stirring eloquence. He was the man too, he said, who of all others seemed, when he was speaking, to see the longest way before him. Dickens thought some speeches which Lyndhurst made when he was chancellor were models of grace and dignity.

I have always found Dickens charming in conversation. He is natural, cheerful, full of knowledge, very easy in his talk, with a gentle touch of humour, and a keen appreciation of it. He is extremely hearty and social, and altogether as excellent a companion as I have ever met.[11]

[Later, reviewing Forster's *Life*, Elwin referred to the blacking warehouse episode, and commented:] The most fastidious observer could never have suspected that he had ever been the comrade of working men and boys, and it was always a marvel how he could have attained to his familiarity with their manners and talk. . . . Time did not permit him to run the immense circuit of literature, but his reading was beyond what could have been

anticipated from his brief and broken studies. He was strongest in
fiction and travels, and, not having gleaned his opinions of books
through books, his judgments of them had a charming directness
and independence. Many of the remarks which he let fall in
conversation upon Shakespeare and others were original and true,
and, had he cared to cultivate the faculty, he would have excelled in
terse, distinctive criticism. . . .

Whatever might be the excess of colouring in parts of the novels
there was none in the conversation and bearing of the man. At the
age of twenty-four he was suddenly elevated to a height of
popularity which has seldom been equalled. Those who have risen
to celebrity without the usual aids from teachers have generally
been noted for vanity and egotism. Dickens, who might well have
presumed upon his fame, kept to his natural simplicity. He never
took up the conversation unless it came to him by right, and he
never made it the vehicle for display. His talk was invariably easy
and unpretentious, interspersed with acute remarks, and lighted up
by a bright and gentle pleasantry. The humour of his novels, which
is of a far higher order than witty repartee, as much higher as the
humorous comedies of Molière are superior to the witty comedies of
Congreve, could not have been exhibited in conversation except he
had descended to be a downright performer for the amusement of
his company. He would have scouted the office. He would be
nothing but himself in his private capacity, and not Sam Weller, or
Squeers, or Mrs. Gamp. No breadth of humour could have been
more exhilarating than the sedater liveliness of his proper
individuality. He carried about with him an atmosphere of
cheerfulness; and his presence, when unconstrained, was like
sunshine. His form and gait expressed his disposition. There was a
spring in his step, and a firmness in his tread, which told both the
airiness and energy of his temperament. It was the same with his
face. The leading lines, especially as he grew older, betokened
resolution, and combined with the determination was a mobility of
muscle, which revealed the sensitiveness of his feelings, and a
vivacity which showed how much he had inherited of his father's
buoyancy. His quick glance announced his penetrating
observation, though so natural was the faculty to him, and so
complete the ease with which it worked, that he had always in
society a disengaged air, and never appeared to be on the watch.[12]

[Frederick Locker, later Locker-Lampson (1821–95), poet, civil servant and man about town, met Dickens occasionally from the early 1840s onwards, but his fullest recollections relate to the novelist's final years. Running into him, at a period between, and failing at first to recognise him, Locker's attention was arrested by his face: 'it struck me as the most animated countenance I had ever seen'. In 1869 he met Dickens again at the publisher Routledge's, at a dinner in honour of Longfellow: and then] Dickens was very friendly; his hearty manner was exceedingly attractive. In March, 1870, we again met at a very pleasant dinner given by my friend, Colonel Hamley, at the Army and Navy Club. Mr. Secretary Walpole, Motley, afterwards United States Minister in London, and Russell Sturgis completed the party.[13] I sat by Dickens. He was remarkably agreeable; his conversation was so affluent, so delightfully alive, so unaffected. When Dickens was in congenial company – and he had the happy faculty of making it congenial to himself – he talked like a demon of delightfulness. At this repast Motley, who was very fond of Dickens, poked a good deal of pleasant fun at him, especially about his *American Sketches*, pretending to be Mark Tapley; much to Dickens's joy, who gave it him back with interest. This was the more diverting as we knew how sensitive Motley usually was as regards America and the Americans, and certainly Dickens had tried him. . . .

A short time before or after this, Alfred Tennyson happening to be in London, and expressing a desire to see Dickens, I invited them to meet at dinner.[14] Just then, however, Dickens was engaged on his readings, and was obliged to decline. About the same time I had been talking to Arthur Stanley of the burials in the Abbey,[15] and he told me that there were certain people who he sincerely hoped would survive him, as, if not, however much their friends might desire it, he should be obliged to refuse them burial in the Abbey. The names of one or two distinguished people were mentioned, such as Carlyle and Mill. Then Dickens's name came up, and the Dean said, 'Oddly enough, I have only only once met Dickens. I do not know him; I have read hardly any of his writings; I should like to meet Dickens'. To gratify this pious wish, I asked Dickens and his daughter to dine, to meet the Dean and Augusta. This was on February 2. . . .

My dinner went off excellently. Arthur said he had had a delightful time, and had found Dickens 'most agreeable'. I afterwards dined *en garçon* with Dickens, Lady Charlotte being out of town, and met the Stanhopes, Edward Hamley, Darnley (his neighbour at Gad's

Hill), Costa, the composer, Strzelecki, and others whose names I forget.[16]

Dickens had much social tact; he was genial and manly; he had a strong personality; he could say 'No', but I should think he had infinitely greater pleasure in saying 'Yes'. He was a jovial fellow, with a most elastic spirit, and apparently an exhaustless vitality. . . . He told me that genuine appreciation of his works was as fresh and precious to him then (1869) as it had been thirty years before; indeed, he was still so sensitive to neglect that, in a railway carriage, if his opposite neighbour were reading one of his novels, he did not dare to watch him, lest he should see the book thrown aside with indifference.

His appearance was attractive; he was not conventionally gentlemanlike-looking – I should have been disappointed if he had been so: he was something better. I shall not quickly forget him at Macaulay's funeral, as he walked among the subdued-looking clericals and staid men of mark; there was a stride in his gait and a roll; he had a seafaring complexion and air, and a huge white tie.

Dickens was fond of dress; he owned that he had the primeval savage's love for bright positive colours. I consoled him with the assurance that it was the poet side of his nature that was so gratified.

Dickens had, as indeed I have already remarked, a wonderfully animated countenance. There was an eager look in his bright eyes, and his manners were as free from *mauvaise honte* as from unseasonable familiarity. He told stories with real dramatic effect; he gave one at my table, as related by Rogers (who made story-telling a fine art), of the English and French duellists who agreed to fight with pistols, the candles being extinguished, in a small room. The brave but humane Englishman, unwilling to shed blood, gropes his way to the fireplace, and discharges his weapon up the chimney; when, lo and behold! whom should he bring down but the dastardly Frenchman, who had crept thither for safety! Dickens said that Rogers's postscript was not the worst part of the story – 'When I tell that in Paris, I always put the Englishman up the chimney!' Dickens mimicked Rogers's calm, low-pitched, drawling voice and dry biting manner very comically.

Dickens admired Smollett; he considered *Humphry Clinker* a highly humorous story, and very originally told. He christened one of his sons Henry Fielding. He did not unduly appreciate Miss Jane Austen's novels. . . .

Dickens was a very good fellow, a delightful companion, warm-hearted, gay-natured, with plenty of light-in-hand fun, and a great capacity for friendship. He was the devoted lifelong servant of the public.[17] . . .

NOTES

1. Edward Wagenknecht, *Dickens and the Scandalmongers* (1965), ch. 4, 'Dickens in Longfellow's Letters and Journals', pp. 85–6; Recollections by 'Cuthbert Bede', in *Pen and Pencil*, p. 161. 'Cuthbert Bede' (the Rev. Edward Bradley, 1827–89), humorous writer, and author of the *Verdant Green* books, 1853–6, published other reminiscences of Dickens in the *London Figaro*, 15 Apr 1874, reprinted in *Dkn*, XII (1916) 208–10, and XXVIII (1932) 300–2.

2. Henry Crabb Robinson on *Books and their Authors*, ed. Edith J. Morley (1938), II 573, 675.

3. R. Shelton Mackenzie, *Life of Charles Dickens* (Philadelphia, 1870) p. 239. Mackenzie's account continues with intriguing, but dubious, assertions that 'Dickens's taste in literature was peculiar. Like Byron, he undervalued Shakespeare. . . . Wordsworth and Dickens did not take to each other . . . ', etc.

4. Sir Frederick Pollock, *Personal Reminiscences* (1887) I, 289.

5. *Lady Jane Russell: a Memoir*, ed. Desmond Macarthy and Agatha Russell, 3rd edn (1926) pp. 108, 119, 213.

6. *Recollections of Lady Georgiana Peel*, ed. Ethel Peel (1920), p. 118.

7. Baroness [Hilda Elizabeth] Deichmann, *Impressions and Memories* (1927) pp. 101–3.

8. *The George Eliot Letters*, ed. Gordon S. Haight (1954), III, 195, 197, 200; see IV, 266–7, for Lewes's account (6 June 1866) of Dickens's 'Curious stories of dreams, etc.'; see also above, p. 27.

9. *The Correspondence of John Lothrop Motley*, ed. George William Curtis (1889), I, 365. On Motley and Dickens, see Frederick Locker-Lampson, later in this item.

10. James Milne, *A Window in Fleet Street* (1931) pp. 183–6.

11. 'Memoir' by his son, Warwick Elwin, prefacing *Some XVIII Century Men of Letters, by the Rev. Whitwell Elwin* (1902) I, 148, 247–50. The Shakespearian recitals of Fanny Kemble (1809–1893) were internationally famous in the 1850s and 1860s. Dickens's anti-feminism was such that he 'delighted' in the quip that 'women's rights' were usually 'men's lefts' – Percy Fitzgerald, *Life of Dickens* (1905) I, 207.

12. [Whitwell Elwin], 'Forster's *Life of Dickens*', *Quarterly Review*, CXXXII (1872) 131, 136, 140–1.

13. Edward Brice Hamley (1824–93), later General Sir Edward Hamley, Commandant of the Staff College, 1870–7, was also a novelist and reviewer; Spencer Walpole MP (1806–98) had been Home Secretary three times; Julian Russell Sturgis (1848–1904), American-born, later became a novelist. On Motley, see above, p. 112.

14. Dickens had known Tennyson (1809–92) since 1843 at least, greatly admired his work, and in 1845 named his fourth son after him; Tennyson acted as godfather. In 1846 Dickens invited him to accompany the Dickens family to Switzerland, '"but", laughed Tennyson, "if I went, I should be entreating him to dismiss his sentimentality, and so we should quarrel and part, and never see one

another any more. It was better to decline – and I declined" '– *The Letters of Robert Browning and Elizabeth Barrett Browning* (1899) II, 116. Tennyson did, however, call on Dickens in Lausanne (*P*, IV, 608, 610), and met him from time to time thereafter. Their facial similarity, after they had both grown beards, was remarkable, as many observers commented. Tennyson himself, on seeing Millais's drawing of Dickens on his deathbed, exclaimed, 'This is the most extraordinary drawing. It is exactly like myself' – J. Comyns Carr, *Some Eminent Victorians* (1908) p. 194.

15. Arthur Penrhyn Stanley (1815–81), clergyman and author of ecclesiastical works, was Dean of Westminster, and conducted Dickens's funeral there. Dickens had greatly admired his *Life of Dr. Arnold* (1844). See A. A. Adrian, 'Dickens and Dean Stanley', *Dkn*, LII (1956) 152–5. Stanley confessed, however, that he 'could not take any pleasure' in Dickens's books – F. Max Muller, *Auld Lang Syne* (1898) p. 110.

16. Lady Charlotte was Locker's wife. The guests mentioned are (probably) Lord Stanhope (1805–75), historian, and his son Edward Stanhope MP (1840–93); Lord Darnley, of Cobham, Kent; Sir Michael Costa (1810–84), director of music at Covent Garden; Sir Paul Edmund de Strzelecki, explorer, of an old Polish family.

17. Frederick Locker-Lampson, *My Confidences* (1896) pp. 321–5.

Working Habits

GEORGINA HOGARTH AND OTHERS

Everything with him [Georgina Hogarth told A. W. Ward] went as by clockwork; his movements, his absences from home, and the times of his return were all fixed beforehand, and it was seldom that he failed to adhere to what he had fixed. [Ward reports, on family authority, that 'Ordinarily, when engaged on a work of fiction, he considered three of his not very large MS. pages a good, and four an excellent day's work.'[1] Elsewhere Georgina recorded that] An average day's work with him was 2–2½ of those sides . . . of MS. A very, *very* hard day's work was 4 of them.[2]

As to his system of work, it was the same wherever he was [reports Dickens's eldest son, Charley, on whom see below, I, 131–40]. No city clerk was ever more methodical or orderly than he; no humdrum, monotonous, conventional task could ever have been discharged with more punctuality or with more businesslike regularity, than he gave to the work of his imagination and fancy. At something before ten he would sit down – every day with very,

very rare exceptions – to his desk which, as to its papers, its writing materials, and the quaint little bronze figures which he delighted in having before him, was as neat and as orderly as everything else in and about the house, and would there remain until lunch time – sometimes, if he were much engrossed with any particular point or had something in hand which he was very anxious to finish there and then, until later. Whether he could get on satisfactorily with the work in hand mattered nothing. He had no faith in the waiting-for-inspiration theory, nor did he fall into the opposite error of forcing himself willy-nilly to turn out so much manuscript every day, as was Mr. Anthony Trollope's plan, for instance. It was his business to sit at his desk during just those particular hours in the day, my father used to say, and, whether the day turned out well or ill, there he sat accordingly. And, very often, I have known a day to have been barren of copy, but to have been a very good day, notwithstanding. Often while I have been in his room while he was at work – as happened not infrequently in the later years of his life – I have seen that he had scarcely written a line, and have heard him report at lunch time that he had had a bad morning, but have known from the expressive working of his face and from a certain intent look that I learnt to know well, that he had been, almost unconsciously, diligently thinking all round his subject; and that the next day's work would result in the comparatively easy production of a goodly number of those wonderful sheets full of blue lines, and erasures, and 'balloonings out', and interlineations, and all kinds of traps for compositors, which you may see at South Kensington.

When he was writing one of his long stories and had become deeply interested in the working-out of his plot and the evolution of his characters, he lived, I am sure, two lives, one with us and one with his fictitious people, and I am equally certain that the children of his brain were much more real to him at times than we were. I have, often and often, heard him complain that he could *not* get the people of his imagination to do what he wanted, and that they would insist on working out their histories in *their* way and not *his*. I can very well remember his describing their flocking round his table in the quiet hours of a summer morning when he was – an unusual circumstance with him – at work very early, each one of them claiming and demanding instant personal attention. And at such times he would often fall to consider the matter in hand even during his walks. There was no mistaking the silence into which he fell on such occasions. It was not the silence only of a pause in conversation, but the silence of engrossing thought, not, one felt, to be broken or interrupted lightly. Many a mile have I walked with him thus – he striding along with his regular four-miles-an-hour swing; his eyes looking straight before him, his lips slightly working, as they generally did when he sat thinking and writing; almost unconscious of companionship, and keeping half a pace or so ahead. When he had worked out what had come into his mind he would drop back again into line – again, I am sure, almost unconsciously – and the conversation would be resumed, as if there had been no appreciable break or interval at all.[3]

[Dickens's elder daughter, Mamie (on whom see below, I, 141–50), gives the most illuminating account of him at work – in front of a mirror.] When at work my father was almost always alone, so that, with rare exceptions, save as we could see the effect of the adventures of his characters upon him in his daily moods, we knew but little of his manner of work. Absolute quiet under these circumstances was essential, the slightest sound making an interruption fatal to the success of his labours, although, oddly enough, in his leisure hours the bustle and noise of a great city seemed necessary to him.[4] . . .

As I have said, he was usually alone when at work, though there were, of course, some occasional exceptions, and I myself constituted such an exception. During our life at Tavistock House, I had a long and serious illness, with an almost equally long convalescence.[5] During the latter, my father suggested that I should be carried every day into his study to remain with him, and, although I was fearful of disturbing him, he assured me that he desired to have me with him. On one of these mornings, I was lying on the sofa endeavouring to keep perfectly quiet, while my father wrote busily and rapidly at his desk, when he suddenly jumped from his chair and rushed to a mirror which hung near, and in which I could see the reflection of some extraordinary facial contortions which he was making. He returned rapidly to his desk, wrote furiously for a few moments, and then went again to the mirror. The facial pantomime was resumed, and then turning toward, but evidently not seeing, me, he began talking rapidly in a low voice, Ceasing this soon, however, he returned once more to his desk, where he remained silently writing until luncheon time. It was a most curious experience for me, and one of which I did not, until later years, fully appreciate the purport. Then I knew that with his natural intensity he had thrown himself completely into the character that he was creating, and that for the time being he had not only lost sight of his surroundings, but had actually become in action, as in imagination, the creature of his pen.

His 'studies' were always cheery, pleasant rooms, and always, like himself, the personification of neatness and tidiness. On the shelf of his writing table were many dainty and useful ornaments, gifts from his friends or members of his family, and always, a vase of bright and fresh flowers. The first study that I remember is the one in our Devonshire Terrace home, a pretty room, with steps leading directly into the garden from it, and with an extra baize door to keep out all sounds and noise. The study at Tavistock House was more elaborate; a fine large room, opening into the drawing-room by means of sliding doors. When the rooms were thrown together they gave my father a promenade of considerable length for the constant indoor walking which formed a favorite recreation for him after a hard day's writing.

At 'Gad's Hill' he first made a study from one of the large spare sleeping rooms of the house, as the windows there overlooked a beautiful and favorite view of his. His writing table was always placed near a window looking out into the open world which he loved so keenly. Afterwards he occupied for years a smaller room overlooking the back garden and a pretty meadow, but this he eventually turned into a miniature billiard room, and then established himself, finally, in the room on the right side of the entrance hall facing the front garden. It is this room which Mr. Luke Fildes, the great artist and our own esteemed friend, made famous in his picture 'The Empty Chair', which he sketched for *The Graphic* after my father's death. . . .

The amount of work which he could accomplish varied greatly at certain times, though in its entirety it was so immense. When he became the man of letters, and ceased the irregular, unmethodical life of the reporter, his mornings were invariably spent at his desk. The time between breakfast and luncheon, with an occasional extension of a couple of hours into the afternoon, were given over to his creations. The exceptions were when he was taking a holiday or resting, though even when ostensibly employed in the latter, cessation from story writing meant the answering of letters and the closer attention to his business matters, so that but little of real rest ever came into his later life. . . .

Despite his regularity of working hours, as I have said, the amount of work which my father accomplished varied greatly. His manuscripts were usually written upon white 'slips', though sometimes upon blue paper, and there were many mornings when it would be impossible for him to fill one of these. . . . This slowness in writing marked more prominently the earlier period of my father's literary career, though these 'blank days', when his brain refused to work, were of occasional occurrence to the end. . . . But, on the other hand, the amount of work which he would accomplish at other times was almost incredible. . . .

I know of only one occasion on which he employed an amanuensis, and my aunt [Georgina] is my authority for the following, concerning this one time: 'The book which your father dictated to me was *The Child's History of England*. The reason for my being used in this capacity of secretary was that *Bleak House* was being written at the same time, and your father would dictate to me while walking about the room, as a relief after his long, sedentary imprisonment. The history was being written for *Household Words* and *Bleak House* also as a serial, so he had both weekly and monthly work on hand at the same time.'. . .

My father wrote always with a quill pen and blue ink, and never, I think, used a lead pencil. His handwriting was considered extremely difficult to read by many people, but I never found it so. In his manuscripts there were so many erasures, and such frequent interlineations that a special staff of compositors was used for his work, but this was not on account of any illegibility in his handwriting. . . . His objection to the use of a lead pencil was so great that even his personal memoranda, such as his lists of guests for dinner parties, the arrangement of tables and menus, were always written in ink. For his personal correspondence he used blue note paper, and signed his name in the left-hand corner of the envelope. After a morning's close work he was sometimes quite pre-occupied when he came into luncheon. Often, when we were only our home party at 'Gad's Hill', he would come in, take something to eat in a mechanical way – he never ate but a small luncheon – and would return to his study to finish the work he had left, scarcely having spoken a word in all this time.[6] Again, he would come in, having finished his work, but looking very tired and worn. Our talking at these times did not seem to disturb him, though any sudden sound, as the dropping of a spoon, or the clinking of a glass, would send a spasm of pain across his face.[7]

[Frederick Chapman, of the publishers Chapman and Hall, told the journalist James Milne:] 'When he had finished a manuscript he warmly interested himself in its publication. He was exacting with himself in his MSS., changing this part and interleaving that part, so that often it was almost indecipherable. Also he made extensive alterations to his proofs up to the moment that, as a book, they went out into the world.'

'Do you happen,' I said, 'to know on what system he wrote his novels, his method of construction and working out?' 'He once told me,' answered his publisher, and who could have been more interested to know? 'After getting hold of a central idea he revolved it in his mind until he had fully thought it out. Then he made what I may call a programme of the story and its characters, drawing up each chapter in skeleton form. Upon this skeleton he set to work and gave it the litereary blood, sinew and vitality of a *David Copperfield* or an *Oliver Twist*.'⁸

[Arthur Locker (1828–93), novelist and journalist, met Dickens through contributing to *All the Year Round*, but he is here drawing on the reminiscences of closer friends – Charles Knight (1791–1873), the radical author and publisher, and his womenfolk, who knew Dickens *en famille*.] Dickens told Miss Knight that he never invented a name for his characters – they were all real. Whenever he saw a queer name he jotted it down, and he used to keep a series of small bags, filled with scraps of paper containing various memoranda of this sort, upon his writing table. . . .

Mr. Knight told me of C. D.'s constant habit of observation as he went along the street. He would say, 'Look at that woman, did you ever see such a face?' – He insisted on being very quiet while working. Between 10 and 2 he would not be at home to an Archbishop. When writing his serials from month to month the labour seemed to tell on him. . . . As I have already said, when preparing for a long novel he would have paper bags full of scraps of character, etc., jotted down. He used to ask Mrs. Knight to tell him of queer names. . . . ⁹

[Forster's *Life*, especially its chapter on 'Dickens as a Novelist' (ix, i, 712–28) which quotes many relevant letters, is a major repository of material about the novelist at work. Here he describes Dickens on one of his special expeditions – comparatively rare – to establish the factual accuracy of settings, etc., for his fictions. He is preparing to write the climactic chapter of *Great Expectations* about Pip's abortive attempt to row Magwitch down the Thames, towards safety from the law.] To make himself sure of the actual course of a boat in such circumstances, and what possible incidents the adventure might have, Dickens hired a steamer for the day from Blackwall to Southend. Eight or nine friends and three or four members of his family were on board, and he seemed to have no care, the whole of that summer day (22 May 1861), except to enjoy their enjoyment and entertain them with his own in shape of a thousand whims and fancies; but his sleepless observation was at work all the time, and nothing had escaped his keen vision on either side of the river. The fifteenth chapter of the third volume [of *Great Expectations*] is a masterpiece.[10]

[David Copperfield speaks for his creator's habit of 'sleepless observation' when he says, 'I looked at nothing, that I know of, but I saw everything' (ch. 27). As other items show – see particularly Arthur Helps, below, II, 332–3 – Dickens's friends were very aware of his remarkable powers of observation, and of the relevance of this habit to his art. Sir Frederick Pollock (on whom see above, I, 111) remarked, 'He could always at a glance take in the contents and furniture of a room, and in this way was able to astonish his friends by performing some of the feats made famous by Houdin the conjurer.' F. G. Kitton, quoting this remark, prints a letter received from Pollock's son, Walter Herries Pollock, whose account has similar recourse to this comparison with Houdin the magician.] Dining at my father's house, Dickens took my mother to dinner. He was deep in conversation through dinner, and never looked about him; yet, in the drawing-room, it came out in some natural way that in the brief time they took going up the dining-room and the moment when the men stood up as the ladies went out, Dickens had noted every picture and every item of interest in the room. I am pretty sure that, on my mother's expressing surprise, he referred to Houdin's description of how he trained himself and his son to observe and remember every object in the shop-windows as they passed down the street. Hence, with a secret code of signals, their astonishing 'second-sight' performances.[11]

NOTES

1. Adolphus William Ward, *Dickens* (1882) pp. 89–91.
2. A. A. Adrian, *Georgina Hogarth and the Dickens Circle*, (1957) p. 204.

3. Charles Dickens, Jr, 'Reminiscences of My Father', *Windsor Magazine*, Christmas Supplement 1934, pp. 24–5.

4. Mamie here quotes Dickens's well-known letters from Genoa, 1844, about how hard it was to write without nightly access to the 'magic lantern' of London (*Life*, IV, v, 346).

5. She was very ill in 1854. Dickens was then writing *Hard Times*.

6. Dickens's son Henry says that he generally worked until 3 p.m. and 'but rarely came in to lunch' – *Recollections* (1934) p. 32. When at Gad's Hill he did join the family at lunch, his niece Emily Barrow reports, 'He would sit at the table oblivious of all seated near him and it was difficult at such times to get him to enter into conversation. It would almost appear as though he was in a temper if anyone spoke to him. He would suddenly push back his chair, leave the table in the middle of a meal, hurry off to his writing, and sit for an hour or two. Members of his family would afterwards go and peep at his manuscript, often coming away laughing at what they had read – Thomas Wright, *Life of Charles Dickens* (1935) p. 311.

7. Mary Dickens, *My Father as I Recall Him* (1897) pp. 46–65.

8. James Milne, *A Window in Fleet Street* (1931) pp. 186–7.

9. Arthur Locker, 'Reminiscences', in *Pen and Pencil*, pp. 173–4. I know of no other evidence for this 'paper-bag' story, but Dickens certainly collected queer names: see his 'Book of Memoranda', *Life*, IX, vii, 747–60, and Howard Paul, *Dinners with Celebrities* (n.d. [c. 1896]) pp. 37–8.

10. *Life*, IX, iii, 736.

11. F. G. Kitton, *Charles Dickens: His Life, Writings and Personality* [1902] p. 419.

The Pace of Serialisation

CHARLES KENT AND HABLOT K. BROWNE

(1) from Charles Kent, *Charles Dickens as a Reader* (1872) pp. 45–6; (2) from David Croal Thomson, *Life of Hablot Knight Browne* (1884) pp. 63, 233–5. Kent (for whom see below, II, 241–50) is at this point in his narrative refuting an apocryphal account of Dickens's being 'nervous' over an early public reading. Hablot Knight Browne, 'Phiz' (1815–82), Dickens's most regular illustrator from 1836 to 1859, left few recollections of his most illustrious employer, and the timetable reprinted below is his most graphic record of the strain to which this remarkably successful collaboration was subjected by the exigencies of last-minute serialisation. Dickens, annoyed by Browne's failure to attend in detail to the text of *Dombey and Son*, wrote to Forster, 'Indeed I think he does better without the text; for then the notion is, made easy to him in a short description, and he can't help taking it in' (*Life*, VI, ii, 478). On this matter, see Frederick G. Kitton, *Dickens and his Illustrators* (1899); Edgar Browne, *Phiz and Dickens* (1913); J. R. Harvey, *Victorian Novelists and their Illustrators* (1970); and Michael Steig, *Dickens and Phiz* (1978). Of Dickens's other

main illustrators it may be remarked that George Cruikshank's reminiscences are highly contentious, and will not be reprinted here. Marcus Stone's are given below, II, 181–9. Luke Fildes, illustrator of *Edwin Drood*, is recorded mainly for his information about how that unfinished novel would have ended – a topic too arcane and, in its intricacies, too boring for the present compilation. Fildes's most significant reminiscence is that he used to go down to Gad's Hill, during the composition of *Edwin Drood*, and Dickens would *act the scenes* he wanted illustrating (*Edwin Drood*, Clarendon Edition, ed. Margaret Cardwell [1972], p. 239). Italics mine, because Dickens's histrionic demonstration strikes me as conveying something important about the spirit he desired in his illustrators, and about his conception of crucial episodes in his novels.

(1) . . . the present writer recalls to recollection very clearly the fact of Dickens saying to him one day, – saying it with a most whimsical air by-the-bye, but very earnestly – 'Once, and but once only in my life, I was – frightened!' The occasion he referred to was simply this, as he immediately went on to explain, that somewhere about the middle of the serial publication of *David Copperfield*, happening to be out of writing-paper, he sallied forth one morning to get a fresh supply at the stationer's. He was living then in his favourite haunt, at Fort House, in Broadstairs. As he was about to enter the stationer's shop, with the intention of buying the needful writing-paper, for the purpose of returning home with it, and at once setting to work upon his next number, not one word of which was yet written, he stood aside for a moment at the threshold to allow a lady to pass in before him. He then went on to relate – with a vivid sense still upon him of mingled enjoyment and dismay in the mere recollection – how the next instant he had overheard this strange lady asking the person behind the counter for the new green number. When it was handed to her, 'Oh, this,' said she, 'I have read. I want the next one.' The next one she was thereupon told would be out by the end of the month. 'Listening to this, unrecognised,' he added, in conclusion, 'knowing the purpose for which I was there, and remembering that not one word of the number she was asking for was yet written, for the first and only time in my life, I felt – frightened!'

(2) When author and artist lived near each other, Dickens would sometimes drop in and read a portion of the novel he was writing, telling the artist that he desired the illustration taken from certain passages, and the whole scene would then be considered and thought out; but at other times, when under extreme pressure, Dickens would stay only a very few minutes, read what was to be

illustrated, and run back to his writing-table without chatting over the points to be brought out particularly. In the latter case it would of course not be very surprising if some discrepancy existed between the letterpress and the plate. At other times, however, Dickens would write out lengthy notes, partly literal extracts from the text and partly condensation.[1] . . .

When 'Phiz' was engaged with the Dickens illustrations, he usually sent the sketch to the author the day following that on which he received the 'copy' with the subject suggested for representation. As there were usually two etchings in hand at one time (because two etchings appeared in each monthly part, and also because it was found commercially economical to have a plate large enough to hold two subjects, which could be printed at little more expense than one), the second sketch was sent immediately afterwards. The following table prepared by Browne himself shows exactly how much time was occupied by the etcher when in ordinary work without extreme pressure, and when etchings for other publications were also in hand. The table was prepared for the publisher's guidance as to how long the month's two etchings should take to prepare.

A DIARY

Friday evening, 11th Jan ..	Received portion of copy containing Subject No. 1.
Sunday.	Posted sketch to Dickens.
Monday evening, 14th Jan .	Received back sketch of Subject No. 1 from Dickens, enclosing a subject for No. 2.
Tuesday, 15th Jan	Forwarded sketch of Subject 2 to Dickens.
Wednesday, 16th Jan	Received back ditto.
Sunday.	
Tuesday, 22nd Jan.	First plate finished.
Saturday, 26th Jan.	Second ditto finished.—Supposing that I had nothing else to do, you may see by the foregoing that I could not well commence etching operations until Wednesday, the 16th.

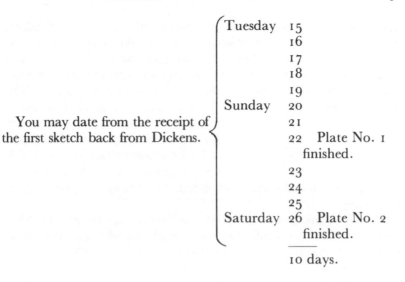

You may date from the receipt of
the first sketch back from Dickens.

	Tuesday	15	
		16	
		17	
		18	
		19	
	Sunday	20	
		21	
		22	Plate No. 1 finished.
		23	
		24	
		25	
	Saturday	26	Plate No. 2 finished.

10 days.

I make ten days to etch and finish four etchings. What do you make
of it?

NOTE

1. Thomson gives us an example Dickens's instructions to 'Phiz' for the *Dombey*
plate entitled 'Doctor Blimber's young gentlemen as they appeared when enjoying
themselves' (*P*, IV. 677–8). There, and in the text of the novel, Dickens specified
that 'The Doctor only takes ten young gentlemen' but Browne carelessly depicted
seventeen. Dickens amended the text to agree with the illustration, but then
restored the 'ten' in the text.

Dickens and his Parents

E. DAVEY

'The Parents of Charles Dickens', *Lippincott's Magazine*, XIII (1874) 772–4.
Mrs Davey met Dickens's parents in 1850, when the novelist requested her
husband, a physician, to attend his sick father. John Dickens, with his wife, went to
live with the Daveys and died next year in their house at Keppel Street, London.

Mr. [John] Dickens was a kind-hearted man, but fearfully irascible. . . . The resemblance between old Mr. D. and Mr. Micawber was very slight. It consisted only in one or two peculiar traits, exaggerated in the description, and in the use of a pet phrase to the effect 'that something was sure to turn up'. . . . The day previous to his death . . . he was taken seriously ill whilst at dinner, . . . and I sent off immediately for Charles. He came as soon as possible. . . . The old gentleman expired about five o'clock in the morning, with little or no pain. Charles Dickens had been with him for hours, standing or sitting by the bedside, and holding his hand. He was much affected, and behaved throughout with great tenderness.

Mrs. Dickens was a little woman, who had been very nice-looking in her youth. She had very bright hazel eyes, and was as thoroughly good-natured, easy-going, companionable a body as one would wish to meet with. The likeness between her and Mrs. Nickleby is simply the exaggeration of some slight peculiarities. She possessed an extraordinary sense of the ludicrous, and her power of imitation was something quite astonishing. On entering a room she almost unconsciously took an inventory of its contents, and if anything happened to strike her as out of place or ridiculous, she would afterward describe it in the quaintest possible manner. In like manner she noted the personal peculiarities of her friends and acquaintances. She had also a fine vein of pathos, and could bring tears to the eyes of her listeners when narrating some sad event. . . . I am of opinion that a great deal of Dickens's genius was inherited from his mother. He possessed from her a keen appreciation of the droll and of the pathetic, as also considerable dramatic talent. Mrs. Dickens has often sent my sisters and myself into uncontrollable fits of laughter by her funny sayings and inimitable mimicry. Charles was decidedly fond of her, and always treated her respectfully and kindly. In the hour of her sad bereavement his conduct was noble. I remember he took her in his arms, and they both wept bitterly together. He told her that she must rely upon him for the future. He immediately paid whatever his father owed, and relieved his mother's mind on that score. . . .

Mrs. Dickens was very fond of her daughter-in-law, Mrs. Charles, and has often told me that she believed 'there was not another woman in all England so well suited to her son'. . . .

Charles Dickens called frequently in Keppel Street, and sometimes stayed to dinner. He was not a very talkative man, but could be extremely pleasant when he chose. Mrs. Dickens does not seem to have foreseen the future celebrity of her son in his childhood, but she remembered many little circumstances afterward which she was very fond of relating. Once, when Charles was a tiny boy, and the family were staying down at Chatham, the nurse had a great deal of trouble in inducing him to follow her when out for his daily walk. When they returned home, Mrs. Dickens said to her, 'Well, how have the children behaved?' 'Very nicely indeed, ma'am – all but Master Charley.' 'What has he done?' 'Why, ma'am, he will persist in always going the same road every day.' 'Charley, Charley, how is this?' 'Why, mamma', answered the urchin, 'does not the Bible say we must walk in the same path all the days of our life?'

The little Dickenses were all fond of private theatricals, and even as children they constructed a small play-house in which the drama was represented by puppets. Charles was the reader, and his brothers moved the marionettes. Those early years were doubtless very sad, for I know the whole family was in very reduced circumstances; and to one so sensitive and imaginative as Charles deprivations and slights must have been indeed hard to bear. I am of opinion that the troubles he met with in his childhood, and the great success won by his genius in after times, made him anxious to have his home so ordered as in some degree to efface his early impressions; and I fear his father's ungovernable temper prevented his being as often received in his son's house as he might otherwise have been. But, whatever may be said to the contrary, his conduct toward both his father and mother struck me as admirable.

The Eldest Son's Recollections

CHARLES DICKENS JR

(1) from his 'Glimpses of Charles Dickens', *North American Review*, CLX (1895) 525–37, 677–83; (2) from his 'Reminiscences of my Father', *Windsor Magazine*, Christmas Supplement, 1934, pp. 8, 23–5. Charles Culliford Boz Dickens (1837–96), 'Charley', the novelist's eldest child, was educated at Eton (at the expense of Miss Coutts). In 1862 he married Bessie, daughter of F. M. Evans (of Bradbury and Evans) – an alliance unwelcome to his father, who had quarrelled with that

firm in 1858; he did not attend the wedding. Charley's business career ended in
bankruptcy in 1868, and Dickens took him on the staff of *All the Year Round*, which
he owned and edited after his father's death. His 'lassitude of character' and lack of
perseverance had cost Dickens much, in worry and cash. In later years he lectured
about his father, wrote introductions to a reprint of the novels, gave public readings
from them, and otherwise exploited the family name. For particulars of the later
lives of him and the other children, see A. A. Adrian, *Georgina Hogarth and the Dickens
Circle* (1957).

(1) My first recollections of my father date from a time when we
were living in Devonshire Terrace, and just after his return from his
first visit to America [in June 1842]. One of the clearest of them is in
connection with a certain American rocking-chair, which I pre-
sume he had brought back with him from the States, and in which
he often used to sit of an evening singing comic songs to a wondering
and delighted audience consisting of myself and my two sisters. *The
Loving Ballad of Lord Bateman*, in the composition of which my father,
and Thackeray, and George Cruikshank were all supposed to have
had some sort of hand, was one of these ditties, and used to be sung
with a prodigious dramatic effect. . . .

Another favorite song of ours – and I think my father enjoyed
them all even more than we did – was one that was concerned with
the history of Guy Fawkes; 'Guy Fawkes, that prince of sinisters,
who once blew up the House of Lords, the King, and all his
ministers.' The beginning of each verse contained some startling
statement of this kind, which was afterwards modified and explained away in what we considered a most artful and humorous
manner. I forget exactly what happened to interfere with the final
stage of Guy Fawkes's nefarious project, but in another verse it was
stated that Guy 'crossing over Vauxhall Bridge, that way came into
London. That is, he would have come that way to perpetrate his
guilt, sir. But a little thing prevented him – the bridge it wasn't
built, sir'. . . . To each verse there was a chorus of the good old-
fashioned sort, with an 'oh, ah, oh, ri fol de riddy oddy, bow wow
wow' refrain, and a great part of the point of the joke lay in the
delivery of the introductory monosyllables; the first 'oh' being
given, as it were, with incredulity, or a tone of inquiry; the second
'ah' strongly affirmatively, and the last 'oh' with an air as of one who
has found conviction not without difficulty. Some of Tom Moore's
melodies also formed part of the repertoire, and there were no doubt
others, which I have forgotten, but the impression of the singer, as
he sat in that rocking-chair with us three children about or on his

knees, has never in the least faded from my mind, though of his appearance at some other and later times the picture may be less vivid.

My first experience, I think, of my father's extraordinary energy and of the thoroughness – the even alarming thoroughness – with which he always threw himself into everything he had occasion to take up, was in connection with a toy theatre of which I was the proud possessor somewhere about the middle of the forties. . . . The size of my theatre fascinated my father, and, in conjunction with Clarkson Stanfield, who had been distinguished as a scene painter before he became a member of the Royal Academy, he set to work to produce the first piece. This, I remember, was a spectacle called the *Elephent of Siam*, and its production on a proper scale of splendor necessitated the designing and painting of several new scenes, which resulted in such a competition between my father and Stanfield that you would have thought their very existences depended on the mounting of this same elephant. And even after Stanfield had had enough of it my father was still hard at work, and pegged away at the landscapes and architecture of Siam with an amount of energy which in any other man would have been extraordinary, but which I soon learned to look upon as quite natural in him. . . .

This extraordinary, eager, restless energy, which first showed itself to me in this small matter, was never absent from my father all through his life. Whatever he did he put his whole heart into, and did as well as ever he could. Whether it was for work of for play, he was always in earnest. Painting the scenes for a toy theatre, dancing Sir Roger de Coverley at a children's party, gravely learning the polka from his little daughters for a similar entertainment, walking, riding, picnicking, amateur acting, public reading, or the every-day hard work of his literary life – it was all one to him. Whatever lay nearest to his hand at the moment had to be done thoroughly. . . .

But, unfortunately, there comes a time at last when . . . never ceasing activity and energy of that kind really deserve Mr. Forster's epithet 'relentless'; and when it becomes of the last importance, for physical as well as mental reasons, to remember that even a virtue carried to an unreasonable excess may become something very like a vice. In my father's case . . . it would have been better if he had been content – or, perhaps, I should say if he had been able – to relax the constant strain, the incessant tension, when the physical and nervous strength were no longer so fit to bear them as they once had been. But he never could be persuaded that that time had come for him, and never would admit in his later days that things were no longer with him as they had been of old.

I shall have to recur several times before I conclude to my father as an actor – both on the boards and on the platform – but I may say now that if ever a man seemed to have been born for one particular pursuit it was my father in connection with the stage. He was, indeed, a born actor, and no line of character that I ever saw him essay came amiss to him. From Captain Bobadil to Justice Shallow, from old-fashioned farce, such as *Two o'clock in the Morning* and *Animal Magnetism*, to the liveliest Charles Mathewsisms, and thence again to the intensest Frederic Lemaître melodrama,[1] from the tremendous power of the *Sikes and Nancy* Reading to the absurdities of *Serjeant Buzfuz*, from the pathos of *Little Dombey* to the broad humors of *Mrs. Gamp*, everything seemed to come natural to him. That he brought to his acting the same earnestness and energy that he gave to everything else is of course true, but no amount of work could have produced the same result if the power had not been there, strongly, unusually strongly, developed. There was a quaint professional touch and yet one easy to understand about the remark which a stage carpenter once made to him during the progress of some amateur performances at the Haymarket Theatre: 'Ah, Mr. Dickens, it was a sad loss to the public when you took to writing.' And, besides his powers as an actor, he had a positive genius for stage management. . . . The celebrated amateur dramatic performances at Tavistock House, which, in their full development with the *Frozen Deep*, were, I have no hesitation in saying, the most extraordinarily artistic and successful things of their kind ever known, had very modest and unassuming beginnings [in the Twelfth Night Children's theatricals which Dickens directed, and played in, in 1854–5]. Of course it was clear that something more important must come of all this, and that something came very soon, only six months afterwards, in fact, in the shape of Wilkie Collins's powerful and ingenious drama, *The Lighthouse*, in which my father, for the first time, I think, displayed that extraordinary melodramatic intensity and force with which his readings were afterwards to make the public so familiar. . . . [Then, in 1857,] the Tavistock House theatricals reached their climax in the production of Wilkie Collins's *Frozen Deep*. This was a very ambitious effort indeed. . . .

In some respects my father's performance in this piece even surpassed that in *The Lighthouse*; and in one particular scene I remember his realism was positively alarming – not to say painful.

In his demented condition in the last act he had to rush off the stage, and I and three or four others had to try and stop him. He gave us fair notice early in the rehearsals that he meant fighting in earnest in that particular scene, and we very soon found out that the warning was not an idle one. He went at it after a while with such a will that we really did have to fight, like prize-fighters, and as for me, being the leader of the attacking party and bearing the first brunt of the fray, I was tossed in all directions and had been black-and-blue two or three times before the first night of the performance arrived.

[Charley then describes the enormous success – and the great strain – of the public readings, given from 1853 onwards for occasional charity performances, and from 1858 to 1870, more intensively, for Dickens's own financial benefit.] For, unfortunately, they did have a distinct bearing upon the end, and must be said to have hastened it even if they did not actually bring it about. It was not only that the work was hard – I have known readers and lecturers who have worked much harder, in so far as mere travelling and number of public appearances are concerned–but there was something of almost willful exaggeration, of a defiance of any possible overfatigue, either of mind or body, in the feverish sort of energy with which these readings were entered upon and carried out. And that they went on long after unmistakable physical signs had given the clearest warnings of serious danger ahead, everybody knows quite well. . . .

Soon after his return [from his American readings tour of 1867–8, Dickens began preparing his new readings item, *Sikes and Nancy*.] We were alone together at Gadshill, I remember, and I was sitting, with doors and windows open, one bright, clear, still, warm autumn day, in the library, engaged upon a mass of papers, as to which I had to report to him later in the day. Where he was I did not know, but, supposing him to be in the Swiss chalet, over in the shrubbery, across the road, took advantage of having the place to myself, and went steadily on with my work. Presently I heard a noise as if a tremendous row were going on outside, and as if two people were engaged in a violent altercation or quarrel, which threatened serious results to somebody. Ours being a country constantly infested with tramps, I looked upon the disturbance at first as merely one of the usual domestic incidents of tramp life arising out of some nomadic gentleman beating his wife up our lane, as was quite the common custom, and gave it hardly a moment's attention. Presently the noise came again, and yet again, worse than before, until I thought

it really necessary to ascertain what was going on. Stepping out of
the door on to the lawn at the back, I soon discovered the cause of
the disturbance. There, at the other end of the meadow, was my
father, striding up and down, gesticulating wildly, and, in the
character of *Mr. Sikes*, murdering *Nancy*, with every circumstance of
the most aggravated brutality. After dinner I told him what I had
seen, and he read me the murder – it was rather a startler for an
audience of one – and asked me what I thought about it. 'The finest
thing I have ever heard', was my verdict; 'but don't do it'. If there
was one thing more than another that my father resented it was any
suggestion from anybody else that his health was failing, or that he
was undertaking anything beyond his strength, so when I was
pressed for reasons I would give none, and merely stuck to my point
without any explanation or argument. Mr. Forster had also
objections to urge; he had, as he tells us, a strong dislike to the
proposal, less, perhaps, on the ground which ought to have been
insisted upon, of the excessive physical exertion it would involve,
than because such a subject seemed to be 'out of the province of
reading', and it was finally resolved that, before the murder was
incorporated in a public programme, there should be a private trial
performance of it at St. James' Hall.

Well, the trial performance was given before a very representative
and critical audience, whose verdict, unfortuanately, confirmed my
father in his opinion of the effect the reading would produce upon the
public, and the moment he spoke to me – eager, triumphant,
excited – at the little supper on the platform which brought the
proceedings to a cheery end, I knew that no advice or expostulation
of mine would avail. 'Well, Charley, and what do you think of it
now?' he said to me as I came up to where he was receiving the
enthusiastic congratulations of such good judges of dramatic effect
as [the actresses] Madame Celeste and Mrs. Keeley. 'It is finer even
than I expected,' I answered, 'but I still say, don't do it.' As he
looked at me with a puzzled expression in his eyes, Mr. Edmund
Yates came up to us. 'What do you think of this, Edmund?' my father
said. 'Here is Charley saying it is the finest thing he ever heard, but
persists in telling me, without giving any reason, not to do it.'
Mr. Yates, an intimate friend and a keen observer, knew more than
most of the people who were gathered about us, and, with one quick
look at me, said gravely, and to my father's intense amazement, 'I
agree with Charley, sir.'

And, indeed, the situation was grave enough to any one who

would look at it impartially. He had altered materially of late. There was no doubt the American work [i.e., the readings tour of 1867–8] had told upon him severely. The trouble in the foot was greatly intensified, and he was gravely out of health. Among other serious symptoms he noticed that he could only read the halves of the letters over the shopdoors on his right. The old elasticity was impaired, the old unflagging vigor often faltered. One night at the St. James's Hall, I remember, he found it impossible to say Pickwick, and called him Pickswick, and Picnic, and Peckwicks, and all sorts of names except the right, with a comical glance of surprise at the occupants of the front seats, which were always reserved for his family friends. But, although his lifelong friend and medical attendant, Mr. Carr Beard, looked very grave at this danger signal, he himself treated it lightly enough, and if he attributed it to any special cause at all, referred it, as he referred the disordered vision I have mentioned, to the effects of the medicine he was taking.

Everything pointed to the desirability of his giving up the more trying part of his work – at the very least to the absolute necessity of not adding to it in any way. But his mind was made up. The new series of readings must be carried through, and *Sikes and Nancy* must be put into the programme as often as possible. . . . [Eventually he broke down, and had to abandon his tour; but he returned to the platform in January 1870 to give] a farewell series of twelve readings at St. James' Hall, and I have no sort of doubt whatever that these completed the work which the murder had practically begun, and, if his death can be attributed to any one thing, killed him. 'I have had some steps put up against the side of the platform, Charley,' said Mr. Beard, who was constantly in attendance. 'You must be there every night, and if you see your father falter in the least, you must run up and catch him and bring him off with me, or, by Heaven, he'll die before them all.' What I felt during those readings, and when I saw the exhausted state of the reader in his dressing-room afterwards, I need not tell you. But, strangely enough, I remember very well that on the very last night of all, the 15th of March, 1870, I thought I had never heard him read the *Christmas Carol* and *The Trial from 'Pickwick'* so well and with so little effort, and almost felt inclined to hope against hope that things had not been really so serious as the doctors had supposed.

My readers know how soon the end came. On that mournful time you will not, I am sure, wish me to dwell. I will only tell you of the last time I was with him before he lay dying in the dining-room at Gadshill – an interview which is curiously illustrative of that reality to him of his ideal world to which I have already referred. He was in town for our usual Thursday meeting on the business of *All the Year Round*, and, instead of returning to Gadshill on that day, had remained over night, and was at work again in his room in Wellington street on Friday, June 3. During the morning I had hardly seen him except to take his instructions about some work I had to do, and at about one o'clock – I had arranged to go into the country for the afternoon – I cleared up my table and prepared to leave. The door of communication between our rooms was open as usual, and, as I came toward him, I saw that he was writing very earnestly. After a moment I said, 'If you don't want anything more, sir, I shall be off now', but he continued his writing with the same intensity as before, and gave no sign of being aware of my presence. Again I spoke – louder, perhaps, this time – and he raised his head and looked at me long and fixedly. But I soon found that, although his eyes were bent upon me and he seemed to be looking at me earnestly, he did not see me, and that he was, in fact, unconscious for the moment of my very existence. He was in dreamland with *Edwin Drood*, and I left him – for the last time.

(2) The only really satisfactory portrait of him that ever was painted – with the single exception, perhaps, of Mr. C. R. Leslie's picture of Captain Bobadil – I mean that by Maclise which was published as the frontispiece to *Nicholas Nickleby*, gives a very good idea of his appearance in these [early] years and for some time later, although it was impossible for the painter quite to catch the brightness and alertness of look and manner which distinguished his sitter in so remarkable a degree. Later, the beard and moustache concealed that wonderfully expressive mouth, but in these days of which I am speaking, the face was clean-shaven, and the firm and yet mobile lips, as well as the keen and vivid light in those eloquent eyes, assisted in conveying the ever-changing expression, grave or gay, humorous or pathetic, which were reflected in that singularly handsome face. Those who only knew him in his later days, when the strong lines and deep furrows, the grizzled beard and moustache, made him look older than he really was, and sometimes conveyed to those who did not know him intimately an exaggerated idea of sternness and severity, can have no idea of the delicacy and

refinement, which were almost as conspicuous as the force and power, in the face of the Charles Dickens of those days. . . .

It was . . . in 1860 that my father finally gave up his house in London and made Gadshill his head-quarters. . . . His personal habits underwent little change in this alteration of his life, however. Whatever his politics may have been, he was conservative enough in his own arrangements. I wonder, for instance, for how many years his breakfast consisted of a rasher of broiled ham; how many dinners were begun with a glass of Chichester milk-punch; how many were finished with a dish of toasted cheese, as to which latter dish it is a fact that when my mother in the old Tavistock House days published, under the name of Lady Clutterbuck, a book of her own daily bills of fare, the critics with one accord agreed that the little work was well enough, but that no man could possibly survive the consumption of such frequent toasted cheese.[2]

In fact, my father's customs as to hours of work and exercise remained practically the same wherever he was, and during all the years he passed at Gadshill it is not too much to say that he never took at all to what most people understand by a country life. . . . [His long walks in the afternoon] were his chief delight, but although his keen observation took in every minutest detail of the scenes through which he passed and of every fluttering rag of every tramp he met, he never acquired, or cared, I think, to acquire, the accurate knowledge of country sights and sounds, the intimate friendship, so to speak, with nature, which comes not always to him who is country-bred and but very, very rarely to the town-bred man who takes at middle age to the woods and fields. There is, you see, a vast difference between a country life and merely living in the country.

It was the same with the gardens, which he always insisted upon having bright and full of colour, as well as well-kept, neat, and orderly, but in which he took none of an expert's individual interest; with the dogs which he appreciated as companions without having any of the sportsman's knowledge or care for breed or points; with the stables, which were only of interest as containing the modest animals which were kept to draw, as they might have drawn in London, the brougham, the basket carriage, or that Irish car which somebody presented to him and which we sometimes had the greatest difficulty in steering through the narrow lanes thereabouts. That he loved Gadshill is true, and that he succeeded in making himself and many other people very happy there, is equally beyond doubt. But I think part of its enjoyment to him was due to the fact that it was very near those streets of London which always had so strong a hold on his imagination. . . .

But you must not suppose that it was all work at Gadshill, or all twelve-mile walks. The house was very snug and cosy in the winter, and the gardens and shrubberies were admirably adapted for idling and loafing in the summer, so that lazy visitors could go their own way in perfect peace, while there was, out of working hours, the brightest and most genial of hosts to keep things going merrily. Music, billiards – he had put a small billiard table into the room which had originally been his study, moving his books and his writing table after leaving Tavistock House into the front room, which so many of you know by Mr. Fildes' picture 'The Empty Chair' – impromptu charades, the drawing-room games in which he took so much delight, the brightest conversation, all these passed the time cheerfully and quickly, and, when the house was full, as it generally was, there was always a very lively time. Of the earnestness and energy with which my father threw himself into everything that came in his way I have already spoken, and it will be enough therefore merely to say that he really did play at these drawing-room games – Spanish merchant; How, when, and where; Yes and no, immortalised in the *Christmas Carol*; and a special memory game which was really hard work by reason of the extreme attention and care which is required – as if his life depended on his success. And I remember him very well in an absurd charade playing a ridiculous sailor who was brought up before a magistrate and could not be restrained from dashing out of the dock, and dancing a preposterous hornpipe on the floor of the court, with as much humorous detail as if he had had days of rehearsal to work it up instead of comparatively few minutes.

NOTES

1. Charles Mathews the elder (1776–1835) was an ostentatiously versatile comic actor, whom Dickens as a young man greatly admired; he was influenced by him, in his writing as well as his acting. Frederic Lemaître (1800–76), the French tragedian, later affected his histrionic style.

2. Catherine Dickens's one attempt at authorship was *What Shall We Have for Dinner? Satisfactorily Answered by Numerous Bills of Fare for from Two to Eighteen Persons, by Lady Maria Clutterbuck* (published by Bradbury and Evans, 1852). The pseudonym was taken from the Character she played in Charles Mathews's comedietta *Used Up*, which Dickens and his friends had lately been performing.

One Apart from All Other Beings

MARY (MAMIE) DICKENS

(1) From *Charles Dickens, by His Eldest Daughter*, 2nd edn (1889) pp. 39–40, 62–5, 76–7, 92–3, 102–3; (2) from her *My Father as I Recall Him* (1897) pp. 11–21, 25–31, 35–9, 46–50, 59–65, 72–5, 78; (3) from *Pen and Pencil*, Supplement, pp. 50–2. Mary Dickens (1838–96), always known as Mamie, second child and elder daughter of the novelist, never married. 'I am so glad I have never changed my name', she wrote shortly after his death; and she begins her 1897 book thus: 'My love for my father has never been touched or approached by any other love. I hold him in my heart of hearts as a man apart from all other men, as one apart from all other beings' (p. 8). Her 'Mild Glo'ster' nickname and nature are mentioned in the Introduction, above, p. xxiii. She stayed with her father after the breakup of his marriage, acting as nominal châtelaine of Gad's Hill (her aunt Georgina Hogarth was more so, in fact). Later the two collaborated in editing Dickens's *Letters* (1880–2). Her earlier book (first published in 1885) appeared in The World's Workers series, intended for children; this helps to account for its tone. Her books and articles on Dickens are repetitive and entirely reverential, but much may be forgiven her for her telling the story of Dickens and the mirror – one of the most illuminating anecdotes about how he conceived and composed his novels: see above, 1, 121–3.

(1) For myself, I cannot say how far back I can actually remember his dear face. But I know I can recollect it without a moustache or beard, when both the sensitive, powerful, and beautiful mouth and the firm chin were visible; and when he grew older and the beard and moustache were grizzled, and his hair became very thin, and the face was lined and worn, it was still the most beautiful and lovable of all faces in the world. It was always delightful to watch him, and the wonderful and quickly changing expression of his face as he talked, sometimes so grave, so earnest, with a searching look in his deep eyes as if he could look into your very heart, and as if it would be impossible to meet those eyes with a bad or mean thought in your own heart, sometimes with a smile and laughing eyes, which seemed to throw sunshine and merriment all about him, but always with a fascination no one could resist, and with the most delightful and most sympathetic voice that was ever heard.

He had a very spirited and characteristic manner of holding his head slightly thrown back – which turn of the head is exactly inherited by one of his sons – and an active, youthful, upright figure, which never changed. . . .

Charles Dickens was always giving funny names to [his] children, and before he started for America they were: 'Mamey (as generally descriptive of her bearing), Mild Glo'ster; Katey (from a lurking propensity to fieriness), Lucifer Box; Charley (as a corruption of Master Toby), Flaster Floby; Walter (suggested by his high cheek-bones), Young Skull.' And each one would be addressed in a peculiar tone of voice, which they recognised perfectly. . . .

And from their very babyhood he was always considerate, always gentle to them about their small troubles and childish terrors. For instance, one of the little girls who slept in 'Auntie's' room for a time, which was on a separate floor from the nursery, would wake up constantly in great alarm, and rush out on to the staircase and cry for help. The faithful 'Auntie'[1] would generally rush up and comfort her; but on one occasion, when, no doubt, the bad dream had been worse than usual, and she could not be pacified, her father took her in his arms, put her back to bed, and sat talking to her with her little hand in his until all fear left her, and she fell asleep. After this the 'grown-up' people often sat in the drawing-room, which was near this bedroom, instead of in the study, which was down-stairs; and the child knew perfectly well why this was done, and why the piano was played for some time after she was put to bed; and though her terrors were often very great, gratitude for her father's sweet consideration helped her, I feel sure, in some measure, to subdue these terrors. . . . He had such wonderful sympathy for all childish fears and fancies, that he never once 'snubbed' his children about such things.

He considered that an intelligent child's observation was accurate and intense to a degree; that such a child should never be needlessly frightened, or sent into the dark against its will, but should be kindly and gently reasoned with, until all such childish fears and terrors should gradually melt away, from the very consideration and sympathy shown to the little creature.

. . . he wrote a *History of the New Testament* for his children. He had written prayers for them, as soon as they were old enough to say them. All through his literary life – and no man in the world ever worked harder than he did, not only for himself, but for others as well, in many, many ways – he never was too busy to interest himself in his children's occupations, lessons, amusements, and general welfare. They were in the habit, at one time, of writing letters to him every morning, or making pen-and-ink drawings of the most primitive kind, and laying them on his breakfast plate. He must have had hundreds of these, but he always expressed much surprise on finding them, and always had something kind or funny to say, about the writing, spelling, or drawing. . . .

The old days in Devonshire Terrace are, to the children of Charles Dickens, full of childish associations and remembrances, in which he is the centre and well-beloved figure. What tender, loving care he showed to them! What pains he took to make their lives happy! There never could have been such parties as those Twelfth Night parties.[2] Never such magic lanterns as those shown by him. Never such conjuring as his: when dressed as a magician, he would make the children scream with laughter at the funny things he said and did, and part of which he has described in a letter to a friend in America, as to how 'a plum-pudding was produced from an empty saucepan, held over a blazing fire kindled in Stanfield's hat without damage to the lining; a box of bran was changed into a live guinea-pig, which ran between my godchild's feet, and was the cause of such a shrill uproar and clapping of hands that you might have heard it (and I daresay did) in America; three half-crowns being taken from Major Burns and put into a tumbler-glass before his eyes, did then and there give jingling answers to the questions asked of them by me, and knew where you were, and what you were doing, to the unspeakable admiration of the whole assembly'. Never such Sir Roger de Coverleys as those he joined in, and danced as madly and as delightedly as any child in the room. Never such suppers as those when he cut up the great Twelfth-cake, and distributed the bonbons and crackers, and waited upon the children like some good fairy, paying attention to all, and making the little cheeks blush, and the eyes sparkle with pleasure, at some kind or funny remark. . . .

[A notably proud and active householder,] he invented all sorts of neat and clever contrivances, and was never happier than when going about the house [Gad's Hill] with a hammer and nails doing some wonderful piece of carpentering. As he had a passion for colour, so the garden was planted with the brightest coloured flowers, the two beds in the front being filled with scarlet geraniums – his favourite flower – which made a splendid blaze of colour all through the summer months. And as he had also a passion for looking-glass, so were there looking-glasses placed in every possible corner of the house.

(2) From his earliest childhood, throughout his earliest married life to the day of his death, his nature was home-loving. He was a 'home man' in every respect. When he became celebrated at a very early age, as we know, all his joys and sorrows were taken home; and he found there sympathy and the companionship of his 'own familiar friends'. In his letters to these latter, in his letters to my mother, to my aunt, and, later on, to us his children, he never forgot anything that he knew would be of interest about his work, his successes, his hopes or fears. And there was a sweet simplicity in his belief that such news would most certainly be acceptable to all, that is wonderfully touching and child-like coming from a man of genius.

His care and thoughtfulness about home matters, nothing being deemed too small or trivial to claim his attention and consideration, were really marvellous when we remember his active, eager, restless, working brain. No man was so inclined naturally to derive his happiness from home affairs. He was full of the kind of interest in a house which is commonly confined to women, and his care of and for us as wee children did most certainly 'pass the love of women'! His was a tender and most affectionate nature. . . .

There never existed, I think, in all the world, a more thoroughly tidy or methodical creature than was my father. He was tidy in every way – in his mind, in his handsome and graceful person, in his work, in keeping his writing table drawers, in his large correspondence, in fact in his whole life.

I remember that my sister and I occupied a little garret room in Devonshire Terrace, at the very top of the house. He had taken the greatest pains and care to make the room as pretty and comfortable for his two little daughters as it could be made.[3] He was often dragged up the steep staircase to this room to see some new print or some new ornament which we children had put up, and he always gave us words of praise and approval. He encouraged us in every possible way to make ourselves useful, and to adorn and beautify our rooms with our own hands, and to be ever tidy and neat. I remember that the adornment of this garret was decidedly primitive, the unframed prints being fastened to the wall by ordinary black or white pins, whichever we could get. But, never mind, if they were put up neatly and tidily they were always 'excellent', or 'quite slap-up' as he used to say. Even in those early days, he made a point of visiting every room in the house once each morning, and if a chair was out of its place, or a blind not quite straight, or a crumb left on the floor, woe betide the offender.[4]

And then his punctuality! It was almost frightful to an un-punctual mind! This again was another phase of his extreme tidiness; it was also the outcome of his excessive thoughtfulness and consideration for others. His sympathy, also, with all pain and suffering made him quite invaluable in a sick room. Quick, active, sensible, bright and cheery, and sympathetic to a degree, he would seize the 'case' at once, know exactly what to do and do it. In all our childish ailments his visits were eagerly looked forward to; and our little hearts would beat a shade faster, and our aches and pains become more bearable, when the sound of his quick footstep was heard, and the encouraging accents of his voice greeted the invalid. I can remember now, as if it were yesterday, how the touch of his hand – he had a most sympathetic touch – was almost too much sometimes, the help and hope in it making my heart full to overflowing. He believed firmly in the power of mesmerism, as a remedy in some forms of illness, and was himself a mesmerist of no mean order; I know of many cases, my own among the number, in which he used his power in this way with perfect success.[5]

And however busy he might be, and even in his hours of relaxation, he was still, if you can understand me, always busy; he would give up any amount of time and spare himself no fatigue if he could in any way alleviate sickness and pain. . . .

In the 'Gad's Hill' days, when the house was full of visitors, he had a peculiar notion of always having the menu for the day's dinner placed on the sideboard at luncheon time. And then he would discuss every item in his fanciful, humorous way with his guests, much to this effect: 'Cock-a-leekie? Good, decidedly good; fried soles with shrimp sauce? Good again; croquettes of chicken? Weak, very weak; decided want of imagination here', and so on, and he would apparently be so taken up with the merits or demerits of a menu that one might imagine he lived for nothing but the coming dinner. He had a small but healthy appetite, but was remarkably abstemious both in eating and drinking.

He was delightful as a host, caring individually for each guest, and bringing the special qualities of each into full notice and prominence, putting the very shyest at his or her ease, making the best of the most humdrum, and never thrusting himself forward.

But when he was most delightful, was alone with us at home and sitting over dessert, and when my sister was with us especially – I am talking now of our grown-up days – for she had great power in 'drawing him out'. At such times although he might sit down to dinner in a grave or abstracted mood, he would, invariably, soon throw aside his silence and end by delighting us all with his genial talk and his quaint fancies about people and things. He was always, as I have said, much interested in mesmerism, and the curious influence exercised by one personality over another. One illustration I remember his using was, that meeting someone in the busy London streets, he was on the point of turning back to accost the supposed friend, when finding out his mistake in time he walked on again until he actually met the real friend, whose shadow, as it were, but a moment ago had come across his path.

And then the forgetting of a word or a name. 'Now into what pigeon-hole of my brain did that go, and why do I suddenly remember it now?' And as these thoughts passed through his mind and were spoken dreamily, so they also appeared in his face. Another instant, perhaps, and his eyes would be full of fun and laughter. . . .

Christmas was always a time which in our home was looked forward to with eagerness and delight, and to my father it was a time dearer than any other part of the year, I think. He loved Christmas for its deep significance as well as for its joys, and this he demonstrates in every allusion in his writings to the great festival, a day which he considered should be fragrant with the love that we should bear one to another, and with the love and reverence of his Saviour and Master. Even in his most merry conceits of Christmas, there are always subtle and tender touches which will bring tears to the eyes, and make even the thoughtless have some special veneration for this most blessed anniversary.

In our childish days my father used to take us, every twenty-fourth day of December, to a toy shop in Holborn, where we were allowed to select our Christmas presents, and also any that we wished to give to our little companions. Although I believe we were often an hour or more in the shop before our several tastes were satisfied, he never showed the least impatience, was always interested, and as desirous as we, that we should choose exactly what we liked best. As we grew older, present giving was confined to our several birthdays, and this annual visit to the Holborn toy shop ceased.

When we were only babies my father determined that we should be taught to dance, so as early as the Genoa days we were given our first lessons. . . . Our progress in the graceful art delighted him, and his admiration of our success was evident when we exhibited to him, as we were perfected in them, all the steps, exercises and dances which formed our lessons. He always encouraged us in our dancing, and praised our grace and aptness, although criticized quite severely in some places for allowing his children to expend so much time and energy upon the training of their feet.

When 'the boys' came home for the holidays there were constant rehearsals for the Christmas and New Year's parties; and more especially for the dance on Twelfth Night, the anniversary of my brother Charlie's birthday. Just before one of these celebrations my father insisted that my sister Katie and I should teach the polka step to Mr. Leech and himself.[6] My father was as much in earnest about learning to take that wonderful step correctly, as though there were nothing of greater importance in the world. Often he would practice gravely in a corner, without either partner or music, and I remember one cold winter's night his awakening with the fear that he had forgotten the step so strong upon him that, jumping out of bed, by the scant illumination of the old-fashioned rushlight, and to his own whistling, he diligently rehearsed its 'one, two, three, one, two, three' until he was once more secure in his knowledge.[7]

No one can imagine our excitement and nervousness when the evening came on which we were to dance with our pupils. Katie, who was a very little girl was to have Mr. Leech, who was over six feet tall, for her partner, while my father was to be mine. My heart beat so fast that I could scarcely breathe, I was so fearful for the success of our exhibition. But my fears were groundless, and we were greeted at the finish of our dance with hearty applause, which was more than compensation for the work which had been expended upon its learning. . . .

But I think that our Christmas and New Year's tides at 'Gad's Hill' [in the 1860s] were the happiest of all. Our house was always filled with guests, while a cottage in the village was reserved for the use of the bachelor members of our holiday party. My father himself, always deserted work for the week, and that was almost our greatest treat. He was the fun and life of those gatherings, the true Christmas spirit of sweetness and hospitality filling his large and generous heart. Long walks with him were daily treats to be remembered. Games passed our evenings merrily. 'Proverbs', a game of memory, was very popular, and it was one in which either my aunt or myself was apt to prove winner. Father's annoyance at our failure sometimes was very amusing, but quite genuine. 'Dumb Crambo' was another favourite, and one in which my father's great imitative ability showed finely. I remember one evening his dumb showing of the word 'frog' was so extremely laughable that the memory of it convulsed Marcus Stone, the clever artist, when he tried some time later to imitate it. . . .

He was a wonderfully neat and rapid carver, and I am happy to say taught me some of his skill in this. I used to help him in our home parties at 'Gad's Hill' by carving at a side table, returning to my seat opposite him as soon as my duty was ended. On Christmas Day we all had our glasses filled, and then my father, raising his, would say: 'Here's to us all. God bless us!' a toast which was rapidly and willingly drunk. His conversation, as may be imagined, was often extremely humorous, and I have seen the servants, who were waiting at table, convulsed often with laughter at his droll remarks and stories. Now, as I recall these gatherings, my sight grows blurred with the tears that rise to my eyes. But I love to remember them, and to see, if only in memory, my father at his own table, surrounded by his own family and friends – a beautiful Christmas spirit. . . .

Outdoor games of the simpler kinds delighted him. Battledore and shuttlecock was played constantly in the garden at Devonshire Terrace, though I do not remember my father ever playing it elsewhere. The American game of bowls pleased him, and rounders found him more than expert. Croquet he disliked, but cricket he enjoyed intensely as a spectator, always keeping one of the scores during the matches at 'Gad's Hill'.

He was a firm believer in the hygiene of bathing, and cold baths, sea baths and shower baths were among his most constant practices. In those days scientific ablution was not very generally practised, and I am sure that in many places during his travels my father was looked upon as an amiable maniac with a penchant for washing. . . .

He loved animals, flowers and birds, his fondness for the latter being shown nowhere more strongly than in his devotion to his ravens at Devonshire Terrace. . . . But I think his strongest love, among animals, was for dogs.

(3) I don't think my Father ever had a single *morbid* thought. In whatever mood he might be, from whatever troubles, anxieties, sorrows, or disappointments he might be suffering, he was never morbid. His was essentially a wholesome mind and nature. He was intensely fond of music, and would listen to playing or singing by the

hour together. The song, *Little Nell*, composed by the late George Linley, was a special favourite. In the play of *The Lighthouse* he wrote words to the music; and the prologue to *The Frozen Deep* was spoken to the accompaniment of the same song. He was very critical as to the proper and distinct pronunciation of words in singing. He greatly delighted in hearing Madame Viardot, Madame Sainton-Dolby, and the late Mrs. Edward Sartoris. The singing, also, of Miss Amelia Chambers (now Mrs. Rudolf Lehmann, and the mother of a most gifted and talented daughter), gave him the greatest pleasure, and the manner in which she spoke her words was 'capital'.

We had a visit at Gad's Hill from Joseph Joachim – 'a noble fellow,' as my Father wrote of him – which is never to be forgotten. Mr. and Mrs. Frederick Lehmann – and *her* beautiful playing always *delighted* my Father – were also with us. The great violinist perfectly enchanted him.[8] I never remember seeing him so rapt and absorbed as he was then, in hearing him play; and the wonderful simplicity and *un*-self-consciousness of this genius went straight to my Father's heart, and made a fast bond of sympathy between these two great men. It was a treat, indeed, to have this friend, with his Art, to ourselves as it were, and I never saw my Father happier.

Excepting the song of *Little Nell* I cannot well specify another as being his favourite, as there were so many he liked. Nor can I specify any particular music. Mendelssohn's 'Lieder' charmed him, as did also Chopin's and Mozart's music. National airs, good dance music, etc., all pleased him. I always regret that he never cultivated singing, for he had a sweet voice and a perfect ear. . . .

Had he lived he would have been an old man now, though not as old as many of our great men, now living. I can never picture him as *old*. And as he could not bear the idea of losing any of his activity, either of mind or body, we must be thankful that he left us in the full power of his strength and genius.

NOTES

1. 'When I write about my aunt, or "Auntie", as no doubt I may often have occasion to do, it is of the aunt *par excellence*, Georgina Hogarth. She has been to me ever since I can remember anything, and to all of us, the truest, best and dearest friend, companion and counsellor. To quote my father's own words: "The best and truest friend man ever had."' (Mamie's footnote, at another point.)

2. Twelfth Night (6 Jan) was Charley's birthday, so its festivities were always vigorously celebrated in the Dickens household.

3. Elsewhere, Mamie describes the 'better bedroom than they had ever had before' which Dickens promised the girls when they moved to the 'far larger and handsomer' Tavistock House: 'it surpassed even their expectations. They found it full of love and thoughtful care, and as pretty and as fresh as their hearts could desire, and with not a single thing in it which had not been expressly chosen for them, or planned by their father. The wall-paper was covered with wild flowers, the two little iron bedsteads were hung with a flowery chintz. There were two toilet tables, two writing tables, two easy chairs, &c., &c., all so pretty and elegant, and this in the days when bedrooms were not, as a rule, so luxurious as they are now' – 'Charles Dickens at Home', *Cornhill Magazine*, n.s. IV (1885) 39.

4. Her sister Katey was recalcitrant to these daily inspections, which even included the girls' drawers. Katey's friend Gladys Storey records that Dickens's remonstrances 'were frequently consigned to notepaper, folded neatly and left by him on their pincushion, which they called "pincushion notes". "Oh dear! – what's up now?" Katie would remark, observing the third in a week! His punctuality was almost painful – Katie being the only one in the family who dared be five minutes late at breakfast-time, when it was noted and remarked upon, to receive in response a light kiss upon the forehead, and a lighter, "Yes, Pa," to his observation that it was the third time that week she had been late for breakfast' – *Dickens and Daughter* (1939) pp. 77–8.

5. See Fred Kaplan, *Dickens and Mesmerism* (1975).

6. John Leech (1817–64), *Punch* artist and illustrator, was a close family friend.

7. This, however, is an instance of Dickens being self-consciously 'Inimitable'. Next morning he told Forster about this bedroom rehearsal, adding – 'gravely', as Forster specifies – 'Remember that for my Biography!' A nice example of the difficulty of behaving unselfconsciously, if one well knows that one's biography will be written, and if one is living familiarly with a friend appointed, decades ahead of need, as one's official biographer! Still, Forster comments upon Dickens's getting out of bed to rehearse: 'Anything *more* characteristic could hardly be told, unless I were able to show him dancing it afterwards, and excelling the youngest performer in untiring vigour and vivacity' (*Life*, VI, vi, 528–9).

8. 'It was the fantastic lyricism of the Tartini "Devil's Trill Sonata" which made the greatest impression on him', Joachim recalled – Andreas Moser, *Joseph Joachim: A Biography 1831–1899*, trs. Lilla Durham (1901) p. 302. Other reminiscences of Dickens appear in *Letters from and to Joseph Joachim*, ed. and trs. Nora Bickley (1914).

'I Loved Him for His Faults'

KATE DICKENS PERUGINI

From Gladys Storey, *Dickens and Daughter* (1939) pp. 93–6, 104–6, 212, 219. Catherine Elizabeth Macready Dickens (1839–1929), Dickens's third child and younger daughter, was generally called Kate or Katey. She was named after her mother and grandmother, and her godfather, the actor W. C. Macready. On her fiery disposition, and on Gladys Storey, see Introduction, above, I, xxiii. Talented, pretty and vivacious, she inherited much of her father's appearance and disposition, and was his favourite daughter, as her sister Mamie acknowledged; when the children wanted a treat or favour, Katey was deputed to ask him for it. She trained in art at Bedford College, and became a modestly successful artist. Both her husbands were painters: in 1860 she married Charles Collins, brother of the novelist Wilkie Collins, and after his death in 1873 she married Carlo Perugini. She was very fond of her father, but too like him to be uncritical. Characteristically, during his experiments in mesmerism, he could easily hypnotise Mamie but failed with Katey. Gladys Storey, whose friendship with Katey was during her later years, describes her as 'an extremely witty woman, a joy to hear talk and to talk to, and if the thrust of her rapier spared few, it was ever aimed at herself' (p.12). See below (II, 354–8) for Katey's account of her father's last days. Other reminiscences by her include 'Dickens as a Lover of Art and Artists', *Magazine of Art*, XXVII (1903) 125–30, 164–9; 'My Father's Love for Children', *Dkn*, VII (1911) 117–19; and 'Thackeray and My Father', *Pall Mall Magazine*, XLVIII (1911) 213–19. The Pierpont Morgan Library, New York, contains a lengthy manuscript by Katey about her relations with her father.

There is no doubt that the children of his imagination came before his children of the flesh, which may have accounted for Mrs. Perugini saying: 'The only fault I found with my father was that he had too many children': a remark far-reaching in its depth of meaning.

'His passionate love of fresh air and sunshine', she said, 'had [by the 1850s] changed his once pale skin to a florid complexion; his hair, formerly chestnut brown and flowing, became almost daily darker and was worn shorter; the beard and moustache he had allowed to grow, which was a mistake for not only did it cover his very mobile sensitive mouth but it seemed in a curious way to detract from the beauty of the upper part of his face and make his features look often grave, though never self-conscious'.

Thus he appeared at the age of forty-six when Miss Ellen Lawless

Ternan, 'the small fair-haired rather pretty actress' (as Mrs. Perugini described her), of no special attraction save her youth, came like a breath of spring into the hard-working life of Charles Dickens – and enslaved him.[1] She flattered him – he was ever appreciative of praise – and though 'she was not a good actress she had brains, which she used to educate herself, to bring her mind more on a level with his own. Who could blame her?' said Mrs. Perugini in her generous make-excuses way. 'He had the world at his feet. She was a young girl of eighteen, elated and proud to be noticed by him.' Happy at first, perhaps, to love and be loved by him, who subsequently brought to her relief from a hitherto hard and precarious life. . . .

'My father was like a madman when my mother left home,' said Mrs. Perugini, 'this affair brought out all that was worst – all that was weakest in him. He did not care a damn what happened to any of us. Nothing could surpass the misery and unhappiness of our home.' . . .

One afternoon, at the commencement of this affair, Mrs. Perugini happened to be passing her parents' bedroom (which stood ajar) when she heard somebody crying. Entering the room, she found her mother seated at the dressing-table in the act of putting on her bonnet, with tears rolling down her cheeks. Inquiring the cause of her distress, Mrs. Dickens – between her sobs – replied: 'Your father has asked me to go and see Ellen Ternan.'

'You shall not go!' exclaimed Mrs. Perugini, angrily stamping her foot.

But she went. . . .

[At an earlier point in her book, Gladys Storey reports Katey as saying:] 'There was nothing wrong with my mother; she had her faults, of course, as we all have – but she was a sweet, kind, peace-loving woman, a lady – a lady born.' [Georgina Hogarth's charge that Catherine Dickens threw the responsibility of her children upon others was] as unkind as it was untrue. When Mrs. Perugini was asked whether she considered it a mistake for a sister to live in the house with a husband and wife, she immediately and emphatically replied: 'Never, never, never – the greatest mistake; she [Georgina Hogarth] was useful to my mother, of course, but that was all. My poor, poor mother.' . . .

Mamie was in love, but Dickens did not approve of the match, so that was the end of it.[2] In any case, she adored her father and no sacrifice would have been considered too great to please him. It may have been out of love for him that she did not go and see her mother, as often as she might have done, both before and after his death. She was very pretty and dainty, always tastefully dressed, and had a soft way of speaking; but though her father nicknamed her 'Mild Gloucester' she did not, when occasion arose, hesitate to express a vehement opinion. Always up to date, she was the first woman to ride a bicycle at Gad's Hill. The sisters used to attend military and other balls at Chatham and in the surrounding neighbourhood of their home, chaperoned by 'Aunty' – Georgina Hogarth. Dickens considered two balls in one season 'excessive'.[3]

Charles Allston Collins, a contributor to *All the Year Round* had, for some time, been paying his addresses to Katie, who, although she respected him and considered him the kindest and most sweet-tempered of men, was not in the least in love with him. Dickens did not desire the marriage, but Katie saw in it an escape from 'an unhappy home', away from which, as a married woman, she considered she could more or less do as she liked, and for these reasons only she accepted Mr. Collins.

There was a great to-do at Gad's Hill over the marriage. Dickens was elated and pleased at the interest shown in the wedding by the villagers, who turned out in great force. . . .[But Katey's mother had, conspicuously, not been invited.] After the last of the guests not staying in the house had departed, Mamie went up to her sister's bedroom. Opening the door, she beheld her father upon his knees with his head buried in Katie's wedding-gown, sobbing. She stood for some moments before he became aware of her presence; when at last he got up and saw her, he said in a broken voice:

'But for me, Katey would not have left home', and walked out of the room. . . .

[Long after Dickens's death, some letters came on to the market, written by her mother and aunt. Embarrassed by Georgina Hogarth's describing her as 'intolerant', she purchased the lot, and remarked:] 'Aunty was not quite straight, and I often stood up to her; *that* is why she called me "intolerant". To build up the reputation of one big person you often have to knock down the reputations of a lot of little people. My father, with all his greatness, was what Aunty called me – "intolerant".'

We frequently sat for long periods in silence. . . . After a time she would look up and give utterance to what appeared to be a decision – a summing-up of her deliberations.

'I loved my father better than any man in the world – in a

different way of course', she observed after one of these long silences. 'I loved him for his faults'. Rising from her chair and walking towards the door, she added: 'My father was a wicked man – a very wicked man.' And left the room.

On her return she continued: 'My poor mother was afraid of my father. She was never allowed to express an opinion – never allowed to say what she felt.' Following another considerable silence, she said: 'Ah! We were *all* very wicked not to take her part; Harry does not take this view, but he was only a boy at the time, and does not realize the grief it was to our mother, after having all her children, to go away and leave us. My mother never rebuked me. I never saw her in a temper. We like to think of our geniuses as great characters – but we can't.'

NOTES

1. Ellen Lawless Ternan (1839–1914), actress, came of a theatrical family. Dickens is said to have first met her, backstage, at the Haymarket Theatre, London, in April 1857. With her mother and her sister, she appeared in his production of *The Frozen Deep* during its Manchester performances, August 1857. Manifestly Dickens felt a passionate desire for her, but not all of his biographers since the 1930s (when this episode in his life was first revealed) believe that she became his mistress. There are allegations, similarly unproven, that she bore him a child, or children (Storey, *Dickens and Daughter*, p. 94, says there was a son, who died in infancy). Ada Nisbet's *Dickens and Ellen Ternan* (1952) is the most useful account.

2. Nothing seems to be known of this matter. Gladys Storey is here writing about events in 1860.

3. Rumours – how well-founded, I do not know – circulated, however, that the Dickens girls were regarded, after the breakdown of their parents's marriage, as badly lacking in decorum. Thus, E. S. Dallas, the critic and reviewer, writes on 3 January 1859 to the publisher John Blackwood about the Garrick Club affair: 'The great fun I think is to see how Dickens backs up Yates, & how his jealousy of Thackeray comes out. Surely that man will one of these days blow his brains out. With the exception of a few toadies there is not a soul to take his part. They cut him at the clubs. His daughters – now under the benign wing of their aunt, Miss Hogarth – are not received into society. You would be excessively amused if you heard all the gigantic efforts the family make to keep their foot in the world – how they call upon people that they never called on before & that they have treated with the most dire contempt. Fancy Dickens & his family going to call on that worthy couple – Mr. & Mrs. Pecksniff [i.e. S. C. Hall, the original of that character], & informing these people upon whom they never called before that they would be happy to see them at Tavistock House. But still better – fancy Pecksniff & his wife in a high moral transport and religious spite informing Miss Hogarth & the Miss Dickenses, that it was with Mrs. Dickens they were

acquainted, that if Mrs. Dickens were at Tavistock House they should be happy to call, but otherwise – afraid – very sorry – but etc., etc. It is a wretched business altogether' (MS, National Library of Scotland; I owe this reference to the M Litt. thesis by C. C. Leahy, ' . . . Selected Letters of E. S. Dallas, with a Critical Introduction', University of Edinburgh, 1969).

Dickens's friend Frederick Lehmann reported in 1866 that Katey ('Kitty') was unhappy in her marriage, and seeking out lovers, and that he saw Mamie behaving with great imprudence at a dinner: 'Kitty looked a spectacle of woe . . . and was quite distracted. She told me that Mamie, who looked round and matronlike, was to be pitied and she could not lead such a life, but added mysteriously, "she takes her happiness when she can, and a few visits to town lately have given her all she cares for". She added, "Of course, it will come out. Sure to". My dear, these two girls are going to the devil as fast as can be. From what I hear from third parties who don't know how intimate we are with them, society is beginning to fight shy of them, especially of Kitty C[ollins]. . . . Mamie may blaze up in a firework any day. Kitty is burning away both character and I fear health slowly but steadily' – John Lehmann, *Ancestors and Friends* (1962) pp. 210–11. Dallas's letter is malicious and may be untrustworthy, but Lehmann was a good friend of Dickens's and remarks in this letter that he still has 'an old kind of affection' for the two girls, so his report may be credited. There is a devastating account of Dickens's behaviour at this time, and of the Gad's Hill atmosphere in 1860, in the forthcoming *Letters* of Harriet Martineau.

'The Kindest and Most Considerate of Fathers'

ALFRED TENNYSON DICKENS

(1) from Raymond Blathwayt, 'Reminiscences of Dickens: An Interview with Mr. Alfred Tennyson Dickens', *Great Thoughts*, 12 Nov 1910, pp. 104–5; (2) from his letter to G. W. Rusden, 11 Aug 1870 (MS., State Library of Victoria); (3) from his 'My Father and His Friends', *Nash's Magazine*, IV (1911) 628, 636–41. Alfred D'Orsay Tennyson Dickens (1845–1912) was Dickens's fourth son. Trained for the army, he proved unequal to the competition for Woolwich and, after two years in a London office, he emigrated to Australia, where he worked at farming and in business, returning to England in 1910, and lecturing there and in America about his father. For his career, see Mary Lazarus, *A Tale of Two Brothers: Charles Dickens's Sons in Australia* (1973), where he is quoted as saying that when he took his schoolfriends home they 'used to go down in awe and trembling, and after being there two or three hours, the verdict was always the same: "By Jove, Dickens, your governor is a stunner and no mistake"' (p. 5). Forty years after his father's death he remarked, 'I never forget my father for a moment. I fancy he is always with me, you know' (p. 178). G. W. Rusden, to whom he was writing in 1870, was a friend of Dickens's in Australia who was keeping an eye on the Dickens boys.

(1) My father never talked about himself and his writings: he would always turn the subject to something else. He would even keep the MSS of his most famous books hidden out of sight on a top shelf so that he might not be thought ostentatious. He was a splendid companion for boys and he dearly loved his children. . . . I used to go snipe shooting in the Christmas holidays in those very Essex marshes which he describes so vividly in *Great Expectations*. We used to row him up from Rochester to Maidstone, when he used to act as coxswain and laugh and chaff us all the time, and that is how he got to know river life so well. He was very fond of the Thames also, and all his accounts of Rogue Riderhood in *Our Mutual Friend*, and the pictures of river-side scenery, were all gathered during the expeditions he used to make with us up the Thames.

(2) It is very hard to think that I shall never see him again, and that he who was so good, so gentle with us, has passed away. . . . There is but one unfortunate incident in our dear father's life, and that was his separation from our Mother. As people will doubtless talk about this may I ask you to state the facts properly for myself and Plorn [his younger brother, also in Australia] should they be misrepresented. When the separation took place it made no difference in our feelings toward them: we their children always loved them both equally, having free intercourse with both, as of old: while not one word on the subject ever passed from the lips of either father or mother. Of the causes which led to this unfortunate event, we know no more than the rest of the world. Our dear mother has suffered very much. My brother's wife in her letter says – 'Poor dear she is better than I dared to hope she would be, and I am sure that in a little time she will be more settled, and even happier than she has been for years, for she says what is true that she has already lived 12 years of widowhood and she feels that there is nobody nearer to him than she is.'

(3) During the time we were in residence at Tavistock House my brother Frank [Francis Jeffery], next older in the family to myself, suffered from a very severe affection of stammering. Although my father at the time was working night and day at a very high pressure, he used to have Frank in the study every morning. He would read him a passage from Shakespeare, and then would make my brother Frank do the same thing over and over again, very slowly and very distinctly. Finally my father made a complete cure of him, and in later life in Canada, where Frank held a high position in the

Canadian Mounted Police force, he was described in the public press of that dependency as being a good and effective speaker. Frank, like my youngest sister, Katie (Mrs. Perugini) bore a striking resemblance in face, gesture, and manner to our father.

As I am writing just on the eve of the centenary of the birth of William Makepeace Thackeray, it is appropriate that I should make some reference to him in connection with my father. . . . Each writer had the most sincere and hearty admiration for the works of the other. . . . At Thackeray's funeral at Kensal Green my father stood as chief mourner by the grave.[1] I drove my father down in the basket carriage from Gad's Hill to Higham railway station on the morning when he was going to London to the funeral, and I know how much distressed he was at the death of his old friend. . . .

I cannot, I think, conclude these detached reminiscences better than by giving a short sketch of the personal characteristics of Charles Dickens in the year 1860. In this year he decided to live permanently at Gad's Hill. He was then fifty years of age, about the middle height, with his hair just grizzled with gray. His face was full of life and intellect. His bright, piercing eyes were very thoughtful and dreamy looking at times, but seemed always to be able to look you through and through. . . . He was the kindest, most thoughtful, and most considerate of fathers, and he was one of the most charming hosts it is possible to conceive. While he had a fund of anecdote and humour, he was never in the least pedantic or bookish in his talk, and if anyone referred to himself or his books, he invariably in a very pleasant way turned the conversation into another channel.

As in his public and professional life he laid down for himself the golden rule that 'Whatever is worth doing at all is worth doing well,' so in his private life he was the most methodical and orderly of men. He could not bear to see anything out of its place. If a book was removed from the library, he looked for the borrower to return it immediately it was done with. I recollect once when I was going to drive with him in the basket carriage to Gravesend to meet either Mr. Spiers or Mr. Pond (I forget which of these two gentlemen it was), who was coming over to see him about the contemplated Australian reading,[2] I was busily engaged brushing my coat in the dining-room, instead of outside. He happened to come in just at the moment, and I never by any chance committed that particular offence afterward. . . .

He was wonderfully good and even tempered, although, as may be easily imagined, of a nervous and excitable temperament. If he did allow his temper to get the better of him for a few moments, which, however, he very rarely ever did, then, like the sun after a passing summer shower, all the most lovable traits of his most lovable character shone out to greater advantage afterward.

That is the Charles Dickens of my loving recollection. In 1865 I went to Australia, and I never saw him again.

NOTES

1. But, according to Maltus Questell Holyoake, 'Dickens was not in mourning [at the Thackeray funeral], and was wearing trousers of a check pattern, a waistcoat of some coloured plaid, and an open frock-coat'–'Memories of Charles Dickens', *Chambers's Journal*, 13 Nov 1897, p. 724.

2. Twice in the 1860s Dickens considered touring Australia, but nothing came of this.

'His Lovable and Great-Hearted Nature'

HENRY FIELDING DICKENS

(1) from 'A Chat about My Father', *Harper's Magazine*, CXXIX (1914) 187–90; (2) from *Memories of My Father* (1928) pp. 18–24, 28–9; (3) from *The Recollections of Sir Henry Dickens, Q. C.* (1934) pp. 16–42. Henry Fielding Dickens (1849–1933), sixth son of the novelist, was the only one who 'did well' – becoming Head Boy at school, going to Cambridge, achieving success at the Bar, and gaining a knighthood. He gave public readings from the novels (for charity), was active in the Dickens Fellowship (founded 1902), and piously promoted and protected the blessed memory. 'I always feel so proud of Harry', his aunt Georgina Hogarth wrote in 1877. 'He is such a *worthy* representative of his Father, thank God! and is growing more like him as he gets older' – quoted by A. A. Adrian, *Georgina Hogarth and the Dickens Circle* (1957) p. 189. His sister Katey always said how good he was, but was amused by his proprietorial attitude; in conversation with her he would refer to 'my father' not 'our' – Gladys Storey, *Dickens and Daughter* (1939) p. 204. For his knowledge of the Ellen Ternan affair, see *Dkn*, LXXVI (1980) 3–16.

(1) Now if I were asked what it was that had struck me most about my father I think I should unhesitatingly say that it was his extraordinary modesty. His nature was of the simplest; his absence of affectation or conceit surprising. When it is remembered how, at

the age of twenty-four, he jumped to the very top of his profession and remained there to the end, no man could well have blamed him if he had shown some slight symptoms of having had his head turned. I can emphatically assert, from my knowledge of him, that there was a total absence of anything of the kind.

The next point about him which I should like to emphasize is his power of work. I do not suppose that there ever was a man who lived a more strenuous life than he did. This can be fairly gauged, to a certain extent, by his manuscripts alone; but no one can thoroughly realize it except those who were constantly in his company and knew his habits well. He had not the faculty or gift – call it what you will – which Anthony Trollope prided himself upon, of being able to 'reel off' his three thousand words before breakfast. On the contrary, Forster has told us of 'the difficulties, physical as well as mental, on which he held the tenure of his imaginative life, which led to frequent strain and unconscious waste of what no man could less afford to spare'.

Much of his work was done when he was far away from his desk during hours which, to others, might be regarded as hours of leisure. This is, I suppose, by no means uncommon with authors at times; but with him it was uncommon in that it was so continuous. I have myself walked with him, over and over again, for two or three hours at a stretch, in company with the dogs, through the lanes and orchards of Kent – in silence. I have accompanied him through the *Great Expectations* country; I have stood by his side in the churchyard where Pip was turned upside down by the convict; I have looked down with him upon the tombstone of 'Pirrip', also 'Georgiana, wife of the Above'; we have wandered together over the marsh country down by the river – that dark, flat wilderness, as he described it – without a word being exchanged between us. And yet, absorbed though he was in his thoughts, I believe my companionship was a source of consolation to him.

With such an imaginative dispositon it is not to be wondered at that his nature was mercurial. He had strange fits of depression from time to time, but his vitality was extraordinary, and, except in those rare intervals, his animal spirits and the brightness of his nature were delightful to see.

He was haunted at times, as I suppose some people know, by a dread of failure, or of a sudden waning of his imaginative powers. . . .

He was generally acknowledged to be one of the best speakers of his day. . . . One great speech of his I well remember. It was the occasion of his delivering his inaugural address as President of the Midland and Birmingham Institute. . . . How well do I remember the visits I paid with him next day to some of the large and important factories in Birmingham, and how the grimy workmen, stained with heat and toil, kept on stopping me as we passed to say, 'Is that Charles Dickens?' This was not in the least to be wondered at, seeing that he was throughout his whole career a true friend of the poor; and that this was fully recognized by themselves the following little story will prove. The day after he died, a workman, walking into a tobacco-shop to buy his screw of tobacco, paid a tribute to his memory which should, in my judgment, rank as high as any one of the glowing tributes paid to him at the time, when, throwing his money on the counter, he said: 'Charles Dickens is dead. We have lost our best friend.'[1] . . .

He used to say – and indeed he has said it to me – that he believed that the man who had influenced him most was Thomas Carlyle. This somewhat surprised me. I could understand this in connection with his book, *The Tale of Two Cities*, but not when taken in its general sense. I gathered, however, that what he most admired in Carlyle was his sincerity and truth.[2]

(2) I have been asked what is my strongest outstanding memory of him, or whether there are any particular phrases or remarks of his which live in my memory. The first part of the question is difficult to answer; but as to my remembering any particular phrases or remarks that fell from him, it is highly improbable that I should do so, for the simple reason that in ordinary conversation he never talked for the sake of mere effect; he never turned a sentence or coined an epigram with a view to its being recorded, as some literary and learned people are inclined to do. He was as simple and natural in his speech as he was in his manner, which was always quiet, refined, and entirely free from ostentation.

Looking back now upon the years that are gone, I find that there are one or two scenes or incidents which arise with astonishing vividness to my mind that may be worth recording. The first is one which I can never forget, as it was so peculiarly personal to myself. I hope it will not be thought that I tell this story vaingloriously, as it was but a small matter so far as I was concerned. Nothing is farther from my thoughts. I do so because it is typical of a strange reticence on his part, an intense dislike of 'letting himself go' in private life or of using language which might be deemed strained or over-effusive;

though, as will be seen later, when he was deeply moved he was at no pains to hide the depth of his emotion. Thus it came about that, though his children knew he was devotedly attached to them, there was still a kind of reserve on his part which seemed occasionally to come as a cloud between us and which I never quite understood.

In the year 1869, after I had been at college about a year, I was fortunate enough to gain one of the principal scholarships at Trinity Hall, Cambridge – not a great thing, only £50 a year; but I knew that this success, slight as it was, would give him intense pleasure, so I went to meet him at Higham Station upon his arrival from London to tell him of it. As he got out of the train I told him the news. He said, 'Capital! capital!' – nothing more. Disappointed to find that he received the news apparently so lightly, I took my seat beside him in the pony carriage he was driving. Nothing more happened until we had got half-way to Gad's Hill, when he broke down completely. Turning towards me with tears in his eyes and giving me a warm grip of the hand, he said, 'God bless you, my boy; God bless you!' That pressure of the hand I can feel now as distinctly as I felt it then, and it will remain as strong and real until the day of my death.

After this the relations between us became closer and warmer than they had ever been before, and when New Year's Eve came, the year before he died, and he clasped my hand to wish me a Happy New Year, there was a steady look in his eye which I read as meaning, 'We understand one another; I trust you to try to do your best in life.' . . .

There is another striking incident in his life which neither I nor anyone present at the time could by any possibility forget. That was the occasion of his Farewell Reading in St. James's Hall in [March] 1870. . . . When he ceased to speak a kind of sigh seemed to come from the audience, followed almost at once by such a storm of cheering as I have never seen equalled in my life. He was deeply touched that night, but infinitely sad and broken. . . .

I do not pause to describe the first reading he gave to an audience of undergraduates at Cambridge at which I was present, except to say that his reception was such as to astonish even himself; but I cannot pass over the impression which was made upon me on the occasion of my youngest brother leaving England for Australia. I accompanied him to Plymouth, and the leave-taking between my father and him was on the platform at Paddington Station. The scene that followed was tragic in its emotional intensity. My father openly gave way to his intense grief quite regardless of his surroundings, and I do not think I had ever fully realised till then the depth of his affection towards his children.

One last impression, a curious one, was of something that took place at Christmas, 1869, the Christmas before his death. He had been ailing very much and greatly troubled with his leg, which had been giving him much pain; so he was lying on a sofa one evening after dinner, while the rest of the party were playing games. I should say here, truly enough, that at this time I had not the faintest idea that he had gone through those terrible days when, as quite a child, he tied up bottles of blacking for a small pittance. I knew, in a general sort of way, that *David Copperfield* to a certain extent portrayed some of his own life; but it never entered my mind that he had gone through this pitiable struggle until Forster's *Life* was published, in which was contained my father's fragment of autobiography.

We had been playing a game that evening known as 'The Memory Game', in which, after a while, my father joined, throwing all his energy into it, as he always did in anything he put his hand to. One of the party started by giving a name, such as, for instance, Napoleon. The next person had to repeat this and add something of his own, such as Napoleon, Blackbeetle, and so on, until the string of names began to get long and difficult to remember. My father, after many turns, had successfully gone through the long string of words, and finished up with his own contribution, 'Warren's Blacking, 30, Strand'. He gave this with an odd twinkle in his eye and a strange inflection in his voice which at once forcibly arrested my attention and left a vivid impression on my mind for some time afterwards. Why, I could not, for the life of me, understand. When, however, his tragic history appeared in Forster's *Life*, this game at Christmas, 1869, flashed across my mind with extraordinary force, and the mystery was explained. [Henry and the other children then learned, for the first time, about their father's childhood privations and his doing manual work in Warren's Blacking warehouse.]

He was intensely human, and I do not suppose it could be said of him that he was freer from the faults and defects appertaining to humanity than most of us are; but he was 'thorough' to the core, absolutely and entirely sincere and earnest in all he did. He had, in fact, if ever man had, an 'infinite power of taking pains', which was, in my judgment, one of his greatest gifts; while his active sympathy for the poor and struggling people was never-ending.

His political views were, of course, strongly radical; he was very intolerant of much that he found in the body politic. Nor did he see much to admire in Parliament or its methods; but he was absolutely loyal, and was never in any sense of the word a revolutionary. In this, I think, Forster rightly appraised him when he wrote of him, 'His wish to better what was bad in English institutions carried with it no desire to replace them by new ones.' He had a very strong love of his country, though he himself used to say, laughingly, that his sympathies were so much with the French that he ought to have been born a Frenchman.

His religious convictions, though he never made a parade of them, were very strong and deep, as appears by the letters he wrote to me and my brothers when we started our careers, as well as in the beautiful words of his will, which are most solemn and impressive in their religious devotion. So strong was this feeling, indeed, that he wrote the simple history of Our Lord's life for us when we were children. The manuscript of this I have in my possession, but my father impressed upon us that, as it was not intended as a literary effort, it was never to be published to the world.[3]

If I were asked, when all is said and done, what is my most abiding memory of him, I should say, beyond all question, it was of his lovable and great-hearted nature – a nature which not only appealed strongly to those who were dear to him, but which also won for him the affection and admiration of all those who were brought into direct association with him.

(3) *Great Expectations* he himself regarded as one of the best of his books. Indeed, I have heard him say that, putting *Pickwick* aside as being a book by itself and quite unlike his other work, he would place *David Copperfield* first and *Great Expectations* next to it. . . .

My father was very orderly in his methods and punctual in his habits; and, as we small boys were somewhat slack and untidy, a system was set on foot which went by the name of 'Pegs, Parade and Custos'. To each boy was allotted a particular peg for his hat and coat; there was a parade from time to time in order to check the stains of grease or dirt which had accumulated on our clothing; and to one boy was allotted the task each week of collecting the sticks, balls and croquet and cricket materials which represented the 'Custos' for the week. We shied a little at this kind of discipline on the first going off, but we soon fell into line and rather enjoyed it than otherwise. . . .

[Reverting to his father's 'deep religious convictions', Henry instances] the simple prayer written by him for his own children when they were very young: 'Pray God who has made everything and is so kind and merciful to everything he has made: pray God to bless my dear Papa and Mama, brothers and sisters, and all my relations and friends: make me a good little child and let me never be naughty and tell a lie, which is a mean and shameful thing. Make me kind to my nurses and servants and to all beggars and poor people and let me never be cruel to any dumb creature, for if I am cruel to anything, even to a poor little fly, you, who are so good, will never love me: and pray God to bless and preserve us all this night and for ever, for the sake of Jesus Christ, our Lord. Amen.'[4]

He taught me shorthand in his spare moments. During the time he was in the gallery of the House of Commons he used Gurney's system; but at the time he taught me he had so radically altered it, from time to time, as to make it practically a system of his own. . . . These lessons were great fun, though I found it was by no means an easy science to learn. . . . To take down a speech quickly and correctly you must have all your faculties in perfect order, and that is where I experienced a special difficulty in my own case. This arose from the kind of speeches which my father delivered for me to practise on, speeches which shortly reduced my mind to a state of wild confusion. They were of the character you would expect from a street tub orator or from a speaker on the hustings or a parody of orations in the House of Commons. These soon reduced me almost to a state of collapse in consequence of the laughter which followed on them; and when I say laughter, I mean laughter on the part of both of us. For he himself, tickled by the ridiculous nature of his own fancies, gave way to fits of laughter only equalled by wild bursts on my part. This part of my training was most amusing, but was not productive of much progress.

NOTES

1. Elsewhere Henry Dickens records how, soon after his father's death, he was recognised by a London cabbie, who exclaimed, 'Ah! Mr Dickens, your father's death was a great loss to all of us – and we cabbies were in hopes that he would soon be doing something to help us' (*Recollections*, p. 61).

2. The 'two most dramatic scenes he could recall' in literature (Dickens told Henry) were Carlyle's account of the march of the women to Versailles, in *The French Revolution*, and the description of the Woman in White's appearance on the

Hampstead Road after escaping from the asylum, in Wilkie Collins's novel (*Recollections*, p. 54).

3. In his will, however, Henry permitted the publications of this *Life of Our Lord* after his death, if the majority of the family favoured it. The book was published in 1934.

4. Another exercise in this kind by Dickens is the (lengthy and flatulent) 'Prayer at Night', for adult use, printed in *Mr. and Mrs. Charles Dickens: His Letters to Her*, ed. Walter Dexter (1935), pp. 266–8.

Charming with Children, Usually

KATE DOUGLAS WIGGIN AND OTHERS

References to sources for this miscellaneous item are given in the Notes, and the authors are identified at the head of the extracts. Dickens evidently had a good touch with children; and his are of course the first English novels to make much of childhood. There are other accounts of his treatment of children in the present collection, by (for instance) his own children and by Thackeray's daughter Annie (see Index). If his relations with his own children are any guide, he was less felicitous with adolescents: see Philip Collins, *Dickens and Education* (1963) ch. 2, 'Father of Nine'.

[His daughter Mamie writes:] He had a wonderful attraction for children and a quick perception of their character and disposition; a most winning and easy way with them, full of fun, but also of a graver sympathy with their many small troubles and perplexities, which made them recognise a friend in him at once. I have often seen mere babies, who would look at no other stranger present, put out their tiny arms to him with unbounded confidence, or place a small hand in his and trot away with him, quite proud and contented at having found such a companion; and although with his own children he had sometimes a sterner manner than he had with others, there was not one of them who feared to go to him for help and advice, knowing well that there was no trouble too trivial to claim his attention, and that in him they would always find unvarying justice and love.[1]

[Edgar Browne, son of Dickens's illustrator Hablot K. Browne ('Phiz'), was less attracted.] Dickens apparently was not much interested in us personally, and we only saw him in uncertain glimpses by no means free from an uncomfortable sense of awe. He appeared to us overwhelming, very splendid as to his clothing, and rather unapproachable. Reflection in afteryears has convinced me that our impression was erroneous. What we saw and felt was the contrast between ourselves and a being of superhuman energy and vigour of expression. Added to that, it is quite certain that he came about business, and on most occasions we were bundled out of the way.[2]

[Leonardo Cattermole, son of another of Dickens's artist friends, George Cattermole, felt more at ease with the great man.] A halo of Charles Dickens surrounds many of my earliest and most agreeable memories, especially as regards certain dinner-parties at our house in Clapham Rise, when Dickens, always accompanied by Forster, used to appear to the delight of juveniles as well as seniors. One of the charms Charles Dickens possessed was his ability to render himself interesting to, and beloved by, children, who felt that he *adapted* himself without 'condescending' to them. Young as I was then, I call to mind the delight I felt on being permitted, at dessert time, to sit by Mr. Forster and listen to the 'talk'. . . . I can fancy I see Charles Dickens now in one of the Byron arm-chairs, holding forth to an admiring audience of both sexes and various ages. When *he* spoke, it was *'conticuere omnes'* [every tongue was still] with the rest of the company. Who could tell a story as he did? Rivetting the attention from 'start to finish', holding his audience magnetically, selecting his subtle tools of narrative and using them always in the right place with effect, carrying his audience entirely with him by means of that power he had of building his story without lumber or extraneous non-important matter, feeding his listeners without *sating* them, leaving them always like his own Oliver, wanting 'more'![3]

[The Rev. C. J. Whitmore recalled in 1877 his work, years earlier, in a costermongers' school in Saffron Hill (the Fagin area in *Oliver Twist*). One of his boys was severely maimed in an accident, losing most of both of his hands.] I went home thinking what I could do to help that poor crippled lad. Just a week before that – I don't know whether any one here will remember it – Charles Dickens had published in *Household Words* an article entitled 'Nobody's Child', and I thought to myself, 'If that is an imaginary sketch it will be worth while to show the author a real specimen.' I wrote to Charles

Dickens, saying that if he would like to see 'Nobody's Child', I would show him to him. He sent me in reply a very kind letter, in which he said he could not be expected to take up all the 'Nobody's' children, but that nevertheless he would see this particular specimen if I would send it to him. Of course I very gladly sent the boy to Devonshire Place, where Mr. Dickens then lived. But when he got up to the house he found it a grander place than he had ever seen before, and so he sat down, like Mordecai at the King's gate, and did not dare to knock at the door. By-and-by Mr. Dickens sent his footman out to fetch him, and he brought him in. The boy said to me afterwards, 'Oh, sir, he did put me through a catechism – he asked me everything; but after I had talked three-quarters of an hour he gave me half-a-crown and this letter to take to his printer.' The boy took the letter to the printer, the printer instantly engaged him, and he remained there till, also through Mr. Dickens's kindness, he obtained employment as a telegraph messenger – a post which, so far as I know, he still holds.[4]

[Lord Redesdale was at Eton with Charley Dickens.] My friendship with him led to my first acquaintance with his great father, who came down to Eton one fine summer's day, with Mark Lemon and, I think, Shirley Brooks, and took several of us up the river to Maidenhead. What a day that was! The great man was full of life, bubbling over with fun, the youngest boy of the party. I often met him in after life, but then, wonderful as he was upon occasions, his face when at rest already showed signs of fatigue; the strenuous work had told upon him; he looked careworn and older than his years. I like to think of him as he was on that day at Maidenhead, brilliant, young and gay, the spirit of joy incarnate.[5]

[Mary Frances Morgan, daughter of Dickens's dear American friend Captain Elisha Ely Morgan, was in England in 1861 with her sister Ruth and brother William – all teenagers. They wanted to meet the great man, and to hear his public readings, which had just recommenced. So they wrote to him, and he asked them to join him in Colchester, where he installed them in his inn. He had ordered a meal for them, and 'Everything that the appetite of sixteen was likely to fancy was there – even to a certain kind of little custards which Mr. Dickens had selected as being sure to please the "young ladies."' They then heard him read *Nicholas Nickleby at the Yorkshire School* and *The Trial from 'Pickwick'*.]

After the reading was over, it was with not a little trembling that our insignificant feet followed the attendant to the dressing-room, where Mr. Dickens, in his shirt-sleeves, was walking rapidly up and down, as a means of getting through with the cooling and calming process which was always necessary after the great excitement and exertion of his reading.

The thing which struck me first, and which has always remained my strongest impression about him, was his power of putting himself in complete sympathy with other people; and I believe that to be the key-note of his genius. During that hour, and the hours which followed it – for we went back with him to the inn and sat beside him while he ate his hearty supper, – he was literally one of us – a boy – only a boy beyond compare in exuberance of mirth, quickness of wit, and inexhaustible capacity for happiness. He was absolutely never still, mentally or physcially; thoughts, words, and gestures followed each other in bright succession, till it was little wonder that my sister and I went to bed thoroughly exhausted, to pass a night of mingled dreams and sleeplessness, under the canopy of our queer old dingy four-poster.

In the morning, we woke to find a smart little snow-storm going on, but none the less cheery was the breakfast with Mr. Dickens; for his was a gayety dependent neither on weather, nor hours, nor people. . . . Through the softly falling snow we came back together to London, and on the railway platform parted with a hearty hand-shaking from the man who will forever be enshrined in our hearts as the kindest and most generous, not to say most brilliant, of hosts. Our gratitude was too exuberant to be satisfied without some speedy and tangible manifestation; so, after some deliberation, we decided to take advantage of our knowledge of Mr. Dickens's special weakness. He was a constant smoker and a connoisseur in cigars, and on the whole, we believed that nothing within our reach would please him more than a box of what he called 'American cigars'. Therefore, the best that we could find was bought and sent to him.[6]

[William Milligan, then a small boy living in Cambridge, Mass., was devoted to Dickens's works and wrote him a fan-letter when he was in Boston early in 1868. Dickens wrote back, 'My dear boy, come Tuesday morning at ten' (to the Tremont House, Boston). But the hotel servants would not believe that Dickens was expecting a little boy, so it was well past ten before he arrived, in some embarassment, at Dickens's door.] After a moment's hesitation I rapped at the door and was told to enter. Opening the door, I passed into the presence of the great author, my heart thumping like a trip-hammer, and my face probably reflecting the perturbation and distress that possessed me. Mr. Dickens was seated at a large, square table, surrounded by books. These he consulted from time to time. There he was, in the flesh, as I had pictured him so often, and I was about to approach him when I was again submitted to a rebuff, and again dumbfounded, for without any apparent interest or cordiality I was unceremoniously ordered to take a seat at the farthest corner of the room, with a significant wave of the hand as if he was done with me. . . . I was kept waiting three quarters of an hour. His continued indifference to my presence did not add to my peace of mind. But I began to realize that there were compensations. Gradually my sense of injury passed, and I found myself observing him, and that I was having an exceptional opportunity and privilege for observation that many an older person would have gone much farther than I did to enjoy. Meanwhile I remained respectfully quiet and awaited my host's pleasure. As I watched him, he appeared to be ill and tired. He had had a severe cold about all of the time he was in this country, made a severe strain upon his vitality in the ceaseless round of festivities and demands upon his nerve forces, and his continuous appearances in his readings. He constantly placed his face in the hollow of his right hand, with the fore finger extended over his cheek, the second finger over his upper lip, and the thumb under his chin, closing his eyes as if resting.

Finally, he laid down his quill pen, and looking toward me, beckoned me to him and pointed to a chair about five feet away from him. When I was seated, he looked at me steadily as if to read me through and through, and sternly said: 'You were late. I do not like people who do not keep their appointments with me.' It was certainly a harsh and cold reception. In later years I learned that he was punctilious to the second in keeping his own engagements, and naturally had no toleration with those who were delinquent with him.

As earnestly and respectfully as possible I related how I had failed in my appointment, and how sorry I was, and his face softened, he became instantly cordial, and drawing his chair close up to mine, instead of making me draw mine to him, took me by the hand, smiled and said he was pleased that it was not my fault, or through any negligence or disrespect on my part. The atmosphere was instantly cleared, and for fifteen minutes there was a rapid fire of questions and answers. It seemed that I could hardly contain myself. I was lifted far above this plane, and I certainly had the time of my life. I tried to be subdued, courteous and alert, and answered his questions about my home, school and social life and my sports. Mr. Dickens had nothing but love in his share of the interview, and was very earnest in all he said and did. His speech was direct, and his questions apt and pertinent. His voice was pleasant and clear, and he was most affable and companionable. From his unaffected laughter and spontaneous hilarity, I felt that he was getting his share of the enjoyment and that my boyish manner and presence did not bore him. At all events he appeared contented, free from restraint, and he certainly made me happy.

Time will never efface from my memory his kindliness and unreserved glee. While his face evidenced, at times, indisposition, there was no reason to suspect that he had lost any of his capacity for portrayal of his emotions, or that his penchant for drollery and fun was in any degree limited. He had many changes of expression in the differing moods of our conversation. He seemed a perfect mimic. . . . It seemed less difficult for him to lower himself to the standard of my presence than it was for me to rise to the height of his. I have often wondered if the same privilege could have come to me in later years, if there could have been greater enjoyment or a differing estimate of his manner and speech. It was impossible not to feel the charm of his company.[7]

[Kate Douglas Wiggin (1856–1923), later author of *Rebecca of Sunnybrook Farm* and other juvenile and adult fiction, was a precocious twelve-year-old when she made herself known to Dickens during his American readings tour. She was then living in a village in Maine, and was thrilled to hear that he was reading (on 30 March 1868) in Portland, sixteen miles away; but 'The price of tickets was supposed to be almost prohibitory' – certainly for a child to attend – so, to her acute mortification, she was not allowed to hear him. But next day she had the good fortune to be on the same train as he. During the journey, she managed to sit next to him, and confess her love for his books, some of which she had read six times.]

'Bless my soul!' he ejaculated. . . . 'Those long thick books, and you such a slip of a thing.'

'Of course,' I explained conscientiously, 'I do skip some of the very dull parts once in a while; not the short dull parts, but the long ones.'

He laughed heartily. 'Now, that is something that I hear very little about', he said. 'I distinctly want to learn more about those very dull parts.' And whether to amuse himself, or to amuse me, I do not know, he took out a notebook and pencil from his pocket and proceeded to give me an exhausting and exhaustive examination on this subject; the books in which the dull parts predominated; and the characters and subjects which principally produced them. He chuckled so constantly during this operation that I could hardly help believing myself extraordinarily agreeable, so I continued dealing these infant blows, under the delusion that I was flinging him bouquets.

It was not long before one of my hands was in his, and his arm around my waist, while we talked of many things. . . . I wish I could recall still more of his conversation, but I was too happy, too exhilarated, and too inexperienced to take conscious notes of the interview. I rememeber feeling that I had never known anybody so well and so intimately, and that I talked with him as one talks under cover of darkness or before the flickering light of a fire. It seems to me, as I look back now, and remember how the little soul of me came out and sat in the sunshine of his presence, that I must have had some premonition that the child, who would come to be one of the least of writers, was then talking with one of the greatest; – talking, too, of the author's profession and high calling. All the little details of the meeting stand out as clearly as though it had happened yesterday. I can see every article of his clothing and of my own; the other passengers in the car; the landscape through the window, and above all the face of Dickens, deeply lined, with sparkling eyes and an amused, waggish smile that curled the corners of his mouth under his grizzled moustache. . . .

'What book of mine do you like best?' Dickens asked, I remember; and I answered, 'Oh, I like *David Copperfield* much the best. That is the one I have read six times.'

'Six times – good, good!' he replied; 'I am glad that you like Davy, so do I – I like it best, too!' clapping his hands; and that was the only remark he made which attracted the attention of the other passengers, who looked in our direction now and then, I have been told, smiling at the interview, but preserving its privacy with the utmost friendliness.

'Did you want to go to my reading very much?' was another question. Here was a subject that had never once been touched upon in all the past days – a topic that stirred the very depths of my disappointment and sorrow, fairly choking me, and making my lip tremble by its unexpectedness, as I faltered, '*Yes; more than tongue can tell.*'

I looked up a second later, when I was sure that the tears in my eyes were not going to fall, and to my astonishment saw that Dickens's eyes were in precisely the same state of moisture. That was a never-to-be-forgotten moment, although I was too young to appreciate the full significance of it.

'Do you cry when you read out loud?' I asked curiously. 'We all do in our family. And we never read about Tiny Tim, or about Steerforth when his body is washed up on the beach, on Saturday nights, or our eyes are too swollen to go to Sunday School.'

'Yes, I cry when I read about Steerforth,' he answered quietly, and I felt no astonishment.

'We cry the worst when it says, "All the men who carried him had known him and gone sailing with him, and seen him merry and bold"' I said, growing very tearful in reminiscence.

We were now fast approaching our destination – the station in Boston – and the passengers began to collect their wraps and bundles. Mr. Osgood[8] had two or three times made his appearance, but had been waved away with a smile by Dickens – a smile that seemed to say, – 'You will excuse me, I know, but this child has the right of way.'

'You are not travelling alone?' he asked, as he arose to put on his overcoat.

'Oh, no,' I answered, coming down to earth for the first time since I had taken my seat beside him – 'oh, no, I had a mother, but I forgot all about her.' Whereupon he said – 'You are a passed-mistress of the art of flattery!' But this remark was told me years afterwards by the old lady who was sitting in the next seat, and who overheard as much of the conversation as she possibly could, so she informed me.

Dickens took me back to the forgotten mother, and introduced himself, and I, still clinging to his hand, left the car and walked with him down the platform until he disappeared in the carriage with Mr. Osgood, leaving me with the feeling that I must continue my existence somehow in a dull and dreary world.[9]

[Mary Angela Dickens (1862–1948), daughter of Dickens's eldest son Charley, was his first grandchild. Her father bought Gad's Hill after the novelist's death.] A child's impressions depend upon sensitiveness to atmosphere, and it must have been a dull child indeed who was not affected by the atmosphere of Gad's Hill. The great place, consequently, which my grandfather holds in my memory – and few people could realise how great it is – is filled by an immense personality, a personality so dominating that it affected everything and everybody with whom it came in contact; that the world in which he moved, so to speak, existed only in order that he might so move at his good pleasure.

This atmosphere I believe to have been partly created by the fact that the saying regarding the honour of a prophet in his own country was never more completely falsified than in the case of my grandfather. Never was a great man more loved by his children, more reverenced in his life, more deeply and enduringly mourned and missed in his death. . . . All my personal recollections of my grandfather – all but one that is to say – belong to his last and best loved home, Gad's Hill – my own home for years after his death. . . .

Four distinct pictures of my grandfather hold their places in my memory, and oddly enough, each one of the four reflects more or less definitely a different phase in his many-sided character. In the first I see the dining-room at Gad's Hill, and a large dinner-party in progress. It is very gay and very glittering, many flowers, much glass, much silver – I have spoken already of my grandfather's love for brightness about him – and every one is in great good humour. I think it must be Christmas Day, as I can imagine no other reason for the presence on the scene of my little brother and myself. My little brother – a mere mite, a great favourite and innocent of the 'seen and not heard' adage – said or did something which caught my grandfather's attention. I can see the figure at the head of the table standing with his glass in his hand, alert, laughing, full of the zest of the moment, and pausing for an instant to say something to the little boy – something which I probably did not understand, and certainly do not remember – which was received with peals of laughter, in which the child joined gleefully without the faintest idea what it was all about! Here then is the social Charles Dickens, the delightful companion whose friends invariably forgot that he had ever written anything, so great was the charm of his capacity for enjoyment, so great was his gift for causing those about him to enjoy. He talked well, because he was so full of spirit, and so keenly observant, and because his sense of humour was wholly irrepressible. But he never talked otherwise than naturally and unaffectedly, and he was never bookish.

My second picture always makes me smile a little. . . . in my second picture, my grandfather and I are certainly confronting one another with an awful fascination. My grandfather is standing in front of a red and roaring fire – again in the dining-room at Gad's Hill. There is a very high and a very narrow mantelpiece, and he is framed, so to speak, against the background of cheery flame. On either side of the fireplace is a window, through which the garden, covered with snow, can be seen. My grandfather, handsome, alert, but for the moment a little at a loss, looks down at me. I, a very small girl in a pinafore look up at him. And I am afraid . . . I never speak a word! For it is an occasion, and I have been sent into the room, alone, with the impression strong upon me that something tremendous is going to happen to me – my grandfather is going to give me a Christmas present himself. The present was one of the few children's Annuals of those days – the *Child's Prize*, and I do not doubt that my aunt had bought it, and had asked him to perform the ceremony of its bestowal. And my grandfather either was not in spirits that morning – let no one suppose that he alone among all geniuses never paid the penalty exacted by his gift – or else my preternatural solemnity seemed to demand a return in kind. So there we stood, the presentation being made, and I always wonder how the interview closed! It seems that it might have gone on interminably.

To his charm in a sick-room I have already alluded, but I must emphasise it, because it forms the frame-work of my third picture. . . . On one of my visits to Gad's Hill, running about where I should not have been allowed to go, I fell over a saucepan of boiling water. Dinner was going on, and my nurse, frightened at the result of her shortcomings, dared not disturb my aunt, and accordingly put me to bed, and told me not to cry! My aunt coming to see me after dinner, instantly discovered my unhappy plight, but to my astonishment it was my grandfather who appeared at my bedside and 'made me better'. And through the unhappy days that followed – for I was badly scalded – the faith that he would always 'make me better' never left me.

In the course of those days he had to go to London, and my childish misery was great. I 'hurt dreadfully', no one knew how much, and no one could possibly know, until 'Venerables' – our childish name for him – came back! I can remember the joy of hearing the pony carriage which brought him from the station drive into the yard, and can see him, almost immediately afterwards, coming into the room to me – a little invalid, waiting in perfect confidence to be 'made better'. . . .

My last picture of my grandfather is connected [with his public readings]. It was my father, I think, who was determined that I should be taken to one of the last series of readings, and he very naturally chose for me the *Christmas Carol*. Curiously enough, I was not in the least elated at such an unusual form of 'treat' – I think the necessity for being very good must have been unduly impressed upon me! But I never went into the St. James's Hall in after years without looking at the place where I sat on that occasion, and feeling again the half-frightened expectation of I knew not what, which I felt then. I see my grandfather now, as I saw him then, standing at the little table, not 'Venerables' at all, but a terrible and unknown personage, a long way off, quite unaware of my existence and speaking in unknown voices. And I count among the most dreadful moment of my childish existence the moment when 'Venerables' cried.[10]

NOTES

1. Mary (Mamie) Dickens, 'My Father at Home', *Cornhill Magazine*, n.s. IV (1885) 33.

2. Edgar Browne, *Phiz and Dickens* (1913) pp. 45–6.

3. *Pen and Pencil*, pp. 177–9.

4. *Ragged School Union Quarterly Record*, July 1877, repr. in *Dkn*, LVI (1960) 185–6. Mr Whitmore was doubtless a veracious man, but he slips up in some of the details of his anecdote. Probably the article he mentions was 'Anybody's Child' (by W. B. Jerrold), *Household Words*, 4 Feb 1854, describing the plight of London's uncared-for children. Alfred Dickens gives another instance of his father's helping such 'ragged' children: he befriended a local crossing-sweeper boy, sent him to a Ragged School at night, and paid for his emigrating to Australia – 'but one of the many hundreds of similar actions which this warm-hearted man performed . . . of which the world knew nothing' – 'My Father and His Friends', *Nash's Magazine*, IV (1911) 628. See also Philip Collins, 'Dickens and the Ragged Schools', *Dkn*, LV (1959) 94–109; and Norris Pope, *Dickens and Charity* (1978).

5. Lord Redesdale, *Memories* (1915) I, 65–6. Dickens wrote a superbly amusing account of this (or some similar) day on the river in a letter of 11 July 1851 (*N*, II, 325–7). For Redesdale's memories of Dickens a few days before his death, see below, II, 350–1.

6. M. F. Armstrong [*neé* Morgan], 'Our Letter', *Saint Nicholas: Scribner's*

Illustrated Magazine for Girls and Boys, IV (1877) 438–41. For Dickens's letter of thanks, 10 Feb 1862, see *N*, III, 286. On Dickens and the Morgan family, see essays by W. J. Carlton, *Dkn*, LIII (1957) 75–82, and LIV (1958) 88–93. The Colchester performance which they attended took place on 1 November 1861.

7. William Milligan, 'How I met Charles Dickens', *Dkn*, XVIII (1922) 211–15. Dickens later wrote to him again, from Gad's Hill. For further particulars of this encounter, see *Dkn*, VII (1911) 249–50.

8. James R. Osgood, Dickens's travelling companion, was a member of the publishing firm Ticknor and Fields, which was managing his American tour.

9. Kate Douglas Wiggin, *A Child's Journey with Charles Dickens* (Boston and New York, 1912) pp. 20–32.

10. Mary Angela Dickens, 'My Grandfather as I Knew Him', *Nash's Magazine*, V (1911) 101–10. She also wrote 'A Child's Recollections of Gad's Hill', *Strand Magazine*, XIII (1897) 69–74, where she specifies that it was over Tiny Tim that Dickens wept (and 'I had never before seen a grown-up person cry'). She also remarks, 'I have no recollection of ever being told that my grandfather was a great man. There is no shadow in my memory of ever having feared him. But all my recollection is pervaded with the sense that "Venerables" – as I was taught to call him – was not as other men.' And, though she did not fear Dickens, 'a vague sense of dread' was associated with his absences, so that when he was writing in the chalet, she used to creep in from the garden, no longer feeling at ease playing there.

'That Curious Life-giving Power of His'

LADY RITCHIE

(1) and (3) from her *From the Porch*, (1913) pp. 33–45; (2) from her *Chapters from Some Memoirs*, (1894) pp. 78–81. Anne Isabella Ritchie (1837–1919), elder daughter of W. M. Thackeray and herself a minor novelist, was the wife of Sir Richmond Ritchie. She ('Anny') and her sister Harriet ('Minny', born 1840) were childhood friends of the Dickens girls, and Katey Dickens in her adult life was particularly close to Anny and her father. His charming verses addressed to her ('K.E.'), 'Mrs Katherine's Lantern', open Anny's chapter 'Charles Dickens as I Remember Him' in *From the Porch*, and she refers to Katey as 'K.E.' in what follows. 'My chief remembrance' of Dickens, she wrote to Kitton in 1888, 'is of the delightfulness and *light* of his enchanting talk and playful spirits, and also of his *great* kindness and warmth of sympathy – something quite apart and not to be forgotten by me – after my Father's Death' (*Pen and Pencil*, Supplement, p. 15).

(1) The first occasion of my meeting Mr. Dickens was at the house of Charles Leslie, a painter for whom my father had a great sympathy and affection. . . . [There] my sister and I first realised Mr. Dickens himself, though only as a sort of brilliance in the room, mysteriously dominant and formless. I remember how everybody lighted up when he entered. [She also recalls an expedition, which started from the Leslies' house, to visit a ship commanded by Dickens's American friend Captain Morgan.[1]] Mr. Dickens seemed to take command of the party. . . . He was talking, arranging everything, in spirits gaily delightful – as I have said, mysteriously dominant. All comes back to my mind as I think of it, and I remember (after forgetting a great deal) that we travelled back in a railway carriage in Mr. Dickens's company late at night, dead tired, enchanted, sleepy, yet somehow carried along by his kindly brilliance. It was soon after this that we went to some eventful children's parties in Devonshire Place, and also later to Tavistock House. . . .

(2) It is curious to me now to remember, considering how little we met and what a long way off they lived, what an important part the Dickens household played in our childhood. But the Dickens books were as much a part of our home as our own father's. Certainly the Dickens children's parties were shining facts in our early London days – nothing came in the least near them. There were other parties, and they were very nice, but nothing to compare to these; not nearly so light, not nearly so shining, not nearly so going round and round. Perhaps it was not all as brilliantly wonderful as I imagined it, but most assuredly the spirit of mirth and kindly jollity was a reality to every one present, and the master of the house had that wondrous fairy gift of leadership. I know not what to call that power by which he inspired every one with spirit and interest. One special party I remember, which seemed to me to go on for years with its kind, gay hospitality, its music, its streams of children passing and re-passing. . . . Somehow after the music we all floated into a long supper-room, and I found myself sitting near the head of the table by Mr. Dickens, with another little girl much younger than myself; she wore a necklace and pretty little sausage curls all round her head. Mr. Dickens was very kind to the little girl, and presently I heard him persuading her to sing, and he put his arm round her to encourage her. . . .

(3) One day, I specially remember [from the period in 1855 when

the Dickenses and the Thackeray girls were living in Paris], when
we had come to settle about a drawing class with our young
companion K.E. (who had already found out what she liked doing),[2]
her father came into the room accompanied by a dignified person –
too dignified we thought – who came forward and made some
solemn remark, such as Hamlet himself might have addressed to
Yorick, and then stood in an attitude in the middle of the room. The
Paris springtime was at its height, there was music outside, a horse
champing in the road, voices through the open window, and
Mr. Macready, for it was he, tragic in attitude gravely awaiting an
answer. Mr. Dickens seemed to have instantly seized the
incongruity, suddenly responding with another attitude, and
another oration in the Hamlet manner, so drolly and gravely, that
Macready himself could not help smiling at the burlesque. . . .

I remember Mr. Dickens, one day long after those early times,
when we were all in London again, and our friend K.E. lay
dangerously ill of a fever in an old house in Sloane Street. We had
gone to ask for news of her. It was an old house, panelled, and with a
big well staircase, on a landing of which we met Mr. Dickens
coming away from the sick-room. He was standing by a window,
and he stopped us as we were going up. K.E. has told me since then
that in those miserable days his very coming seemed to bring healing
and peace to her as she lay, and to quiet the raging fever. He knew
how critical it was, but he spoke quietly and with good courage –
that curious life-giving power of his struck me then no less than
always before. . . .

There is one other meeting, a very memorable one, which I
should like to note here, even though I cannot quite place it with its
date and its time. About eighteen months after my father's death
this same K.E. said suddenly one day to my sister and myself, 'I
know you will shrink from it, but I want to take you to the reading of
Copperfield in St. James's Hall. It is the last London reading. I have
your places; I asked for them to be kept for you.' She was so
affectionately insistent that we could not help agreeing, for she
spoke with the true friend's voice, and looked with eyes that
compelled us. I have always been glad to think that we went with
her on that occasion. As I have said, I had only once before heard
Mr. Dickens read – on that wasted occasion in the Paris studio,[3] but
on this special evening in London, it was for all the rest of my life
that I heard his voice. We sat in the front, a little to the right of the
platform; the great Hall was somewhat dimly lighted, considering

the crowds assembled there. The slight figure (so he appeared to me) stood alone quietly facing the long rows of people. He seemed holding the great audience in some mysterious way from the empty stage. Quite immediately the story began: Copperfield and Steerforth, Yarmouth and the fishermen and Peggotty, and then the rising storm, all was there before us. . . . It was not acting, it was not music, nor harmony of sound and colour, and yet I still have an impression of all these things as I think of that occasion. The lights shone from the fisherman's home; then after laughter terror fell, the storm rose; finally, we all were breathlessly watching from the shore, and (this I remember most vividly of all) a great wave seemed to fall splashing on to the platform from overhead, carrying away everything before it, and the boat and the figure of Steerforth in his red sailor's cap fighting for his life by the mast. Some one called out; was it Mr. Dickens himself who threw up his arm? . . . It was all over, we were half-laughing, half-crying with excitement; being at that special time still very much wrought up, remembering the past, naturally our emotions took shape.

NOTES

1. Dickens had a great affection for Captain Morgan, who appears as Captain Jorgan, 'a frank, open-hearted American shipowner', in *A Message from the Sea* (1860). On Morgan, see above, 1, 176, note 6.

2. Katey had some talent as an artist, and both of her husbands, Charles Collins and Carlo Perugini, were professional artists.

3. She had heard him giving a private reading in the artist Ary Scheffer's studio, but was 'wool-gathering in those days', so she hardly listened or noted it.